Programming with Java IDL

Geoffrey Lewis
Steven Barber
Ellen Siegel

WILEY COMPUTER PUBLISHING

John Wiley & Sons, Inc.
New York • Chichester • Weinheim • Brisbane • Singapore • Toronto

Publisher: Robert Ipsen
Editor: Robert Elliott
Managing Editor: Brian Snapp
Electronic Products, Associate Editor: Mike Sosa
Text Design and Composition: Benchmark Productions, Inc.

The content of this book is based on an early-access version of Java™ IDL. There have been changes made to the product and code since this release. Therefore, screen shots and examples may not be identical to any final product.

Library of Congress Cataloging-in-Publication Data:
ISBN: 0-471-24797-9

Printed in the United States of America

10 9 8 7 6 5 4 3 2 1

About the
Authors

Steven Barber is a principal consultant with Fusion Systems Group, a firm specializing in the design and implementation of multitiered Java and CORBA systems.

Geoffrey R. Lewis was formerly manager of strategic alliances for Sun Microsystems' Object Products, including NEO and Joe. He managed Sun's activities at the Object Management Group and represented Sun on OMG's Technical Committee, Architecture Board, and Board of Directors. In 1994, he received OMG's Distinguished Service Award and in March 1997, he was awarded OMG's first Fellows Honor.

Ellen Siegel is a member of the Internet Client Server group at Sun Microsystems, Inc. She was technical lead for the Joe 1.0 and 2.0 product releases as well as the initial Java IDL development, and currently holds a position focusing on Web technology. Prior to joining Sun, she worked at Xerox PARC and held visiting posts at national computer science research laboratories in France, Germany, and Portugal. Dr. Siegel holds a Ph.D. degree in Computer Science from Carnegie Mellon University.

About the Contributors

Henry Balen has been working with Object Technologies since the mid-1980s. During that period, he architected and implemented numerous distributed object systems for major financial institutions. He was a technical director for the Fusion Systems Group in the New York office from 1995 to 1997. Henry can be contacted via e-mail at balen@computer.org.

Pierre Delisle is a staff engineer at SunSoft where he has worked on distributed application models for SunSoft's Joe and NEO products. Since joining Sun Microsystems in 1990, Pierre has been involved in a variety of projects based on distributed object-oriented technologies. He led the software team responsible for the development of the load-balancing system used by Sun Microelectronics for the design and verification of the UltraSparc and Java series of microprocessors.

Bruce Martin is a senior staff engineer at Visigenic Software in San Mateo, California. Previously, he was at SunSoft and HP Laboratories where he worked on distributed object technology since the late 1980s. He is the principal author of five of the OMG's CORBA Services specifications. He has authored numerous papers on object-oriented distributed computing. Bruce received a Ph.D. in Computer Science from the University of California, San Diego.

Patrick McTurk is a developer of distributed object systems in the financial services industry. A graduate of Brown University, his interests include distributed systems and object-oriented methodologies and languages.

Gordon Palumbo has been a proponent of the adoption of technology and its integration in everyday life ever since he began programming at the age of eight. Since joining Fusion, he has been entrenched in the CORBA front lines, and has designed and implemented CORBA- and Java-based systems for major financial institutions.

Jeff Nisewanger is a staff engineer at SunSoft where he has developed CORBA products since 1994. Together with Graham Hamilton and Peter Kessler, he implemented the first CORBA-compatible Java ORB, which was demonstrated in September 1995 at SunSoft's NEO product announcement. He has played a key role in subsequent releases of Joe and Java IDL and led the definition of the standard OMG Java IDL mapping. Prior to 1994, he worked on X and NeWS window system technology at Sun. Mr. Nisewanger is a graduate of Hellgate High School in Missoula, Montana.

Larry Pass is an applications engineer in Sun's Internet Client Server group, where he has worked on customer applications of Sun's distributed object technology. Before coming to Sun, Larry held a similar position at Taligent, Inc., and before that, a varied career from mainframe MIS to shrink-wrapped applications.

Mary Ann Rayner is a senior technical writer at Sun Microsystems with experience writing about JOE, NEO, Java IDL, and distributed object-oriented technology.

Marvin Wolfthal has been technical director for Fusion Systems Group's Boston office. Marvin has architected and developed many CORBA-based distributed object systems for financial institutions and insurance companies, and has been an active participant in the OMG's financial domain task force.

Contents

Introduction

The example programs in *Programming with Java IDL* have been written and tested to work with Sun's Java JDK 1.1. At the time of this writing, the next version of Java, currently known as JDK 1.2, has not been released. However, according to an examination of the preliminary specifications available, the code in this book will be compatible with JDK 1.2.

Who Should Read This Book?

This book is a guide to programming CORBA distributed objects in Java with Java IDL. This book is for developers who need to understand and work with systems that use both Java and CORBA. It's not only for people who work directly with the Sun Java IDL package, but also for people working with any CORBA Object Request Broker that conforms to the new OMG IDL-to-Java mapping specification. In this book, you will learn how to build systems using the technology that will become part of the foundation of future systems. CORBA object implementers will find this book useful for creating new shared services implemented in Java. Project managers and systems architects will find that this book is helpful in communicating the use of Java IDL without having to absorb all the minutiae in the specification itself. We hope that you will find the material in the book useful for both learning this technology and as a reference when you go on to build such systems of your own.

What's in the Book?

Here are overviews of each chapter:

Chapter 1—Java IDL and CORBA
This chapter provides both an overview of the need for distributed objects and a framework for understanding Java and CORBA and how they fit together.

Chapter 2—Java Fundamentals
This chapter provides an extensive overview of Java and has enough information in it for you to understand and write the Java applications dealt with in the following

chapters. It is a good reference guide to the features of Java used later within this book, and also describes other Java references for further study.

Chapter 3—Introduction to CORBA

This chapter presents a description of the OMG's CORBA standard. After reading it, you will have a good idea as to where the standard is today and where the technology is heading tomorrow. You will learn what an Object Request Broker is and how it is used, get a description of the services and facilities defined by the OMG and the technology that allows ORBs from various vendors to interoperate (IIOP). The chapter ends with a brief description of some CORBA services.

Chapter 4—Distributed Architecture Concepts

What issues arise when designing a distributed system using CORBA and Java? How does IDL fit into the design process? The importance of standards is highlighted. The analysis and design processes used to build distributed systems and, in particular, CORBA-based systems, are very briefly covered in this chapter.

Chapter 5—Getting to Know Java IDL

This chapter contains a description of Java IDL. There is a description of the API supplied with Java IDL that enables the construction of Java IDL applications and applets, and abstracts some of the CORBA services. The relationship of Java IDL to the new OMG Portable Object Adapter specification (POA) is also described. After reading this chapter, you will be ready to build your own Java IDL application.

Chapter 6—A Basic Java IDL Applet and Server

No programming book is complete without the requisite "Hello, world!" program, and here it is. This example makes use of Java IDL to provide a client/server distributed object version. You will be shown how a simple Java applet can be turned into a client/server program using Java IDL.

Chapter 7—Internet Polling

We now delve into more detail and provide a more-extensive application. This application is a good demonstration of the capabilities of Java IDL for Internet or intranet polling, running surveys over the Internet, and providing a mechanism for real-time analysis to participants. You will be taken through the design process and shown how the application was developed. This chapter provides an extensive treatment of designing service interfaces using IDL.

Chapter 8—InterPoll Shared Services

This chapter gives a description of how to write servers that support calls to distributed CORBA objects in Java. This is done by presenting some details of the server side of the polling application presented in Chapter 7.

Chapter 9—The Network Pricing System: Building a Distributed Financial Services Application with Java IDL

We provide an implementation of a common function found in almost every financial services firm: the distribution of financial instrument pricing information to customers and end users in a reliable manner. You will be taken through the business problem and shown how this is realized with the design. We discuss issues of network bandwidth, security, and accounting. We present the high-level system architecture and design, and map that design into IDL. Finally, the client side of the application is presented in full. The implementation of the architecturally more-interesting server side is covered in Chapter 10.

Chapter 10—Server Objects for the Network Pricing System

Details of the server side of the application described in Chapter 9 are presented here. This application makes use of the CORBA event service to provide a simple publish and subscribe mechanism, remembers user profiles, and implements a simple user authentication mechanism.

Chapter 11—Summary

We bring the book to a close and give a glimpse of what to expect in the future of CORBA and Java IDL.

Appendix A—IDL/Java Language Mapping

Contains excerpts of the IDL-to-Java mapping specification as ratified by the OMG.

Appendix B—What's on the *Programming with Java IDL* Web Site?

A brief guide to the Web site for this book.

How To Read This Book

While it is not necessary to read this book from beginning to end, the book has been structured so that it starts with brief descriptions of Java and CORBA, concentrates on the specifics of Java IDL, and then presents several extended programming examples. Readers familiar with Java basics can comfortably skip Chapter 2 entirely, and readers already familiar with CORBA fundamentals can briefly skim Chapter 3. Issues relevant to the architecture and deployment of systems are dealt with in Chapters 3 and 4, so these may be worth a read even if you are familiar with CORBA. Chapters 5 and 6 form an introduction to the Java IDL package itself, while Chapters 7, 8, 9, and 10 present substantial programs written with Java IDL.

Java IDL
and CORBA

With the recent growth surge of the Internet and the World Wide Web, distributed applications have become mainstream. More and more businesses are prototyping and deploying distributed applications and are looking for tools and programming models that allow them to compete in the rapidly evolving world of the Internet and the Web without losing their large existing investments in legacy software. The combination of Java and CORBA technology embodied in Java IDL allows such enterprise computing solutions.

Java IDL exists in a world of rapidly developing technologies and ever-evolving terminology. To start learning Java IDL, you will need to master some basic terms and definitions.

Java IDL, a Sun Microsystems technology, gives Java programmers a way to develop multi-tier enterprise applications using CORBA distributed objects. CORBA is the Object Management Group's Common Object Request Broker Architecture—a standardized way to distribute objects across networks and between varying hardware, operating system, and language platforms. Java is the object-oriented programming language and cross-platform runtime environment originated by Sun and now in wide use as a way to deploy interactive content and other distributed systems on the Internet, intranets, and the World Wide Web.

Why Use Java IDL?

Why would anyone want to use Java IDL and CORBA? Isn't Java already a distributed system? Well, yes and no. Java 1.0 is distributable in the sense that it is designed to have applets download from Web servers into client machines where the applets execute. Java programs can also talk to other programs via sockets, so distributed systems can be built in this traditional bytestream-oriented way. Two Java programs talking to each other in this manner, however, have little to do with actually being able to distribute objects across machines; socket programming requires each application to define its own intra-application protocols, which must then be implemented using application-specific logic to stuff data into bytestreams and then remove it laboriously on the other end. Distributing objects (that is, being able to directly invoke the methods of remotely located objects) allows an application to be distributed at a higher level of abstraction without ever having to stop using the object-oriented paradigm and allows the way the application is distributed to be changed with relative ease.

Another technology related to distributing Java objects is Sun's RMI, or Remote Method Invocation. RMI is included as a core package in Java 1.1, so it is legitimate to ask: Why bother with CORBA at all? The CORBA architecture adds some complexity and is also more heavyweight than RMI. The key advantage to CORBA is that it allows the integration of systems written using multiple languages and paradigms, while RMI allows the distribution of objects only between Java programs. It is very hard to point to a system that will exist in isolation from all other existing systems: At some point, or at many points, the new programs written in Java will have to interface with some other previously existing systems. CORBA excels as an integration technology: Language mappings to the CORBA distributed object model exist for quite a few languages, such as C, C++, Smalltalk, and now Java.

Java IDL provides an OMG-standardized Java mapping to CORBA. Java IDL supports the CORBA 2.0 IIOP (Internet Inter-ORB Protocol) standard, which allows Java IDL programs to be used with any CORBA 2.0-compliant Object Request Brokers across TCP/IP networks.

If you don't have experience working with CORBA you may find some of the terms used in this discussion unfamiliar. That's all right: It's the job of the rest of this book to teach Java programmers about CORBA and Java IDL. It's not as difficult as it might sound at first, and when you're done, you too will know some new acronyms to throw around.

Living in a Heterogeneous World

Internet technology has exploded in the past couple of years, as evidenced by the appearance of Web URLs (Universal Resource Locators) on everything from movie advertisements to cereal boxes. Plenty of articles are being written on the new technologies as firms rush to capitalize on the promise of the Web and Java.

It has only been three years since the introduction of Mosaic, the first Web browser. Mosaic and HTML were developed as a means to share information within the research community. The Net has now become something more. The Internet used to be viewed as the domain of computer aficionados, the technological elite who would stay up late in the glow of the fluorescent tube. Now the Internet has become user friendly; all you need is a browser to ride the virtual waves of the new information ocean.

Today the capitalists have arrived on the Net, and the gleam of gold lights the eyes of companies eager to stake a claim, to set up an island in the network. Some trends are obvious: more commercial use of the Internet, greater interactive content, and more and more commercial and consumer services.

As a result of these trends, the ever-proliferating number of different systems and technologies, consisting of a mix of different hardware and software, need to interoperate. Systems have become more complex and diverse. Because building new systems from the ground up is costly, there is a demand to leverage existing systems so that their disparate parts work cooperatively.

These trends are pushing the business community to be more productive and profitable and to encourage a highly competitive environment. All this activity means that applications need to be more flexible to accommodate sudden and continuous change. These new applications can be realized by flexible three-tier or multi-tier architectures, simplifying the maintenance of application program logic and supporting reusability.

Essential Building Blocks

Object-oriented systems support the needs of business. They provide a paradigm that encourages reuse, rapid application development, and systems that adapt well to change. Constructing systems with objects allows the packaging of software capabilities into manageable units and supports the building of applications as a series of cooperating components.

Distributed Objects

An *object* is a self-contained software module encapsulating both code and data. An object describes both the behavior and the information associated with it. All interactions with objects are performed through well-defined interfaces. An object can map to a real entity from the point of view of both the programmer and the user. Programs constructed using objects can better model the real world.

A distributed object can reside anywhere on the network. It is independent code that can be accessed by remote clients via method invocation. Clients do not need to know where the distributed object resides nor the programming language in which it is implemented. Communication between distributed objects happens in a transparent manner.

A three-tier architecture is a natural embodiment of distributed objects: The first tier is the user interface, the second holds the business logic, and the third provides access to persistent storage such as databases or files. Services provided by distributed objects are publicized through well-defined interfaces. To realize the benefit of these distributed objects, interfaces need to be independent of operating system, programming language, and network protocols.

Java IDL helps us implement systems that provide the benefits of distributed object systems. They help to realize systems that fill the demands of both modern-day corporate information systems and the increasingly important global Internet infrastructure.

Java

Java is a platform-independent, object-oriented programming language and runtime environment from Sun Microsystems. It arrived on the scene with its release in the autumn of 1995. Since then, there has been more growth in Java development tools, environments, and applications making use of this new language within its first year than for any similar time period for any previous language.

Java has given us the ability to provide more interactive content on the World Web Wide, with dynamic Web pages that are no longer limited by the capabilities of HTML and CGI scripts. Java programming provides a more natural form for writing interactive content for the Net. It has also enabled the "write once, run everywhere" paradigm; with the soon-ubiquitous deployment of Java-enabled Web browsers and operating systems, developers can be assured that their applications will run on the target machines with minimal distribution costs.

Java as a programming language is relatively simple, portable, and architecture neutral. With the wide adoption of Java by software vendors it is becoming ubiquitous: from Web browser to network computer, from operating system to Java chips. It seems that everyone is using this "cool" technology, increasingly for serious production work.

The future, however, cannot ignore the past. We need to incorporate the old with the new. Many years of development have gone into existing systems. Corporations want to protect their investment in such development. Business logic is encapsulated within these systems. Existing databases will need to be reused. How do we glue all this together and preserve the existing investment while also building for the future? Currently, Java on its own has distributed object services and no support for integrating legacy applications across networks.. With the introduction of RMI comes some support for building distributed systems using Java and only Java. Java IDL holds the promise of providing a common Java interface to CORBA-compliant Object Request Brokers.

To build systems for the future, technologies must conform to industry standards, provide a natural mapping between old and new systems, and offer services that support the business process. One such technology solution is described by this book: Java IDL provides the glue between Java and existing systems by making use of an open industry standard, the Common Object Request Broker (CORBA).

Three-Tier Architectures

To date, client/server systems have been implemented with a two-tier model. The two-tier model consists of "fat" clients talking to servers that contain the data logic. Critical business logic becomes embedded within the front-end application, the database server, or both. The user interface implementation ends up containing application logic, or the server contains business logic in the form of schema and stored procedures. This drastically limits the ability of the application to adapt to change as businesses evolve.

Applications that put three tiers within a single monolithic application, using paradigms such as model-view controller, provide better adaptability but still produce "fat" clients and suffer from high distribution costs.

The modern enterprise receives demands from locations around the globe. The distribution and deployment of client applications have become important considerations when developing information systems. These systems need to adapt to rapid change to keep up with modern business demands, which change so rapidly that the costs of repeated software distribution and manual installation can dwarf the cost of developing the software system in the first place.

Three-tier architectures are better suited to the demands of the modern business environment. They provide a flexible model within which services and components can easily be added or changed to match changing business requirements.

A three-tier architecture is made up of the following parts:

- *User interface.* The user interface is embodied within the client application; typically there are no business rules within this application.

- *Business logic.* Business rules are implemented as a series of cooperating objects, which can be viewed as network components. Often this business logic tier has multiple levels itself, resulting in so-called N-tier or multi-tier system architectures.

- *Data access.* Persistent information is accessed via data servers.

Incorporating application-specific business knowledge within application servers allows the servers to be used by a wide variety of client programs. New client programs can make use of preexisting application servers. The application server itself can be viewed as a distributed object.

An existing application can be incorporated into such an architecture by wrapping it so that it appears as another application server or as a component within the system. This technique preserves investment in currently developed products.

Three-tier architectures provide an information system with flexibility—the ability to grow and adapt. By making use of "object wrappers," existing systems can be incorporated into distributed object systems. Products such as Java IDL provide the infrastructure to design, develop, and deploy distributed components, the building blocks of three-tiered architectures.

CORBA and Object Request Brokers

An *Object Request Broker* (ORB) brings the object paradigm to the network. This is the technology that allows corporations to realize the benefits of distributed objects: All the benefits of object-oriented systems can now be applied to three-tier and multi-tier architectures.

The Common Object Request Broker Architecture (CORBA) has been specified by one of the largest standards bodies currently in existence, the Object Management Group (OMG). The OMG (http://www.omg.org) has more than 700 members. CORBA is an open standard that is both machine and language independent. ORB products developed to conform to the CORBA 2.0 standard can interoperate with each other, bringing the promise of componentware to reality.

A CORBA object advertises its services through an interface, defined in the programming language-neutral Interface Definition Language (IDL). An IDL interface provides the ORB infrastructure with information about the contents of messages to and from the object and provides for transparent access to the object. A distributed object is referenced via a handle called an *object reference*, which contains information to locate the remote object so that a client can access its services.

CORBA provides an object bus on which each object is a node with a well-defined interface that can be identified by a unique handle. CORBA provides both cross-platform and cross-language communications, contrasted with Java RMI, which provides cross-platform communication between programs written in only a single language. A client of a distributed object does not care what language that object is implemented in: It is interested only in the interface to the methods providing services. ORBs provide a clean separation between interface and implementation.

By providing an interface via IDL and wrapping the existing code, we make an existing application appear as a component on the object bus. IDL provides us with a natural mechanism to produce object wrappers. Once existing systems have been wrapped, they look like distributed objects on the object bus. Thus, by using object wrappers we can integrate existing nondistributed, nonobject applications into a flexible CORBA-based distributed object system.

The CORBA 2.0 standard specifies one of its common communications protocols, the Internet Inter-ORB Protocol (IIOP), to be based on TCP/IP. All CORBA 2.0-compliant ORBs need to provide an implementation of this protocol. This makes CORBA 2.0 ideally suited for Internet- and intranet-based applications.

CORBA also defines a rich set of distributed object services that include, among others, such functionality as object persistence, life cycle, relationship, transactions, and security. These services support the development of enterprise architectures and allow developers to concentrate on the actual business problems that need to be solved.

ORB-based architectures provide an excellent framework for building three-tier and multi-tier client/server applications.

Java IDL

Java IDL connects Java-based Web applications to servers provided by an IIOP-compliant ORB such as Iona's Orbix or Visigenic's Visibroker products. Java IDL supports location-independent Web clients and servers with all the benefits of the Java programming language, giving users access to server applications regardless of their location or computing platform. While it isn't necessary to use a separate ORB product in conjunction with Java IDL, many ORBs provide services that are important in constructing robust, flexible, and scaleable multi-tier systems.

Java IDL applications are more dynamic than HTML forms, combining the dynamism of Java applets with the multi-tier architectures provided by ORBs. Java IDL extends the capabilities of Java, providing for the instantiation of and method invocation on remote objects. These remote objects can be written with another language, for example, C++. Because Java IDL is CORBA 2.0 compliant and implements the interoperability standard (IIOP), it can also talk to any other CORBA 2.0–compliant ORB.

Java IDL combines the ease of distributing Java "thin" clients (applets) with the capabilities of a distributed object system. Making use of the strengths of the Java environment and combined with an ORB based on an industry standard (CORBA), Java IDL helps realize applications that will help businesses build with the future and leverage the past: Java IDL enables multi-tier applications with true "thin" clients and enterprise server components supplied via CORBA-based services.

Putting It All Together

Technologies that make it easier to navigate the information ocean of the Internet have grown tremendously in the last few years. These same technologies are being used within the corporate world for similar purposes: to provide information over a private intranet or to provide a corporate interface to the Internet.

The Internet enables great opportunities to be dreamt of and realized. It is a malleable, constantly changing, and increasingly complex environment. As such, applications built for this environment need to be adaptable. Java, with its "write once, run everywhere" capability, is part of the solution to building such applications. Java IDL extends Java with its ability to build clients that can integrate with ORBs and hence provide the rest of the solution. We now have the infrastructure to build three-tier and multi-tier architectures.

With the ability to integrate existing applications comes the realization that future systems can be built on past investments. We can now realize component-ware for the Web that is truly open. This is the technology that will provide a rich foundation for future enterprise systems.

Java Fundamentals

This chapter is a brief overview of the Java language and environment. It is intended as a review and a ready-reference rather than a complete language tutorial; however, it should be possible to use and understand the rest of the book through study of this chapter alone. Of course, in such a short chapter, only a subset of the Java language, APIs, and virtual machine can be discussed. A number of important topics in the Java programming language and its libraries are omitted because those features are not used in the examples in this book.

For readers who want a more thorough, or more gentle, introduction to Java programming, there is no shortage of excellent books from which to choose. Unfortunately, most of the definitive works on the market as of this writing (June 1997) cover only Java 1.0 at a time when Java JDK 1.1 is the current version. Among the best of the books available are the following titles:

- Ken Arnold and James Gosling's *The Java Programming Language* (Reading, MA: Addison-Wesley, 1996). This book covers only the language and its standard libraries, but it covers it in a way that takes Java seriously as a general-purpose programming language. This seminal book has gone through multiple printings; the fourth printing contains an appendix that captures the revisions to the language as of the 1.1 version.

- An in-depth treatment of applet programming and the Abstract Window Toolkit (AWT) for Java 1.0 is presented in David M. Geary and Allen L. McClellan's *Graphic Java: Mastering the AWT* (Mountain View, CA: SunSoft Press/Prentice-Hall, 1996). For coverage of AWT programming in JDK 1.1, refer to John Zukowski's *Java AWT Reference* (Sebastapol, CA: O'Reilly & Associates, 1997).

- An effective and thorough integrated treatment of both the language and applet programming is contained in Gary Cornell and Cay S. Horstmann's *Core Java, Second Edition* (Mountain View, CA: SunSoft Press/Prentice-Hall, 1997).

- For those in a hurry, Peter van der Linden's *Just Java, Second Edition* (Mountain View, CA: SunSoft Press/Prentice-Hall, 1997) is an entertaining and valuable read. Michael C. Daconta's *Java for C/C++ Programmers* (New York: John Wiley & Sons, 1996) also provides a fine and quick path to the Java JDK 1.0.2 language for C and C++ programmers.

- The hard-core Java programmer will want both David Flanagan's *Java in a Nutshell, Second Edition* (Sebastapol, CA: O'Reilly & Associates, 1997) and James Gosling, Frank Yellin, and The Java Team's *The Java Application Programming Interface, Volumes 1 and 2* (Reading, MA: Addison-Wesley, 1996) beside their monitors at all times. The API reference books cover only the 1.0.2 release at this point; it would be wise to check with the publishers to see when updates are scheduled.

- An extensive and well-conceived treatment of Java's thread facility and related issues appears in Doug Lea's *Concurrent Programming in Java* (Reading, MA: Addison-Wesley, 1996). For the truly hard core, James Gosling, Bill Joy, and Guy Steele's *The Java Language Specification* (Reading, MA: Addison-Wesley, 1996) and Tim Lindholm and Frank Yellin's *The Java Virtual Machine Specification* (Reading, MA: Addison-Wesley, 1996) provide more information than any sane person needs to know about the details of Java circa version 1.0 and includes some crucial information on the semantics of threads that isn't well specified elsewhere.

- Sun's JavaSoft subsidiary makes available a wealth of information through its Web site at http://java.sun.com, including, at the time of this writing, the Java

Language Tutorial, complete API reference documentation, and some, if not all, of the language and virtual machine specifications. Additionally, this site has up-to-date information on the state of Java according to Sun, as well as some software and extensive information on future plans for the Java programming environment.

What Is Java?

Sun and JavaSoft have done an amazing job positioning Java as a way to animate Web pages. Unfortunately, many people have gotten this message all too well and do not realize that the Java language and the Java Virtual Machine are serious tools for implementing multi-tier, platform-independent, enterprise-wide distributed object architectures.

Even though many products and components are associated with the Java name, for the purposes of this book, Java consists of the Java programming language itself, the Java Virtual Machine that executes Java bytecodes, and the set of standard classes that compose the Java API and that are required to be distributed with every virtual machine runtime. The version of the Java Development Kit, which is JavaSoft's reference implementation of Java, that was most widely deployed when the sample code in this book was written was JDK 1.0.2, and this is the version of Java this chapter discusses. This subset of Java, however, was stable between JDK 1.0.2 and JDK 1.1, so this chapter is useful for both environments. The sample code in this book, however, has been verified to compile and execute using JDK 1.1, which had just been released at the time this book was submitted to the publisher. Some of the applet code presented in this book, especially in the area of AWT event handling, requires JDK 1.1 or later.

The Java Programming Language

The Java programming language is a general-purpose, object-oriented programming language. As explained in more detail later in this chapter, object orientation is a way of constructing software systems such that programs are defined in terms of programmatic objects, which encapsulate some state information and generally are operated on by the invocation of methods that manipulate that state. Readers who are familiar with the C and C++ programming languages will find Java relatively easy to learn because Java is very strongly influenced by these languages, even down to many details of syntax.

Whether Java is a simple language, as its creators claim, is a fairly subjective question. Those used to creating entire applications using nothing but an Excel spreadsheet and a few canned libraries will not find Java simple, and Visual Basic programmers will have to endure some acclimation. Even some C programmers will have to jump into object-oriented programming in a hurry. Because Java goes to great lengths to eliminate common C and C++ features such as dangling pointers, explicit storage management, multiple inheritance, and operator overloading, many programmers find that Java can be a very productive development environment. As a language, Java immediately forces the programmer into an object-oriented frame of mind: It is difficult, not to mention counterproductive, to write a Java program that adheres to a procedural code-and-data paradigm.

Java places great emphasis on portability and platform independence. Its primitive datatypes are defined to have the same representation on all platforms, a feature that eases communication between disparate platforms. It does not allow the programmer to explicitly manipulate memory references. Although it is possible to access platform-specific native code and data from a Java program, the interface to that native information is well defined and tightly controlled. However, these features are not what gives Java programs their inherent cross-platform capabilities. To explore these capabilities, it is necessary to understand the Java Virtual Machine and the runtime environment.

The Java Virtual Machine

While the Java programming language is a language that can, in theory, be compiled into native machine instructions, the reference implementation of the Java compiler compiles Java programs into platform-independent bytecodes targeted for execution on the Java Virtual Machine (JVM). The JVM is a program implemented on top of whatever native facilities exist on the user's machine. For example, Sun provides implementations of the JVM for Solaris, Windows 95, Windows NT, and the Macintosh operating system.

The JVM is what gives Java its "compile once, run everywhere" capabilities. The idea of linking a programming language to a virtual machine is far from new. Smalltalk, for example, has been associated with a virtual machine implementation almost from its creation more than 20 years ago. One of the first structured languages available for personal computers, UCSD Pascal, was primarily executed using virtual machine technology. What makes the Java Virtual Machine approach interesting is that the Java environment has been constructed in such a way as to solve, or at least mitigate, some of the problems associated with previous virtual machine-based technologies.

First, Java does not require that compiled bytecodes be simultaneously and permanently loaded into a monolithic virtual machine image. Java compiles into relatively small class files, which are stored as regular files in the host operating environment, that are loaded into the virtual machine only at runtime. This approach, well suited to the load-on-demand predilections of the World Wide Web, also eliminates the coordination problems inherent in maintaining large images on multiprogrammer projects. It also means that huge image files don't have to be moved around, which is a great advantage when bandwidth is limited.

Second, Java Virtual Machines that contain Just-In-Time (JIT) native compiler technology are becoming available, and they promise to be available on most platforms. A JIT compiler compiles Java bytecodes into native machine instructions just before the code is run for the first time after being loaded into the virtual machine. This approach mitigates the relative slowness of virtual machine technology while maintaining Java bytecodes in permanent storage in their machine-independent format.

Finally, the JVM provides an innovative framework for solving some of the security problems that arise when programs of potentially unknown and untrusted origin are downloaded dynamically from the public Internet and executed on a personal computer or other intelligent device. The JVM acts as a sandbox in which Java programs may play to their potentially malicious heart's content, but outside of which the user's resources cannot be permanently affected. This aspect of Java's security model is explained in more detail in a later section, "Java Security Model."

Java APIs (Utility, Streams, AWT, Networking)

Implementations of the Java Virtual Machine typically are packaged with a set of standard classes, or libraries, that provide support to the language and to a graphical user interface (GUI)-oriented and networked runtime environment. These classes provide support for I/O streams; network socket programming; threads; GUI elements, such as buttons, scrollbars, windows, and user interface events; and low-level utility objects, such as dates and mathematical functions. The set of standard classes is expected to grow and change with each subsequent release of Java technology. This chapter describes only the bare minimum of the APIs that the examples in this book require. Accordingly, the File and file I/O classes will not be covered. Similarly, only small portions of the streams classes and AWT will be described.

Execution Environments: Applets and Applications

Programs intended to be run on a Java virtual machine are usually intended for particular execution environments. Because the JVM is relatively portable, new Java execution environments will probably continue to be developed. These environments may be traditional operating systems such as Unix or MS-DOS, or they may be "hosted" environments such as Web browsers or Web servers, or they may even be standalone or embedded environments. These execution environments differ not in the way Java programs operate, but in the kinds of facilities and resources that the program can access and, very importantly, in the level of access the program has to those facilities and resources.

As of this writing, the most important execution environments are traditional operating systems and Web browsers. Programs that run as standalone programs on an operating system—typically invoked from a command line—are called Java *applications*. These programs are relatively trusted in that they have to be installed through some explicit action by the user of the system or by an administrator, and they execute with the privilege level of the invoking user. Therefore, Java applications can use the file system, open network sockets, examine its environment, and invoke code written in other languages ("native methods").

A Java *applet*, however, is usually dramatically restricted in the facilities it may access. An applet is a Java program that is intended to be loaded and executed on a user's machine dynamically while browsing Web pages on the public Internet. Thus, there is absolutely no reason to trust such a remotely loaded program, and so the Web browser's Java virtual machine will typically enforce a very restrictive policy so that even a malicious, virus-carrying applet can do little or no damage to the local host. The particular security policies enforced are specific to the browser's implementation and configuration, but an applet typically cannot access files, open network sockets to machines other than the one from which its code was loaded, examine local environment variables, or invoke native code. The most notoriously restrictive browser implementation is Netscape's, which currently does not allow the user or administrator to configure security policies for applets at all; Microsoft's Internet Explorer and Sun's HotJava are considerably more flexible and allow for the designation of trusted sources for applets. Applets downloaded from trusted or authenticated sources may access some local resources. The support for digitally signed applets in JDK 1.1 will provide all Java virtual machine implementations with a basis on which to relax security restrictions selectively.

One very practical difference between an applet and an application is that they are started differently. Execution of a Java class as an application always begins with that class's `main()` method, while applet execution begins with the class's `init()` method.

Java Security Model

Java programs are likely to be executed in interorganizational networked environments where the level of trust between network participants varies dramatically. It is therefore important that security features be integrated into the Java execution environment from the ground up. As discussed previously, Java users may select various execution environments with differing security characteristics. However, all Java virtual machines have a number of security mechanisms through which they can protect their own integrity and also the integrity of and access to the resources of the host machine.

Computer system security is a multifaceted concept. As of Java 1.0, Java's built-in facilities have addressed only some of those aspects. Some security facilities, such as applet source authentication, will be added in future Java releases or by third-party virtual machine implementations. Some general security features will be left to third parties to provide. For example, Java provides no built-in security mechanisms to support the CORBA security specification or encryption. However, Java does provide a solid foundation for the construction of such facilities.

Java's security features are directed toward two primary areas: virtual machine integrity and resource access control. Java addresses these security areas through four separate components: the compiler, the bytecode verifier, the class loader, and the runtime security manager.

By eliminating such error-prone areas as pointer (memory reference) manipulation and the need for explicit deallocation of temporary storage, the Java compiler helps programmers avoid integrity-compromising mistakes. Further, Java's strict typing model allows the compiler to disallow some operations that would let users override security measures by exploiting the inherent flexibility of object-oriented inheritance. For example, Java provides a mechanism to disallow the subclassing of particular classes or the overriding of particular methods within a class.

Even though the standard Java compiler enforces many rules, there's no guarantee that a given set of Java virtual machine bytecodes was generated by the standard compiler. They could have been developed using some other language or even coded directly in JVM assembly language. They might have been corrupted in storage or transmission. They might maliciously attempt to violate the integrity of the virtual machine by overflowing the stack or performing some other illegal operation. Therefore, all Java virtual machines incorporate a bytecode verifier that analyzes classes after they are loaded and before initial execution. The verifier screens out bytecodes that might attempt to perform illegal operations in the JVM, such as undefined instructions, unmatched or incorrectly sized stack operations at the exit and entry to methods, illegal data conversions, or illegal field access attempts. Some of the checks performed by the verifier are redundant to those performed by the compiler. This redundancy is necessary because the virtual machine operates independently of the compiler.

The class loader's primary function is to find and load classes into the virtual machine, not to enforce security. However, it plays an important role in regulating access to the virtual machine. The class loader's responsibility to find Java classes means that it has to select, from a variety of potential sources, the best place to find the implementation of each class. Separate namespaces are maintained for classes that are loaded from different sources. For example, the default class loader will prefer sources local to the virtual machine's host over those that are remote, perhaps across a network, on the theory that the local classes were installed by someone whose interests are closely aligned with the user of the local host machine. The default class loader also prevents the spoofing of fundamental classes with replacement implementations that might affect the integrity of the virtual machine or might attempt to send private information back to the spoofer.

Finally, each Java virtual machine has a security manager. Its services are called routinely by standard Java classes to control access to various system and network resources. For example, the security manager checks each file open request and either allows or disallows the request based on criteria set by and relevant to the execution environment. For example, remotely loaded classes cannot access local files at all in Netscape Navigator 3.0.

Java's emphasis on security is unusual in a general-purpose programming environment. This emphasis makes sense when we consider that the public Internet will be a predominant environment for the deployment of Java programs. Also, by building in security-related features from the beginning, Java may find wide acceptance where other technologies, such as CORBA, have had difficulty because security has long been treated as an afterthought. It is also important to consider the effect of Java's security model on the kind of system architectures Java favors. Some of these implications will be illustrated by the example systems presented in this book.

For more information on Java security, see the Java Security White Paper at http://java.sun.com/security/whitepaper.ps or the Java specification books listed in the first section of this chapter (including *The Java Language Specification* Sections 12.2, 20.14, and 20.17). For an instructive account of some problems with the Java security model, see Gary McGraw and Edward W. Felton's *Java Security: Hostile Applets, Holes and Anecdotes* (New York: John Wiley & Sons, 1997).

Important Java Language Concepts

Let's go over the terminology and object model used by Java, even if object-oriented concepts are very familiar to you. Object models tend to use very similar terminology for concepts that differ significantly between models. Also, because Java's object model differs somewhat from CORBA's object model, you should have the definitions firmly in mind when reading the rest of this book.

Object Orientation in Java: Concepts and Terminology

Java is an *object-oriented* programming language and environment. Objects provide a very useful model for constructing computer programs. Object orientation leads to the grouping of conceptually related code and data, and it provides a mechanism for encapsulating information. Encapsulation encourages the building of systems that maintain their architectural integrity over time and over subsequent revisions.

In an object-oriented environment, the fundamental computational unit is an *object*. Each object may have a state that is local to it and that is often private. Every Java object is associated with a class. A *class* provides a place for defining things that are common to every object of the class. An object's state is accessed by, or manipulated through, executable logic called *methods.* The set of methods that may be used with reference to an object is not specific to the object itself; rather, every object in the same class uses the methods associated with that class, and only those methods. A class can be thought of as a template for an object because the set of data that each object will have, as well as its methods, is declared through the class's definition. Conceptually, this template is used whenever a new object is created.

When a new object is created according to the rules of a particular class, that object is said to be an *instance* of that class. The process of creating a new instance is sometimes called *instantiation.*

To provide for reuse of existing classes, object-oriented systems typically support *inheritance,* and Java is no exception. Inheritance allows the programmer to define a new class using another class, termed the *superclass, parent,* or *base* class. The newly defined class, called the *subclass, child,* or *derived* class, consists of all the data and methods (collectively, *members*) of the parent class plus whatever new members are defined by the new class. A class may also redefine some or all of its parent's methods so that the implementations of those methods are different when invoked on objects of the new class (but not when invoked on objects that are instances of the parent class). This redefinition is known as *overriding.* In Java, a class may have only a single parent for its implementation—multiple implementation inheritance is not supported. Java does, however, support the multiple inheritance of interfaces.

An *interface* is a named collection of method signatures and constants that can be used in Java as a type. Why do we need interfaces when we already have classes? Interfaces support the notion that the interface to an object, or rather to the set of services an object provides, can and often should be separable from the implementation of those services. Interfaces provide a direct and unambiguous mechanism to support delegation of function within an object-oriented design, and provide an alternative to implementation inheritance, which is often overused, as a fundamental building-block for object and class reuse.

Java also supports the notion of *packages.* A package is a way of segmenting the Java namespace into a hierarchy of dot-separated components. For example, all of the classes that are fundamental to the Java language are in the `java.lang` package. Setting up classes in packages makes it possible for programmers in different organizations to avoid name collisions without having to continually negotiate detailed agreements about naming conventions—everyone stays within their own part of the package namespace, and everything is fine. The convention that seems to be evolving is that providers of Java classes use package names that correspond to their organization's Internet domain (DNS) names. For example, programmers at XYZ Corporation, whose domain is xyz.com, would put their publicly available Java widgets in the `com.xyz` package. Packages have other effects on Java programs besides just segmenting the namespace: certain access control mechanisms recognize package scope as distinct from other kinds of scope. This will be explained in more detail later in this chapter.

Strong Typing

Java is a strongly typed language. This means that the Java environment expends a great deal of effort to ensure that the values stored in variables of a given type are compatible with that type. It also means that operations cannot be invoked on a value that is not allowed to use that operator. Most of these problems are checked for, and caught, at compile time, but some end up being detected by the runtime. Strong typing not only catches some errors relatively early in the development cycle, it also provides a foundation for maintaining the integrity of the environment.

Not all previous object-oriented systems have been strongly typed. Smalltalk, for example, is notorious for performing almost no type checking, except that it checks the types of primitive operations at runtime. Also, Java is much more strongly typed than its procedural language predecessors, C and C++. Java's strong typing can give it a flavor similar to Pascal, Modula-3, or CLU.

Portability

Java is intended, and to a great extent actually is, a "compile once, run everywhere" language. It is Java's wide portability and the platform independence of its bytecodes that will encourage its broad use. This is the feature that really appeals to corporate information managers trying to keep distribution, updating, and maintenance costs down. Most of the other features of the language and environment have an appeal that is primarily technical; wide portability makes Java interesting for business reasons as well. Many languages, notably C, have taken on portability as a goal, but Java makes portability almost its *raison d'être.* Java, the programming language, eliminates access to facilities that are machine- or platform-specific. Java's primitive types have rigidly defined lengths and byte ordering. The standard Java compiler emits not machine-specific object code, but bytecodes targeted to a virtual machine. It is expected that the virtual machine will be ported to all significant platforms (and indeed this is very close to true at this writing). The virtual machines implement a standard set of APIs in a machine-independent manner. The replication of this set of APIs across Java virtual machine implementations is enforced through Sun's licensing policies, so the likelihood of their presence is fairly high.

Java Language Overview

Even though the Java programming language is object oriented, it is not a pure object-oriented language. In a pure object-oriented language, everything is an object, and every program is formed solely by performing method invocations with respect to some receiver object. In Java, certain primitive data types exist that are not objects, and the basic syntactic constructs of the language are not tied to object semantics. In these ways, Java reflects its procedural C/C++ heritage. It differs from C++, however, in that it is not easy to write a program that does not use objects. A C++ programmer can go for years writing C-like code that does not exploit the object-oriented paradigm; a Java programmer is forced to structure all programs using object-oriented concepts.

Java Types

Java has two general kinds of data types: primitive types, such as simple numbers and characters, and object types.

Primitive Types and Literals

Java supports a number of primitive types that can be used in situations where using objects would be inefficient. Other than the primitive types discussed in this section, everything else in Java is an object of some kind. Each Java primitive type is defined to have identical size and byte-orders in all Java implementations, regardless of the underlying processor's natural type sizes. While these types generally map very naturally to the types defined by CORBA IDL, there are some minor differences that will be identified later in this book. For now, it is enough to be aware that the types described in this section are Java types and that the CORBA IDL types may be a little different.

Booleans

The `boolean` type consists of only two possible values: `true` and `false`. Java, unlike C and C++, does not use integers to indicate truth values. Note that these boolean literals are in lowercase, unlike the `TRUE` and `FALSE` macro definitions familiar to C and C++ programmers.

Whole Numbers

Java has an unsurprising set of types to represent whole numbers:

`byte`	8-bit signed two's complement integer
`short`	16-bit signed two's complement integer
`int`	32-bit signed two's complement integer
`long`	64-bit signed two's complement integer

These types are declared and initialized as follows:

```
byte b = 7;
short s = 6;
int i = 8;
long l = 9L;
```

Floating-Point Numbers

Java has two types of floating-point numbers:

`float`	32-bit IEEE 754-1985 floating-point number
`double`	64-bit IEEE 754-1985 floating-point number

They are declared as shown:

```
float f = 4.23f;
double d = 0.0;
```

Characters

Character values in Java are 16-bit Unicode 1.1.5 characters. Unicode is a relatively new character-encoding standard that attempts to include characters from most known languages and dialects. Java's use of Unicode for the character type differs from practically all other popular languages, which typically represent characters with eight bits. Adoption of the emerging Unicode standard is very forward-looking and should ease internationalization; however, it's something that is, for now, a bit unintuitive and warrants careful attention by the programmer. It is also worth noting that while the Java language fully supports Unicode characters, many if not all current virtual machine implementations do not do anything very useful with characters whose values exceed the range of values that can be represented in seven or eight bits.

Character literals are enclosed in single quotes and support the backslash escapes familiar to C and C++ programmers. For example:

```
char c = 'a'; // normal character
char n1 = '\n'; // escape sequence: newline character
```

Arrays

Arrays in Java are ordered collections of values of a particular type. The values are called elements of the array and are accessed by index. Arrays are actually objects (in fact, the superclass of any array is the Object class), and they can be treated as such in almost all situations. The number of elements an array contains—its length—is fixed at the time of the array's creation (for "arrays" whose length can vary at runtime, Java provides the Vector class). Arrays have a single named data member, called `length`, that a program can use to discover the length of the array. The first element of an array has index 0; the last element has index `length`-1.

Variables that hold references to arrays are declared with no length specified; the length of the array is declared in the array creation expression. This idiom is illustrated as follows:

```
int x[] = new int[3];
```

After execution of this statement, x contains a reference to a newly created array with three integer elements. Each of the elements is initialized to 0. Note that x does not contain the array itself; x holds only the reference to the array object.

Arrays can also be created using initializers:

```
double ratios[] = { 1.2, 4.7, 3.6 };
```

Arrays of arrays can also be created:

```
int matrix[][] = new int[3][3];
```

Strings

String is another specialized type of object for which the language provides special support. String literals are enclosed in double quotes, for example, "red". When the Java compiler sees a string literal, it automatically creates a new String object whose contents are the characters enclosed in quotes.

A String object is immutable; that is, once created, its contents cannot be modified. (Java provides the StringBuffer class to allow for modifiable, varying-length strings of characters). Note that a String is represented internally as a sequence of Java char values, which are 16-bit Unicode quantities. Strings are immutable primarily for performance reasons: Immutable objects never have to be locked when used by multithreaded programs.

Object Wrapper Types

Although Java's primitive types are not objects, there may be times when it is convenient to treat them as though they were. Therefore, Java's standard libraries provide a set of object wrapper classes, which allow a primitive value to be placed inside an object and then be manipulated as a first-class Java object. This approach is most useful when some other class or method has been written to manipulate generic objects. Using the wrapper classes eliminates the need for special code to handle each primitive type.

The wrapper classes are also a convenient locus for a variety of utility methods, such as type conversions, and useful constants. Each wrapper class has a name similar to its corresponding primitive, except that the first letter of the wrapper class is capitalized: For example, the wrapper class for long is Long. Some are slightly different: The wrapper class for int is Integer.

To create an object wrapper for a primitive value, create an instance of the wrapper class and pass the value as an argument to the wrapper's constructor:

```
Double piwrapper = new Double(3.14);
```

To extract the primitive value from the wrapper, use class's *type*Value() method:

```
double pi = piwrapper.doubleValue();
```

Language Syntax and Constructs

The syntax of the Java language is modeled closely after that of C and C++. The control constructs are very procedural in style.

Comments

Java provides three styles of comments:

```
// single line comments
```

```
/* multiple
    line
    comments
*/
```

```
/** documentation comments (to be processed by
    automatic documentation tools such as javadoc) **/
```

Identifiers

Java identifiers are used to name variables, labels, methods, and classes. An identifier must begin with a letter, an underscore (_), or a dollar sign ($) character. Subsequent characters may also be digits. Identifiers are case sensitive and have no maximum length. Remember that Java characters are Unicode characters; thus, identifiers need not be limited to ASCII characters.

Although not a formal part of the Java language, a set of conventions is in common use in the Java programming community. Variables, methods, and labels begin with lowercase letters and use capital letters at the beginning of each embedded word in the identifier, as in `endingPosition`. Class names begin with a single capital letter (`Pixel`), and the names of constants are rendered all in uppercase (`PI`).

Variable Declarations

Declarations define and sometimes cause the creation of a variable. A *variable* is a named piece of runtime storage. Declarations consist of optional modifiers, a type, a list of identifiers, and an optional initializer. Modifiers specify access, storage class, or some other attribute: For example, an identifier whose value is declared to be `final` cannot be changed after it is initialized, and an identifier declared to be `static` within the scope of a method retains its value after the method returns. An initializer specifies the initial value for the variable, which is preceded by an equal sign in the declaration.

An example of a variable declaration with an initializer is:

```
final int i = 12;
```

Declarations may appear at any point in a program's code: They need not, for example, appear only before executable statements within a method.

Operators

Java has a full complement of operators, most of which have equivalents in C and C++. To specify the operators completely would take many pages and would teach most readers of this book very little. Thus, in Table 2.1 we will simply list the operators and their precedence and note that all binary operators are left-associative except for assignment (=), which is right-associative.

Non-C programmers should note that Java's logical operators do not guarantee the evaluation of all arguments. instanceof is an operator peculiar to Java that returns true if the object reference in its left argument is an instance of the class specified by its right argument. >> is a signed right bit shift, and >>> is an unsigned right bit shift. == is the comparison operator for identity, while = is the assignment operator. It is common to confuse the two. + means addition when applied to numbers and concatenation when applied to Strings. The *op=* set of operators are binary operators that provide a shorthand for assignment and the operator when performed on a single variable; for example:

```
a += 1;
```

Table 2.1 Operator and Precedence Table

[] . (params) expr++ expr--

++expr --expr +expr -expr ~ !

new (type)expr

* / %

+ -

<< >> >>>

< > >= <= instanceof

== !=

&

^

|

&&

||

?:

= += -= *= /= %= >>= <<= >>>= &= ^= |=

is roughly equivalent to

```
a = a + 1;
```

Java expressions are evaluated left to right and have types that are determined by their component parts. The order of evaluation can be modified using parentheses.

Simple Control Statements

Java supports a variety of statements to allow the programmer to control the flow of execution within a program. The precise syntax of these will be very familiar to anyone who knows C or C++, and they won't be mysterious to anyone who is familiar with any procedural programming language.

if-else Statement Java's conditional statement is very conventional: The `if-else` statements allow different blocks of code to be executed depending on the value of a Boolean expression:

```
if (boolean-expression) {
    // statement block 1;
}
else {
    // statement block 2;
}
```

switch Statement The `switch` statement allows the selection of which block of code to execute based on the value of an expression, which is matched against the value of a constant expression in each case clause:

```
switch (expression) {
    case constexp1:
        // statement block 1;
        break;
    case constexp2:
        // statement block 2;
        break;
    case constexp3:
    case constexp4:
        // statement block 3;
        break;
    default:
        // statement block;
        break;
}
```

The break statement at the end of each statement block keeps execution from falling through each case clause into the next statement block. By making the statement block null, two or more case clauses can be used to enter into a given block, as illustrated by constexp3 and constexp4, in the preceding code. The default: block is executed when none of the case expressions matches the initial expression of the switch. Execution resumes with the statement following the entire switch construct after a break statement is encountered.

Loops

Java has a conventional set of looping constructs: while, do-while, and for.

while Loops The while loop construct executes a block of statements repeatedly until the loop's Boolean expression evaluates to false.

The statement

```
int i = 0;
while(i < 4) {
    System.out.println("Hello world!");
    i = i + 1;
}
```

will cause

```
Hello world!
Hello world!
Hello world!
Hello world!
```

to be printed on the Java process's standard output.

do-while Loops A do-while loop is similar to a while loop, except that the loop termination test is performed after the body has executed, rather than before. Therefore, a do-while loop is guaranteed to execute its body at least once.

```
int i = 0;
do {
    System.out.println("Hello world!");
    i = i + 1;
} while (i < 4)
```

will also print Hello world! four times.

for Loops The basic `for` loop follows C conventions:

```
for (initialization-expr; test-expr; increment-expr) {
    // statements;
```

is roughly equivalent to

```
initialization-expr;
while (test-expr) {
    // statements;
    increment-expr;
}
```

except that (1) the increment-expression is always executed if a `continue` occurs within the statements and (2) the fine points of variable scoping for variables declared within the loop's own expressions differ slightly.

Other Flow Control

Java has a few other flow control constructs, which should be familiar to C and C++ programmers:

Labels Any statement may be preceded with a label:

```
stuff:    i = 7;
```

Labels are used as targets for the `break` and `continue` statements.

break Statements A `break` statement transfers control out of an enclosing statement.

If the `break` statement does not specify a label, then the break terminates the innermost enclosing `switch`, `while`, `do-while`, or `for` statement.

If the `break` statement specifies a label, then control is transferred to the enclosing statement with that label. The labeled statement need not be a `switch` statement or a loop construct; `break` will terminate any block.

As an example,

```
public class breakTest {
    public static void main(String args) {
        int a[] = { 6, 3, 0, 2, -4, 9, 1 };
        for (int i = 0; i < a.length; i++) {
            if (a[i] < 0) {
```

```
                    System.out.println("Negative.");
                    break;
              }
            System.out.println("a[" + i + "] is " + a[i]);
            }
        }
    }
```

prints out:

```
a[0] is 6
a[1] is 3
a[2] is 0
a[3] is 2
Negative.
```

continue Statements The continue statement skips to the end of an enclosing for, while, or do-while loop's body. The continue statement can specify a label, which will cause a breakout of any loops inside the loop with the specified label on the way to skipping the rest of the labeled loop's body. A continue statement without a label refers to the innermost enclosing loop.

For example,

```
int a[] = { 4, 2, 3, -5, 6 };
int total;
for (int i = 0; i < a.length; i++) {
    if (a[i] > 0) {
        total += a[i];
    } else {
        continue;
    }
}
```

return Statements The return statement causes the execution of a method to halt and return to its caller. If the method returns no value, then the return statement must specify no return value:

```
return;
```

If the method requires a value to be returned, the return statement must contain an expression that is assignable to a variable of the declared return type of the method:

```
int ex() {
        int x = 2;
```

```
        return x + 3;
    }
```

Objects and Classes

Java is a language of objects and classes. Objects have private state, and this state is where a program's data resides. Methods operate on the objects and can modify their state. Methods are defined inside class definitions, as are data declarations. In fact, everything in Java is declared inside a class. A class is really a template for objects, and it defines the way the objects are structured.

Members

A class definition contains members. These members can be either executable statements or data. Code members are called *methods*; data members are called *fields*. The members can refer either to the objects created from the class or to the class itself. Data members for which there is only one instance shared among all the instances of a class are called *static fields* or *class variables*; other data members have a separate and unique instance of the member for each object.

Here is a simple class definition:

```
class Car {
    String color;
    int vehicleId;
    Engine engine;
    static int nextVehicleId = 0;

    public start() {
        engine.start();
    }

    public static getNextVehicleId() {
        return nextVehicleId;
    }
};
```

The name of this class is Car. References to instances of the Car class are assignable to variables of type Car. A variable that contains a reference to a Car object would look like this:

```
Car myMother;
```

Note that declaring this variable does not create a new Car object. It merely allocates storage to hold a reference to an object.

Fields

Fields are the data variables that are associated with a class and with the instances of that class. The `Car` class just shown has four fields declared: `color`, `vehicleId`, `engine`, and `nextVehicleId`. The first three fields are instance fields: Each instance of the `Car` class has a separate copy of the field. The `nextVehicleId` field is a static field: Only a single copy of this field exists and is not associated with any particular instance, although it can be accessed using a reference to any instance. Some people find it helpful to think of static fields as being akin to class-level variables.

Methods

Methods contain code that has access to and manipulates the internal state of an object. Methods perform the role usually handled by functions or procedures in nonobject-oriented languages. Java has no free-standing procedures: Every method is associated with some class. Methods, like fields, can be either static or nonstatic. A method must be invoked as an operation on some object reference and cannot be invoked in isolation—even the main method refers to some top-level class. Nonstatic methods generally have access to the fields of the object against which it is invoked; however, a static method does not. A static method has access only to the static data members of the class. As a result, a static method need not be invoked only with respect to an instance of a class—it can be invoked against a reference to the class itself. There are also special methods called *constructors* that are used when new objects are created. Constructors are explained in detail in the *Creating New Objects* section later in the chapter.

In the sample `Car` class, there are two methods. `start()` is a nonstatic, or instance, method. Because starting a car is usually a simple matter of starting the car's engine, it simply invokes the `start()` method of the `Engine` class with respect to the object referenced by the `engine` field of the invoking object. To invoke the `Car start()` method, the following statement would be used:

```
myMother.start();
```

The . (dot) operator is used for method invocation.

Parameters and Arguments

Java methods, like functions and procedures in other languages, can declare *parameters* so that the method may perform operations using a range of input values.

The particular values passed to the method at runtime are called *arguments,* and these become assigned to the method parameters and are referenced as such during the execution of the method.

Suppose the `Car` class declared this method:

```
class Car {
    . . . .
    public accelerate(int acceleration) {
        for (int i = 0; i < acceleration; i++)
            engine.rev();
    }
}
```

and the main method of the program contained

```
myMother.accelerate(4);
```

In this example, `acceleration` is an int parameter to the `accelerate()` method, and 4 is the argument to that particular invocation of the `acceler-ate()` method. The value of the `acceleration` parameter would be 4 throughout the execution of `accelerate()`.

Static Members

A field may be declared with the `static` modifier to tell the compiler that the field will not be an instance field, but will instead be affiliated with the class as a whole. For data members, this means that all instances in the class share a single copy of the field. For methods, a static method is one that need not be invoked on an instance but can be invoked directly on the class itself. Static methods, therefore, may not access any instance variables because no instance is guaranteed to have been instantiated prior to invocation. Static members are useful for manipulating data that is "global" to the class; for example, a static `instanceCount` field could be incremented by the constructor and thus would hold a count of all the instances created by the class, and a static `getInstanceCount` method would return the count to the caller. A static method is useful not only for referencing static members, but also for providing functionality that isn't specific to any instance.

Object References and null

An *object reference* is the final fundamental type in the Java language. All variables whose types are not primitive contain object references. An object reference is not the object itself, but, as the name implies, it is merely a reference to an object. The analogous concept from the C language would be a pointer. Another analogy could be made to the concept of a handle in operating environments such as Microsoft Windows.

This is perhaps an appropriate point to debunk one of the myths surrounding Java. Java's proponents often claim that Java has no pointers, and this claim can cause the uninitiated to wonder how Java is able to do anything complicated with any efficiency at all. The truth is that Java does have "pointers"—these pointers are object references. What Java does not have is the ability to perform arithmetic on these pointers. Pointer arithmetic was always an artifact of particular hardware platforms' memory architecture, and it has no place in a language that aspires to be portable.

All object references, save one, are references to objects that are instances of a particular class. That single exception is the object reference null. null is a reference to nothing, and as such it can legally be used in any situation that calls for an object reference to any type of object at all.

this and super

During the execution of any instance method, two fields are implicitly defined and assigned a value. The this field always contains a reference to the object on which the method was invoked. this is useful to have around, usually either to pass as an argument to a method that might require it or to distinguish between fields and parameters that may have the same name:

```
class Car {
    private Color color;
    public setColor(Color color) {
        this.color = color;
        PaintGun.paint(this, color);
    }
}
```

The super reference also refers to the current instance (this) but refers to it as if its type were that of the superclass of the instant object's class. That's quite a mouthful, but it becomes simpler when we consider how it is used. Usually, the super reference is used to invoke a method as defined in the superclass, as opposed to that method's definition in the object's own class. Often, super is used when overriding a method and extending its functionality:

```
class Car extends Vehicle{
    public paint(Color color) {
```

```
super.paint(color);
engine.paint(color);

    }
  }
```

In this way, it's certain that the `paint()` method of the `Vehicle` class is invoked as part of the `Car` class's `paint()` method. If `Car`'s `paint()` method were invoked instead, it would result in an infinite recursion.

Creating New Objects

Java objects are most commonly created using the `new` operator. For example, this statement creates a new instance of the class `Car`:

```
Car c = new Car("blue");
```

The left-hand side of the assignment declares a variable `c`, which is to contain a reference to an object that is an instance of class `Car`. This declaration does not itself create the new object: The variable `c` holds only an object reference, which is initially `null` prior to assignment. An object reference can be thought of as a pointer to an object and is distinct from the object itself.

It is the right-hand side of the statement that actually creates and initializes the object. The `new` operator allocates sufficient memory from an area of storage in the Java Virtual Machine called the *Java heap* to contain all the instance data members and any other storage associated with the instance. Every use of `new` to create an object must be followed by a *constructor* invocation in the same expression. A constructor is a specialized method whose job is to initialize the fields of the new object using the parameters specified when the constructor was invoked. The name of a constructor method is always identical to the class's name.

```
public class Car extends Vehicle {
private String color;
public Car(String clr) {
    color = clr;
}
}
```

When an object is created, its data fields are initialized to either `null` for object references or to the zero value appropriate for the type of the field for primitive types. (`boolean` types are initialized to `false`.) The body of the constructor is then entered. The first thing the constructor does is implicitly or explicitly call a constructor for its superclass (unless the object's class is `Object`, which has no superclass). If the superclass constructor's invocation is implicit, then the constructor invoked is the superclass's default, or zero-argument, constructor.

After the superclass constructor has finished, the constructor processes any initializers that the class may have defined for its fields. Then the statements in the constructor's body are executed. Finally, when the initialization is complete, a reference to the newly created object is returned. Note that even though the constructor looks like a method, no return type is explicitly declared for it—the name of the constructor itself indicates the class of the object returned.

Just like other methods, Java constructors may be overloaded. It is common for a class to have a set of constructors that allow the programmer to specify initial values for various data members and that allow the programmer to accept default values for parameters that have not been explicitly specified.

Every class has at least one constructor—the zero-argument, or default, constructor. If the class does not contain a definition for any constructors, the Java compiler will create a default constructor for the class implicitly.

Every class has two more implicitly defined constructors at its disposal: `this()` and `super()`. The `this()` constructor is simply a convenience, a way to invoke the constructor of the class from within any constructor of that class without referring to the class by name. The `super()` constructor invokes the superclass's constructor. It is often used when the superclass performs some field initialization that the subclass wants to perform and is a convenient shorthand.

Getting Rid of Objects: Garbage Collection and Finalization

Java frees storage by using garbage collection. This means that the programmer need not, and cannot, explicitly free storage allocated to an object that is no longer in use. The Java Virtual Machine contains a garbage collection mechanism that will automatically reclaim an object's storage sometime after the program no longer holds any references to the object. Garbage collection frees the programmer from the chore of explicitly tracking objects and freeing them, eliminating common programming errors that often cause memory leaks in production systems. This freedom comes at the cost of some overhead imposed by the garbage collection mechanism and, depending on the garbage collector's implementation, some unpredictability in the execution time of Java programs because the garbage collector may run at any time to reclaim storage. Also, the Java specifications do not detail the garbage-collection algorithm. This is left to the implementors of each virtual machine.

Another popular myth about Java is that the existence of garbage collection frees the programming from ever having to worry about memory management. Adherence to this myth by treating memory as if it were infinite and free can cause pretty serious performance problems. Garbage collection merely frees the programmer from having to explicitly deallocate memory once it is used. The programmer of all but trivial Java programs must thoughtfully and intelligently consider the use of memory and should strive to keep object creation to a minimum to keep Java performance crisp for the user and reliable for the system as a whole.

Sometimes it may be appropriate for an object to do some cleanup processing before relinquishing its storage. To allow for this, Java classes may declare the instance method `protected void finalize()`, which is guaranteed to be invoked prior to the destruction of the object by the garbage collector. Note, however, that Java does not guarantee when or if the garbage collector will ever actually reclaim any particular object. Therefore, the finalization mechanism should not be relied on to return resources to the system at any time prior to the virtual machine's termination.

Access Specifiers

All members of a class are declared using one of the following four access specifiers, which control access to the member from other classes and inheritance by subclasses.

The following definitions are from *The Java Programming Language* by Ken Arnold and James Gosling (Reading, MA: Addison-Wesley, 1996, p. 31).

public Members declared public are accessible anywhere the class is accessible, and they are inherited by subclasses.

private Members declared private are accessible only from within the class itself.

protected Members declared protected are accessible to and inherited by subclasses, and they are accessible by code in the same package.

<none> Members declared with no access modifier are accessible only to code and inherited only by subclasses in the same package. This is often referred to as *package* scope.

Exceptions

Exceptions are a mechanism for handling exceptional conditions that occur apart from the normal flow of control of a program. These may be errors or simply unusual conditions. When an exception occurs, it is thrown to a block of code called an *exception handler*, which catches the exception. Once the handler has finished executing, the program continues. The existence of the exception mechanism eliminates the need for methods to return out-of-band error values and eliminates the need to check for these codes in the main line of a program's logic, which can simplify the structure of the program.

Java has a well-defined exception-handling mechanism. Exceptions, like most things in Java, are objects. Each type of exception has a class of its own, which is derived from the `java.lang.Exception` class. Individual occurrences of exceptions are instances. To cause an exception to occur, the program creates a new instance using the `new` operator and throws the exception using the `throw` statement. The `try-catch` statement handles exceptions. Each execution environment has a predefined default exception handler, which typically causes the program that threw the exception to print the exception and a stack trace and then terminate.

Catching Exceptions

Here is the simplest form of the `try-catch` statement:

```
try {
    // code that might throw an exception
} catch (exceptionType e) {
    // code to handle exceptionType (or subclass)
    // exceptions
}
```

If a statement within the `try` block throws an exception, Java skips the remainder of the statements in the `try` block and looks for a `catch` clause that will handle the type of the exception that occurred. If there is no handler for that type within the enclosing `try-catch` statement, the method terminates and returns to its caller, then searches the methods in the method call stack for a handler for the exception.

A try-catch statement may have multiple catch clauses. Each catch's exception type is tested against the current exception in the order in which the catch clauses textually appear in the method. The first clause that matches against the exception's class (either an identical match or a superclass) will handle the exception. This implies that general exception handlers should appear in the last catch clause, or else the more specific clauses will never be invoked.

A try-catch statement can have a finally clause, which must be the last clause of the try-catch statement. The finally clause is guaranteed to execute, no matter what path is taken through the try-catch statement itself.

A Java user can create his or her own exception types by subclassing either Exception itself or some other existing exception. Such user-defined exceptions are treated just like the predefined exceptions.

The Exception class has two very useful debugging methods: toString() and printStackTrace().

Threads and Synchronization

Java is a general-purpose programming language, but it will often be used as a platform for interactive, distributed network applications. In this environment, it is natural and effective to use multiple threads of execution to solve the types of problems that commonly arise. Programs often use one thread to handle user-input event processing, one to handle each network interface that might pend for indefinite times, one to render each complex graphic, and one for each lengthy computation that the user might initiate. The Java Virtual Machine itself typically uses about a half dozen threads to perform various tasks. Java programmers get used to thinking of their programs as collections of relatively simple but autonomous threads that cooperate, rather than as the kind of monolithic, single-threaded programs that have dominated much of programming practice in the past. Other languages and programming environments support multithreaded programming, but Java's direct support of threads within the language makes concurrent programming as easy as it can be.

Threads are the primary way Java supports concurrent programming. Java programs use threads frequently. Threads should not be confused with processes. Java processes are really an abstraction to help deal with other programs that run outside of the Java Virtual Machine. A process has its own copy of the data it uses, but a thread typically must coordinate access to a single set of data with other threads in the same process. Threads typically consume far fewer resources than processes because the creation of a thread does not imply the copying of a lot of data—the only data specific to each thread is the execution state of the thread and some other housekeeping information. The execution state storage is used to keep track of the state of the virtual machine registers and program counter while the thread is suspended and some other thread is currently executing.

It is useful to remember that each new Java program that executes in a virtual machine executes in its own thread. That thread was created immediately prior to the execution of the program's main routine, or during applet initialization.

Java has two other classes closely associated with the management of threads. `ThreadGroups` provide a mechanism for managing related threads and for classifying threads separately for security purposes. `ThreadDeath` provides a way for threads to have very fine control over their own extinction; a `ThreadDeath` is a `Throwable` object similar to an exception. The details of these two classes and their uses are beyond the scope of this book.

Thread Basics

A *thread* is a single sequential flow of control. Threads enable, or give the appearance of enabling, multiple, concurrent flows of control within the Java Virtual Machine. The management of Java threads is to a large degree left to facilities provided by the virtual machine and the Java runtime environment. The Java programmer usually has only to create the thread, specify its tasks, start it up, and let it run.

Things are a bit more complicated than that in practice. The programmer must also provide for the orderly termination of the thread, take care to properly set the runtime priority of the thread, and ensure that each thread does not hog the processor. It is easy to write a Java thread that allows other running threads to become starved for processor time; a well-behaved thread yields the processor periodically to ensure that other threads get an opportunity to run. The thread will yield the processor automatically when it pends waiting for a resource or I/O; threads that are computation-intensive should explicitly yield the processor using the `yield()` method after some fairly short amount of time (not more than 100 milliseconds or so) or else run at a very low priority.

Communication and synchronization between threads are accomplished using the `synchronized` keyword and the Java monitor facility provided through the `wait()` and `notify()` methods of the Object class, described later in this chapter.

Creating Threads

There are two ways to create threads: by subclassing or by specifying an object whose class implements the Runnable interface as the target argument to a Thread constructor. Selecting the appropriate method depends on the design of the other classes in the Java environment or the programmer's preference; further, it is possible to mix both styles within the same program.

The Thread that creates a new thread is referred to as the new thread's parent. A thread can have a name that can be specified to the constructor or set later with the setName() method. The primary use for the name is to allow a debugger or other Java development tool to print it out.

By default, a newly created thread belongs to the same ThreadGroup as its parent. Subject to Java security restrictions, however, the programmer can specify to which ThreadGroup the thread will belong.

Creating a Thread by Subclassing To create a Thread using subclassing, the new class must extend the Thread class or a subclass of Thread. For the thread to actually do anything, the subclass must override the run() method. The run() method is the "main" routine of the thread and contains the top-level code that is to be executed by the thread. Because the default run() method has a null body, if run() is not overridden, the thread will still be created, but it won't do much.

Next, create an instance of the new class and call the start() method using the newly created instance. For example:

```java
public class MyThread extends Thread {

        public MyThread() {
            // initialization code goes here
        }

        public void run() {
            // thread body goes here
        }

        // program startup
        public static void main(String args[]) {
            MyThread mt = new MyThread();
            mt.start();
        }
    }
```

In this example, the `start()` method returns immediately to the next statement within `main()`. By the time `start()` exits, however, a new thread of execution has been created and made known to the scheduler. When the new thread has an opportunity to execute, it will begin with the first statement in the `run()` method and proceed from there. Even though, in this example, there is nothing more for `main()` to do after calling `start()`, the virtual machine won't exit until the `mt` thread has stopped.

Creating a Thread with the Runnable Interface The Java `Thread` class (`java.lang.Thread`) implements the `Runnable` interface.

To start a thread using a `Runnable` object instead of a `Thread` subclass, use the following paradigm:

```
public class Stuff extends . . . implements Runnable {
    public void run()
    {
        // thread body goes here
    }

    public void static main(String args[]) {
        Stuff stf = new Stuff();
        new Thread(stf).start();

        // rest of main method code goes here, if any
    }
}
```

Stopping Threads

Threads can be stopped five different ways: by calling the thread's `stop()` method; by returning from the thread's `run()` method; if the thread is a daemon thread, then by stopping all nondaemon threads in the virtual machine; by throwing a `ThreadDeath` object; or by shutting down the Java Virtual Machine.

Thread Priorities

Each thread has a runtime priority level. The virtual machine's thread scheduler uses the priorities to help it determine when each thread will get a chance to execute. For user-created threads in the Java Virtual Machines currently available, priorities range from `Thread.MIN_PRIORITY` (typically 1) to `Thread.MAX_PRIORITY` (typically 10). If no other action is taken by the programmer, new threads are created with their priority set equal to the priority of the parent thread. A higher priority number means that a thread will be given preference over threads with lower priority levels. Thread priorities in Java are not strict: While threads with higher priorities are generally executed in preference to threads with lower priorities, there is no guarantee that the highest priority runnable thread will always be executing.

Daemon Threads

Each thread has a property that declares whether it is a daemon thread. The only difference between daemon threads and nondaemon threads is that the virtual machine will exit when only daemon threads are left running. Daemon threads perform housekeeping for the virtual machine, such as garbage collection, finalization, screen updates, and input processing. The initial setting of a newly created thread's daemon property is set equal to that of its parent thread.

Synchronization

Java uses the `wait()` and `notify()` methods of the Object class to provide locking and synchronization semantics similar to C.A.R. Hoare's monitor abstraction. The basic idea is that each object has a lock and a set of waiting threads associated with it. It is important to realize that this is an unordered set, not an ordered queue. Methods and code blocks may be designated *synchronized* via a Java language keyword. Synchronized code acquires a lock before beginning execution and releases the lock at its end. A synchronized method attempts to acquire the lock of the method's receiver object; a synchronized code block specifics the object to lock as a parameter to the block. If the object is already locked, the thread that is attempting to execute the synchronized code becomes a member of the object's wait set. Once the lock is released, one of the waiting threads is given a chance to try to acquire the lock.

   `notify()` and `wait()` are intended to be executed only by threads that actually have locked the object prior to executing those methods. Inside a synchronized code block, a thread may call `wait()`, which releases the lock and adds itself to the object's wait set. Another thread may invoke `notify()` to yield the processor and to wake up exactly one thread that has been waiting on that object, or it may use `notifyAll()` to wake up all the threads currently in the object's wait set. Note that Java does not specify which thread in the wait set gets awakened by `notify()`.

   `notify()` will take one thread that is waiting in the object's wait set and make it runnable by placing it on the scheduler's runnable thread queue. At this point, the notifying thread still has the object locked. It's up to the notifying thread to release the lock, which it does by exiting from the synchronized code block it was in when it called `notify()`. The thread that was just awakened is not given the lock automatically: It has to compete for it and obtain it in order to continue. Once it has obtained the lock, the thread will return from `wait()` and continue execution.

The discussion of threads in this chapter has been greatly simplified from the threading model detailed by the Java language specification. That specification provides for Java implementations that might distribute each thread to separate processors, a situation that violates the assumption that each thread shares the same copy of a process's data. The specification, however, makes it so that it appears to the programmer that all threads are running in a single address space on a single processor; thus, the presentation in this chapter is sufficient to give a conceptual background for the rest of this book. For more details on Java's threading, refer to Chapter 17 of *The Java Language Specification* by James Gosling, Bill Joy, and Guy Steele (Reading, MA: Addison-Wesley, 1996).

The Abstract Window Toolkit

Java's Abstract Window Toolkit (AWT) is a set of classes coupled with a platform-specific runtime implementation that provides a platform-independent way to interact with a user via a graphical user interface. Although many of the facilities of the AWT are familiar to anyone who has programmed a GUI, the AWT takes a decidedly least-common-denominator approach. AWT provides only a minimal set of user interface widgets, such as buttons and scrollbars, but it is designed to be extensible in Java.

AWT has one uncommon feature: layout managers. Because screen real estate between platforms and machines is unpredictable and varies widely, it isn't practical to assume that a display can access a screen area of a certain size. Rather, the layout manager mechanism provides a way for a GUI to specify the location and size of its widgets only in terms of its desired relationship to other widgets and allows the local platform to determine the final layout for the user at runtime.

The AWT also provides facilities for handling keyboard and pointing device input, and it provides a simple two-dimensional drawing package for graphical applications. Much of the AWT is designed to optimize its behavior in the situation, very common on the Internet, where large graphical images are being loaded across a relatively slow communications channel.

Java includes the `applet` class, which provides an interface to the runtime facilities for programs that run as part of Web pages within Web browsers.

The AWT is the part of Java that changed most between JDK 1.0.2 and JDK 1.1. In particular, the processing of user interface events is quite different. This chapter presents a subset of AWT common to both JDK 1.0.2 and JDK 1.1 AWT, and we've left out many of the details because they would require another book, or at least another chapter. The sample code presented later in this book conforms to the JDK 1.1 API specification. We apologize in advance if we've left in any JDK 1.0.2 methods that have been depreciated. For more current information on the state of AWT and the JDK, see www.javasoft.com.

This section gives only the barest conceptual overview of the AWT. For further information, refer to one of the books listed at the beginning of this chapter.

Components and Containers

Components are the fundamental building blocks of AWT screen displays. A *Component* can be thought of, from the programmer's perspective, as an area of the screen that knows how to draw itself and that can process input events that occur within the area of the screen that it controls. The Component class is an abstract class; that is, objects of the `Component` class can't be instantiated directly. Particular subclasses of `Component`, such as `Frame` or `Button`, can be instantiated and can inherit all the members and semantics of the abstract Component class.

Containers are components that can contain other components. Containers have a layout manager associated with them, and they know how to communicate with the layout manager to determine and control how any contained objects will be positioned and sized when drawn inside the container. Containers are also useful for grouping components within other Containers. The `Container` class is also an `abstract` class.

`Container` has two important methods: `setLayout()` and `add()`. `setLayout()` simply sets the layout manager for the container. Containers have default layout managers, so there's no need to call `setLayout()` if you're happy with what the Java runtime provides. `add()` adds a component to the container at the logical end of the `Container`. `add()` also allows a `String` name to be associated with the component; the name is used by some layout managers to help figure out where the component will be positioned.

Events

AWT `Component`s can receive events from the Java runtime. The runtime typically generates events in response to some action by the user, usually a mouse movement, mouse button click, or keyboard event. The `Component` that receives the event can either process the event itself with an event-handler method, or it can choose to ignore it, in which case the event will be presented to the component's container (sometimes called the component's *parent*). Events that aren't explicitly handled by any component are quietly absorbed by the runtime.

Simple Components

AWT provides a number of simple components that are the building blocks for most kinds of user interaction with a Java program. We don't have the space here to go into detail, so here's a quick list of the components you'll see used in the sample programs in this book:

- *Button.* A button for the user to press. The button can have a label, and an action event for that button is sent to the program whenever the button is pressed.

- *Label.* Displays a string at a location.

- *List.* Scrollable list of `String`s. One or more of the `List`'s strings can be selected, and the program can be notified with an action event.

- *TextArea.* An editable multiple-line area of text. An action event is generated when the user indicates that editing is finished, usually by pressing the Return key.

- *TextField.* A single-line text area.

Panels

`Panel`s are concrete `Container`s; that is, instances of `Panel` can be created. A `Panel` occupies a certain amount of screen real estate and can contain other `Component`s, including other `Panel`s. GUIs are typically created by nesting `Panel`s; the subpanels identify distinct areas of the screen. For example, an applet (which is itself a `Panel`) may have two subpanels: one for a data display area, such as a List, and another for a row of buttons.

Nested subpanels often have their own layout managers. The combination of `Panel`s and `LayoutManager`s provides enough flexibility to create arbitrarily complex GUI screens.

Applets

An `Applet` is a `Panel` that is associated with some runtime context. Typically, this means that their display area is embedded inline in a Web page. Because they are so often embedded in Web browsers, `Applet` has an API that allows the browser to control applets as the user navigates the Web.

Four `Applet` methods are collectively called the life-cycle methods. These methods are called by the browser at various times in the life cycle of the applet. `init()` is called only once, soon after the applet is loaded into the Java virtual machine, and is useful for doing off-screen initialization. `start()` is called each time the browser enters the applet's page. This is often a good place to start any threads the applet might create. `stop()` is called whenever the browser leaves the applet's page and is a good place to stop threads created by the applet. `destroy()` is called when it is time for the applet to release its resources prior to being removed from the virtual machine.

Applets can do other things, such as get parameters defined in the HTML tag that caused their invocation or load images or sound clips to be used during their execution.

Applets begin execution in a new thread, created just for the applet.

Applets are usually associated with a Web page via the APPLET HTML tag. The APPLET tag has three required attributes: CODE gives the name of the Applet's .class file; HEIGHT and WIDTH define the initial screen area allocated to the applet within the Web page. The APPLET tag can have PARAM tags embedded within it to supply parameters to the applet so that the applet can modify its behavior at runtime. PARAM tags have NAME and VALUE attributes. Here's a sample bit of HTML that shows how to make a Web page that shows the Hello applet:

```
<APPLET CODE="Hello.class" HEIGHT=100 WIDTH=120>
<PARAM NAME=Color VALUE=blue>
</APPLET>
```

Streams

Java supports streams through the `java.io` package. A *stream* is an ordered sequence of data elements that has a source or a destination. Streams are usually used to perform input or output to or from a data program.

Java's stream classes are numerous and varied, and they provide powerful and flexible functionality to the programmer. Streams can be chained and can have files associated with them. Streams can be used to transmit any Java primitive type, and they can be buffered to enhance performance in some situations. Streams can be associated with a variety of input and output sources, such as files, pipes, or byte arrays.

A full description of Java's stream and input/output facilities would be lengthy and, ultimately, unnecessary for this book. The Java programs presented here use only a very small subset of the stream class's functionality directly: logging error messages to the user's console. Therefore, this chapter will present only enough information about streams to enable you to understand the logging code.

All Java streams are instances of subclasses of either the abstract `InputStream` or `OutputStream` classes. `OutputStream` has three methods that are interesting for the purposes of this book: `write()`, `close()`, and `flush()`. The `write()` method has three overloaded forms, but its essential purpose is to place its argument byte or bytes on the stream. When a byte is written to an instance of some subclass of `OutputStream`, it is ultimately transferred to the destination to which the stream is connected.

Filter Streams

A `FilterOutputStream` is an abstract subclass of `OutputStream` that filters bytes as they are written to the stream. It is easy to build chains of streams using filter streams that can arbitrarily transform the input stream.

PrintStreams

A `PrintStream` is a `FilterOutputStream` that supports methods to output most Java primitive types in a character format that is intended to be readable by humans. In addition, `PrintStream` has a number of `println()` methods, one for each primitive type, that output a line terminator to the stream after the representation of the argument is output to the stream. A `PrintStream` can also be set on creation to flush the stream automatically after every newline or after being asked to output a byte array.

A Brief Detour into the System Class

The `java.lang` package contains the `System` class. `System` provides a locus for `static` items that represent the state of the current runtime environment.

System has three static member variables of interest here: in, out, and err, which are by default connected to the standard input, output, and error streams, respectively, of the Java Virtual Machine's process. The destination for out and err will depend on the particular runtime even though their purpose remains constant—these are places for Java programs to write simple text messages, usually for debugging purposes. For a standalone Java virtual machine, out and err are often connected to the user's screen or terminal. For a virtual machine embedded in a Web browser, out and err are often connected to a Java Console window.

For example, to send a text message to somewhere the user has a chance of seeing it, use the following line:

```
System.err.println("Help me, I'm sinking!");
```

This is simply an invocation of the println() method on the standard error stream. This mechanism, coupled with Java's automatic string conversion semantics for the + operator, makes it easy to generate useful debugging output.

That's it. That's all you need to know about streams to use this book.

Chapter Summary

We've presented quite a lot of the Java programming language in this chapter. Because this isn't really a book on Java programming, we won't be presenting many extensive example Java programs that don't use Java IDL. If you are new to Java and want to get a taste of the language itself before moving on to CORBA and Java IDL, take a look at Chapter 6, "A Basic Java IDL Applet and Server." The first section of that chapter presents a pure Java applet that will help you tie together most of the pieces of the Java language presented in this chapter.

Java is a rich language that can be used for general-purpose programming in a platform-independent manner. Its "compile once, run everywhere" properties and its object orientation not only make it an excellent choice for applications that run on the Internet, but also make it almost ideally suitable as an implementation language for CORBA objects and as a language from which CORBA can be easily and naturally accessed.

Introduction to CORBA

The Common Object Request Broker Architecture (CORBA) is a vendor-independent standard for integrating and unifying distributed, object-based systems. CORBA is just one piece of an overall object architecture, but it is perhaps the most important piece. As the communications core of the system, it is the foundation on which the entire infrastructure rests.

This chapter is an introduction to the various components of CORBA. It gives a brief description of the parts that work together to make up an Object Request Broker as well as the standard CORBAServices. It is not a detailed analysis of CORBA, and it is included in this book to help the Java IDL user understand how CORBA works. For a more detailed description of CORBA, see Jon Siegel's excellent book, *CORBA Fundamentals and Programming* (New York: John Wiley & Sons, 1996). If you're really interested, you can take a look at the CORBA specifications themselves. They're available on the Web at www.omg.org or from the Object Management Group, 492 Old Connecticut Path, Framingham, MA 01701, USA, e-mail info@omg.org.

The Object Management Group

The Object Management Group (OMG) is the world's largest software consortium with a membership of more than 750 vendors, developers, and end users. Established in 1989, its mission is to promote the theory and practice of object technology (OT) for the development of distributed computing systems.

A key goal of the OMG is to create a standardized object-oriented architectural framework for distributed applications based on specifications that enable and support distributed objects. Objectives include the reusability, portability, and interoperability of object-oriented software components in heterogeneous environments. To this end, the OMG adopts interface and protocol specifications, based on commercially available object technology, that together define an Object Management Architecture (OMA).

The details of the Object Management Architecture were first published to provide a reference model for developing distributed object standards. This was followed by the original CORBA 1.1 specification in 1991, providing a key piece of that architecture. Today, the OMG has adopted and published an impressive array of standards that extend and complement the base CORBA architecture. Many more are working their way through the OMG standardization process, going a long way toward making the OMA a reality.

For more information about OMG, visit the OMG's homepage at www.omg.org.

Object Management Architecture

The Object Management Architecture (OMA) reference model is an architectural framework that identifies the key components of a distributed object system. By defining these components, the OMA simplifies the problem of characterizing a system. It does not itself specify the behavior of these components. This is done by the individual standards that compose the OMA framework. The individual components of the OMA reference model are shown in Figure 3.1 and are described in the text that follows.

Object Request Broker

The Object Request Broker (ORB) can be thought of as the foundation of the OMA. It handles all communications between objects within a distributed object system. The ORB accepts requests from clients, locates and activates the target

Figure 3.1 The OMA reference model (Source: OMG).

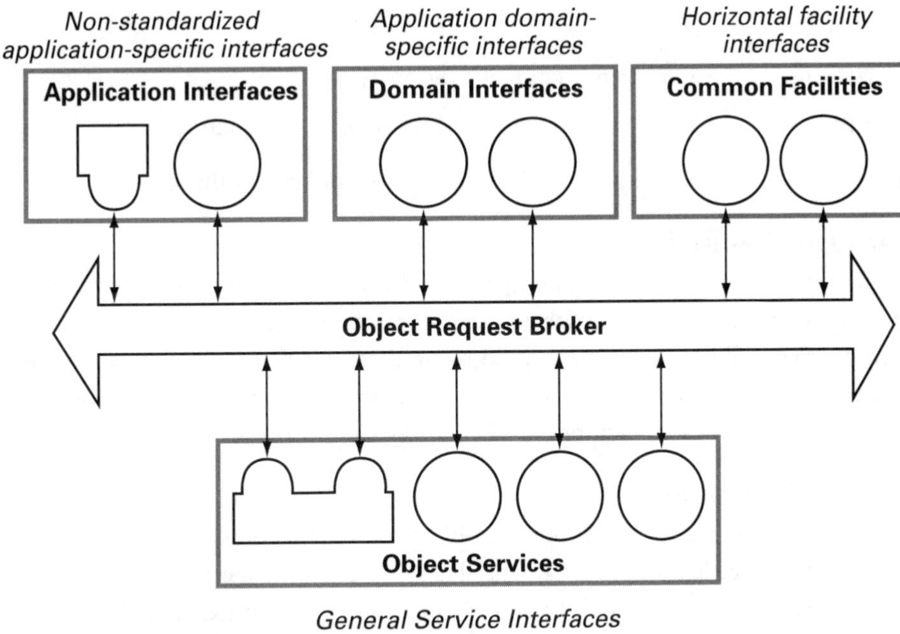

General Service Interfaces

objects, and forwards the requests. All other system components depend on the base set of services provided by the ORB. It supplies the infrastructure that allows other components to work together to provide an integrated distributed object system.

Object Services

The ability to communicate, while important, is only a part of the overall solution. In order for objects to work effectively together, additional services need to be provided. Objects need to know where to find each other, whom to trust, and how to manage their life cycles. The OMG has defined a set of standard object services, known as *CORBAServices*, to address these issues. Services such as Naming, Security, Persistence, and Transactions are essential to developing robust client/server applications. By providing such services and defining consistent interfaces to them, application developers can quickly make use of components that distributed object applications need. The CORBAServices that have already been defined by the OMG as of this writing are listed in Table 3.1.

Table 3.1 CORBAServices

Lifecycle	Naming	Events	
Persistence	Relationships	Externalization	
Transactions	Concurrency control	Security	
Property	Query	Licensing	Time

Some of these services will be described in more detail later in this chapter.

Common Facilities

CORBAServices are system-level components; Common Facilities are application-level components. They cover such services as printing, document management, and electronic mail, all of which can be used by applications rather than forcing each application developer to reconstruct them using low-level system components. OMG-adopted Common Facilities are known as *CORBAFacilities*.

Domain Interfaces

Domain interfaces are specifications for objects or system components that are useful to a specific vertical market segment. They provide very specific functionality useful to users in a certain field. Examples include components designed for markets such as finance, medicine, and manufacturing.

Application Interfaces

Even though application interfaces are a component of the OMA, they are not explicitly defined by the OMG. They are intended to represent the objects written by various end users to meet their needs. They make use of all the other OMA components, ensuring reuse and rapid development.

CORBA

The CORBA specification defines several key pieces that together make up the foundation of the entire OMA infrastructure. Perhaps the most important is the OMG *Interface Definition Language* (IDL). To be able to create distributed objects, we must first be able to describe them, and IDL provides a formal mechanism for specifying an object's interface in a way that is independent of its implementation. This is one of the key reasons for the flexibility of the CORBA architecture. By separating the object's interface from its implementation, portability and interoperability can be ensured.

Of course, an interface definition is useless without a concrete object implementation. To this end, the OMG defines several implementation language mappings that allow a developer to create an actual object from the abstract IDL interface specification. The language mapping describes in detail the conversion from IDL-defined types to native language constructs. This conversion allows the programmer to work with familiar language idioms rather than having to learn a completely new style of programming.

The final piece of the puzzle is the ORB itself. Conceptually, the ORB can be regarded as a single component, but it is, in fact, a combination of several different parts. The ORB is defined by its interfaces, which are, in turn, specified in pseudo-IDL. These are used by both client and server objects to access all of the functionality necessary for them to communicate easily, independent of their location and implementation.

Object Request Broker

Figure 3.2 illustrates the structure of an ORB, with several components arranged in layers. This layering provides generality and allows for a wide range of different implementations to suit different needs. At the bottom is the ORB core, which provides the basic functionality of the ORB itself. This consists of the underlying communications mechanism and object representation. The upper layers are designed to decouple the underlying mechanisms and the application interface. In doing this, CORBA allows a wide range of different implementation styles. For example, this is what allows a Java client application to communicate with a Smalltalk object using familiar Java constructs.

The ORB provides two methods of communication: static and dynamic. *Static* method invocation allows clients to call object methods using client-side stubs specific to that object type. These stubs are generated from the object's IDL specification by an IDL compiler and are linked with the client application at compile time. They provide the client with an interface to the object's methods while hiding all of the communication details.

Dynamic invocation allows requests to be constructed on the fly and sent to a target object. This is useful when the type of the target object will vary at runtime. The client does not know the exact type of the target, but using the object reference it can query the interface repository to determine the methods supported and their associated parameters. A request can then be dynamically constructed and sent to

Figure 3.2 The Object Request Broker (Source: OMG).

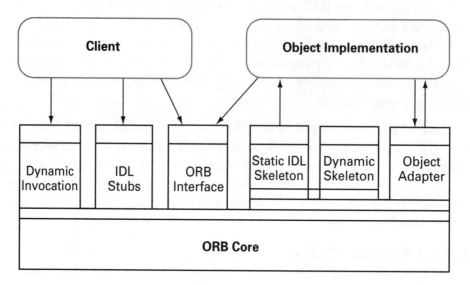

the object. This allows extremely flexible and dynamic applications to be created that make use of the CORBA communications mechanism.

The interface repository mentioned earlier is a part of the ORB core and is not shown in Figure 3.2. For the ORB to be able to talk to different objects, it needs to be able to determine the types of those objects. This is where the interface repository comes in. All objects in a CORBA system store their type information in a database known as the *interface repository*. The ORB uses this information to forward requests, to check that parameters are correct, and to support dynamic invocation.

In addition to the interface repository, CORBA provides an *implementation repository*. This is where the ORB stores information about each object's implementation. The information in this database depends heavily on the particular implementation and can include such things as the location of the server executable, the machine on which to run the server process, and startup arguments.

We will now look at what happens when a request is made. Starting at the client we will follow a request as it goes through the ORB and up to the target object. This will give you a firmer understanding of the abstract terms discussed so far.

Client

Before a client application can invoke a method on an object, it must first obtain a handle to that object. In CORBA, these handles are called *object references*. An object reference usually contains the information that allows the ORB to locate and forward a request to that object. What exactly that information is depends on the ORB implementation and does not concern us here. The ORB is solely responsible for generating and interpreting object references.

Once in possession of an object reference, the client must choose an invocation mechanism. Depending on the situation and requirements, the client application will use either static or dynamic invocation, as described earlier. Regardless of which client-side mechanism is chosen, the request will be the same at the server.

If static invocation is used, the request is made by calling the desired method of the client stub object. The stub will convert the method parameters into a format that can be understood by the server and package them into a request structure to be sent to the server. This process is known as *marshalling*. After marshalling, the request is passed to the ORB core to be sent to the target object.

With dynamic invocation, the situation is slightly different. Rather than have a stub object perform the marshalling transparently, the application programmer constructs the request manually using functions provided as part of the ORB client-side interfaces. Naturally, the programmer needs to know the object type and parameters to each method to do this. To get this information, the programmer can query the interface repository using a well-defined interface. Even though this may seem unusual at first, it is quite possible that the client application could be passed an object reference of an unknown type at runtime.

After being issued by the client, the request is passed to the ORB. Once the ORB has the request, it determines the target object and how to contact it using a combination of the object reference and the interface and implementation repositories. The request is then transmitted to the target machine using an underlying transport such as TCP/IP (see Figure 3.3).

Server

On the server side, the ORB must perform a number of functions before the request reaches the server object for processing. Usually the server-side ORB components receive the request over a network connection. The ORB needs to unmarshall the header data from the transmission format and determine which of the objects on

Figure 3.3 Client-ORB interaction.

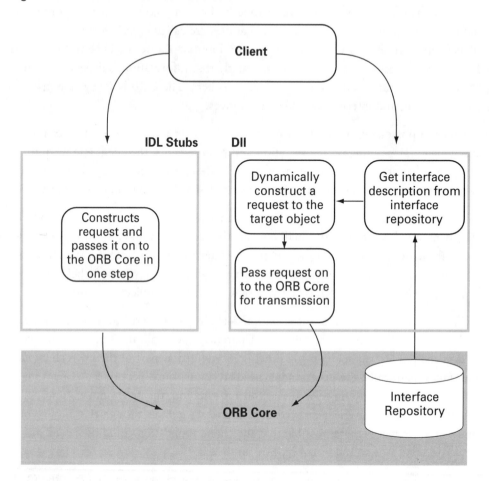

that machine is the target. Having located the object, the ORB must prepare the object to receive the request. This could mean a number of things ranging from starting the server process that contains the object to retrieving the object from persistent storage, such as a database or a file.

Next, the ORB passes the request up to the object. This is done through an up-call to the object implementation from the ORB layer. The ORB core, however, does not talk directly to the object. Communication between the ORB and an object is handled by an *object adapter*. The object adapter provides an interface that allows a common ORB core to support a wide variety of different object implementations. For example, an object could be implemented using a library, a server process that contains the object, or a different process for each object method. The object adapter insulates the ORB core from these differences and allows those implementations access to the ORB core through the most appropriate mechanism. This flexibility is one of the primary strengths of the CORBA model.

Two up-call interfaces to the object lie above the object adapter layer: the static IDL skeleton interface and the dynamic skeleton interface. They are the server-side analogs of the static and dynamic stubs and provide essentially the same functionality to the ORB. They are used internally by the ORB to make calls up to the object implementation to perform a request and return the results to the ORB. These are usually internal components, and they are not directly relevant to the application programmer.

The static IDL skeleton is generated by an IDL compiler and provides an interface for the ORB to make up-calls to a specific object type. Like the client stubs, they provide functions that allow the ORB to call specific methods of the target object.

The dynamic skeleton interface provides more flexibility and allows the ORB to make up-calls to any object regardless of type. The ORB can construct a request from information received across the network and pass it up to an object using the dynamic skeleton interface.

The object receives the up-call from the ORB and processes it according to its implementation. Any return values are passed back through the ORB to the client, using the same mechanisms described previously (see Figure 3.4).

IDL

An understanding of the CORBA Interface Definition Language is central to understanding CORBA objects. Objects in CORBA are defined by their interfaces, and those interfaces are defined using IDL. Using IDL allows objects to be specified independently of the implementation language. An object defined using IDL can be implemented using any programming language as long as an IDL mapping exists for that language.

CORBA IDL is an object-oriented, declarative language that is used to define the operations, parameters, types, and exceptions of a distributed object. It is used

Figure 3.4 Server-ORB interaction.

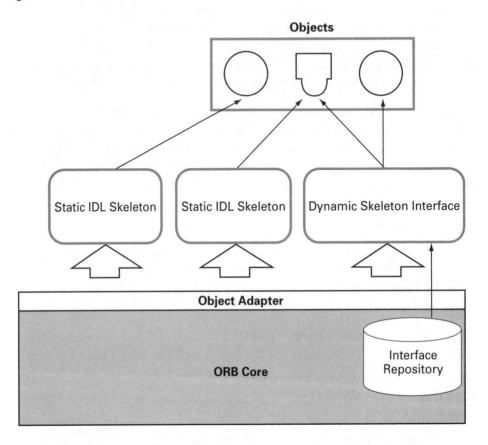

strictly for describing objects and their interfaces and says nothing about their implementation. IDL defines a set of built-in types and provides facilities for defining additional types. It is loosely based on C++, and most of the constructs should be familiar to any Java programmer. Others will need some explanation. Table 3.2 lists the basic IDL types and their definitions.

Using these built-in types and the IDL constructs for extending them, virtually any desired data type can be created. IDL provides several mechanisms for defining structured data types to allow more complex data to be transmitted between clients and objects. The simplest of these are the string and enumerated types. Others include structs, discriminated unions, and sequences. All are discussed here in more detail.

Table 3.2 IDL Types

IDL Type	Definition
short	$-2^{15} .. (2^{15} -1)$
unsigned short	$0 .. (2^{16} -1)$
long	$-2^{31} .. (2^{31} -1)$
unsigned long	$0 .. (2^{32} -1)$
float	IEEE single precision
double	IEEE double precision
char	ISO Latin-1 character for graphic characters, ASCII for NULL and formatting characters
boolean	TRUE or FALSE
octet	8-bit uninterpreted
any	Expresses any IDL type

String

The `string` data type is exactly what it sounds like. To be more precise, an IDL `string` is a null-terminated character array. Strings can be either bounded or unbounded. A bounded string has a specified maximum size, as shown here.

```
string <64> Sentence;
```

Strings can also be defined without a maximum size. Such strings are unbounded, and their size must be set at runtime. An unbounded string declaration follows:

```
string Message;
```

Enumerated Types

Enumerated types will be familiar to most programmers. They are no different in IDL and simply consist of an ordered list of identifiers. A maximum of 2^{32} identifiers can be specified. In addition, the order in which the identifiers are named defines their relative order.

```
Enum Colors {
    Red,
    Green,
    Blue
};
```

Struct

`Structs` are similar to C language `structs`. They define a data structure that is made up of other data types. Here is an example of an IDL `struct`.

```
struct Point {
        long x;
        long y;
};
```

Discriminated Union

A *discriminated union* is a mixture of the C language union data type and `switch` statement. IDL unions need to be able to determine what data type the union currently contains. This is done with an additional data member known as a *discriminator*. The discriminator is used in the `switch` statement to determine the current type of the union. Here is an example:

```
union NumValue switch (long) {
        case 1: long x;
        case 2: double y;
        default: Any z;
};
```

Sequence

Sequences are arrays of a single data type. Here is an example of a sequence:

```
sequence<octet> SoundClip;
```

Like strings, sequences can be either bounded or unbounded. An unbounded sequence can be any length. Its size is specified at runtime. The sequence just shown is unbounded. A bounded sequence has a specified maximum length. This is a bounded sequence:

```
sequence<Point, 100> Curve;
```

Exceptions

Exceptions are used to indicate error conditions in a particular method call. They are structured in a similar manner to exceptions in languages such as Java and C++. The exception is a `struct`-like data structure for which data members can be defined. These data members can be used to indicate what the error might have been.

```
exception MathError {
    string Reason;
}
```

Exception types are used only in IDL method declarations to indicate the various exception conditions that may occur when calling a function.

Any

The `Any` data type is classified as one of the simple data types, but it really isn't that simple and it does need some explanation. The `Any` data type can be used to represent any other IDL data type. Why is this necessary? It provides a more dynamic runtime environment by allowing data of various types to be passed as a single generic type. This can be extremely useful, and it is widely used in the Event Services specification to provide very flexible interface specifications.

Interface

Perhaps the heart of IDL is the `interface` declaration. This is what allows distributed objects to be created. Distributed objects are specified in IDL using the `interface` keyword. An IDL interface defines an object, its operations, and the parameters and return values of those operations. Here is a simple IDL interface:

```
interface Calculator {
    void add(in long a, in long b);
};
```

This declaration shows a simple object that supports one function that takes two parameters. The function will look familiar to Java programmers except for the "in" specifier. This is provided as a hint to the IDL compiler in optimizing the transmission of data. By specifying both parameters as "in," the developer indicates to the ORB transport that they need only be sent from the client to the target object and not vice versa. Other valid specifiers are "out" for those that will only be return values and "inout" for parameters that need to go in both directions.

Notice that the Calculator interface definition itself shows no details of the Calculator object's implementation. Further, no member data nor code for the single method is shown. IDL and CORBA consider these to be implementation details best left to the object implementor or to the implementation language. Note also that there are no indications of public or private methods as in Java: All CORBA

IDL interface methods are public by default. Private methods would be hidden away in the object's implementation.

Although no member data is allowed, an object can have attributes in its `interface` specification. Attributes can be read/write or read-only and look like data member declarations. However, they actually map to accessor methods in the implementation language. Here is a more complex interface declaration:

```
interface SavingsAccount : Account {
    void deposit(in long amount) raises AcctErr;
    void withDraw(in long amount, out long balance)
        raises AcctErr;
    readonly attribute float balance;
};
```

This interface demonstrates inheritance syntax. The `SavingsAccount` type inherits from the `Account` type. `SavingsAccount` supports two methods and any others inherited from the `Account` object. Both of the `SavingsAccount` methods raise exceptions in response to error conditions. In addition, the object supports one read-only attribute of type `float`.

An important point to remember about IDL inheritance is that it is interface inheritance and not implementation inheritance. With a traditional object-oriented programming language such as C++, a subclass inherits the interface and implementation of its superclass. Not so with IDL. The `SavingsAccount` object inherits the method declarations of the `Account` object. The methods themselves must be reimplemented in the `SavingsAccount` object. This is almost identical to the Java notion of implementing an interface. The inheritance implied by the Java `implements` keyword is closer to IDL inheritance than that denoted by the Java `extends` keyword.

Interoperability and IIOP

So far we have discussed communication within a single Object Request Broker. However, a CORBA environment could span multiple ORB implementations. A client using an ORB from one vendor may need to access an object hosted by one developed by another vendor. To be able to communicate easily in such an environment, there must be a way of passing information around such that each distinct ORB environment preserves its own policies and semantics. In CORBA terms, this problem is known as *interoperability*.

Interoperability, as defined by the OMG, is more than just getting different ORBs to communicate with one other. A single ORB environment could consist of multiple administrative departments, security levels, and network protocols. The differences between them present different problems when an object request crosses the boundary between any two of them. How is a request from a TCP/IP-based ORB handled if the requested object is hosted by a Novell IPX-based ORB? How is security information passed between ORBs? The concept of interoperability is designed to address just those problems.

The first key component of the OMG's solution is the ORB interoperability architecture. This is a conceptual framework for describing and addressing the problem of interoperability. In an attempt to describe the problem, it introduces the notion of domains. At an abstract level, a domain is simply a collection of objects that conform to a given set of rules. For example, ORBs with different implementations represent different technological domains, Two departments within a company are different administrative domains within that company.

The problem of interoperability then becomes one of "bridging" between different domains. Objects in different domains communicate by using a bridge that serves as an intermediary between them. The bridge provides transparency, making the differences between the domains invisible to users. This is a very abstract definition and is not very useful to us here. In this section, we will stick to discussing interoperability of technological domains, that is, getting different ORBs with different protocols to talk to each other.

For bridging to be an effective solution, there must be support within the CORBA architecture for its implementation. Application Programming Interfaces (APIs) must be provided that allow requests to pass from one ORB to another transparently. These include the dynamic invocation interface, the dynamic skeleton interface, and APIs for handling object references. These have been described previously.

Another key piece of the interoperability specification is the *Interoperable Object Reference* (IOR). All CORBA objects are accessed using object references. It is therefore very important that the semantics of an object reference are preserved as it passes from one ORB to another. The IOR specification defines a standard format for encoding those semantics, which may include how to contact the object, what network protocol the object uses, and what object services it requires.

At a lower level, CORBA defines the GIOP and IIOP protocols as a concrete step toward interoperability. These are directly relevant to Java IDL because they give Java IDL power and flexibility. GIOP stands for General Inter-ORB Protocol and defines a standard for sending ORB requests over some lower-level communications protocol. The GIOP consists of three components:

- *Common Data Representation* (CDR). The CDR defines a format for transmitting data in request buffers. It specifies a byte-order-independent representation of each IDL type for transmission.

- *Message Formats*. GIOP also specifies the types of messages that can be sent and their format. In total, there are seven GIOP messages: Each one has a specific format that must be followed.

- *Transport Assumptions*. GIOP makes several assumptions about its underlying transport. GIOP assumes the use of a reliable connection-oriented transport where transmitted data can be viewed as a bytestream.

The GIOP is designed to be implemented over a wide variety of network protocols. The only requirements for the chosen transport are that it support the assumptions just mentioned. GIOP was designed to work with TCP/IP, but it could just as well be used over Novell's IPX or a future protocol.

Obviously, the GIOP by itself is not very useful. It is designed to be implemented on top of a lower-level protocol. This is where IIOP comes in. The IIOP (Internet Inter-ORB Protocol) is the implementation of GIOP over TCP/IP. It consists of the GIOP protocols, CDR, and the GIOP messages, plus the IIOP Message Transport. The IIOP Message Transport defines the mapping of GIOP messages to TCP/IP connections and addressing.

You don't need to understand all the gory details of GIOP and IIOP unless you are implementing an ORB, so they won't be discussed in this book. They are discussed in detail in the CORBA specifications.

For any ORB to be CORBA 2.0-compliant, it must implement the IIOP protocol. This does not mean that the ORB must use IIOP as its native protocol, although it could. It simply needs to provide a half-bridge to IIOP. A *half-bridge* is a module that translates between the ORB's internal protocol and IIOP. It guarantees that it could interoperate with any other CORBA 2.0–compliant ORB.

CORBAServices

This section briefly discusses some of the CORBAServices relevant to this book. As noted before, there are many CORBAServices. Some have already been defined; others are still going through the OMG standards definition process. Although several Object Request Broker implementations are currently on the market, implementations of the various CORBAServices have lagged significantly and are only now becoming available. This section describes the following CORBAServices: Naming, Events, Properties, Relationship, and Lifecycle.

Naming Service

The CORBA Naming service provides a directory that allows client applications to find objects using simple names. When an object is created it can put a reference to itself in the Naming service under a name of its choosing. Any client that wishes to find that object can simply look up the name and get back a reference to the object. Like a telephone book, the Naming service makes it easy to find and contact objects with which we want to communicate.

The Naming service is accessed, like all CORBAServices, through its interface. This interface was designed to be as simple as possible while allowing for a wide range of implementations. Such flexibility is especially important for naming because a wide variety of naming standards are already in existence. The CORBA Naming service was specifically designed so that its implementation could support any other standard.

The Naming service interface does not enforce any particular rules about the interpretation of the namespace other than that it be hierarchical. In its simplest form, the Naming service provides a mapping between string names and object references. The representation of those names to the user is irrelevant to the Naming service. At a lower level, the Naming service defines the concept of a `NameComponent`. A `NameComponent` is, for our purposes, an abstract structure that represents a part of a name. A name therefore consists of a sequence of `NameComponents`. Consider the following pathname:

`/user/fred/file.txt`

This path is a visual representation of a path. Each occurrence of text between the slashes represents a `NameComponent`. A name, therefore, is a sequence of

NameComponents. Objects are added to the namespace by using the bind()
method of the Naming interface (see Figure 3.5). This method takes a name and an
object reference.

The Naming service also supports a concept analogous to the directory in a file
system. In CORBA these are known as *contexts* and represent the initial and intermediate components of a full pathname. A context is a container object within the
namespace and has a name just as a directory in a file system would. Figure 3.6
shows a naming context with two name bindings: one names a Stock object as
"SUNW" and the other binding names another Stock object as "SGI."

Naming contexts support the bind operation, which creates a binding between a
name and an object in some Naming context. The bind operation was used to add
the SUNW and the SGI bindings in the Naming context in Figure 3.6.

The resolve operation returns an object reference, given a binding. In Figure
3.6, invoking the resolve operation with "SUNW" as a parameter will return an
object reference to the Stock object for SUNW.

The list operation returns all the bindings (pairs of names and object references) in the Naming context. In Figure 3.6, the list operation would return
"SUNW," the object reference for SUNW, "SGI," and the object reference for SGI.

Figure 3.5 A typical namespace.

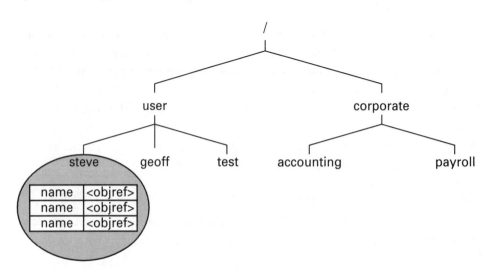

Figure 3.6 A Naming context with two name bindings.

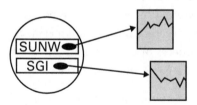

Because Naming contexts are themselves objects, they can be named in other Naming contexts, forming naming graphs. Clients can provide compound names to traverse a naming graph. Typically there are multiple naming graphs in a CORBA environment; there is no requirement that all Naming contexts be connected.

The `bind_new_context` operation creates a Naming context and binds it into another context. In Figure 3.7, a context with "IBM" and "HWP" was bound in a context by "NYSE"; a context with "SUNW" and "SGI" was bound in a context with "NASDAQ."

Event Service

Even though the typical request-response cycle of CORBA communications is quite effective, it is not universally applicable. Consider an object that needs to notify

Figure 3.7 Naming contexts are objects and can be named in other contexts.

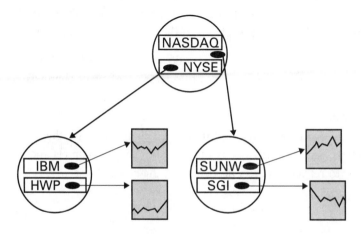

other objects of any changes to itself. The only way to do this would be to invoke a method of each of those objects. This can involve considerable overhead in the time required to make those calls and for the storage required by each object reference. The situation gets worse as more objects, requiring different notification messages, are added. A separate entity to handle the whole process of collecting and distributing messages is needed, and this is the purpose of the CORBA Event service.

Events are application-specific data defined by the application developer; they can be any valid IDL-defined data type. The Event service acts as an intermediary between producers of events and consumers of events. These intermediaries are referred to as *event channels*. Event consumers get data from the event channel, and event producers add data to the event channel. An application that needs to distribute information in this way creates an event channel, and other applications subscribe to that channel. Any event that the producer sends to the channel is forwarded to any consumers connected to it. The channel itself does not need to know what the type is because all data is sent through the channel as the any data type. What is important is that both producer and consumer applications know what data is being sent. Usually, such knowledge is contained in the implementations themselves. The actual type of the object will be defined somewhere in IDL, however, usually as an IDL struct.

Event channels support two modes of operation: push and pull. In the push mode, data is "pushed" from the producer to the event channel or from the event channel to the consumer. In pull mode, data is "pulled" from the producer by the event channel or from the event channel by the consumer. These different modes provide a lot of flexibility in the implementation of event channel clients. In some situations, one may be simpler to implement or may have a better fit with the application model (see Figure 3.8). The choice is left up to the application developer.

Now that we know what event channels are, how do we use them? CORBA defines IDL interfaces for using the various modes of operation of event channels:

Event Service Interfaces

- *PullConsumer*. A PullConsumer is an event channel client that uses the PullConsumer interface. This interface is supported by event channels and allows the consumer to retrieve data as needed from the channel.

  ```
  interface PullConsumer {
      void disconnect_pull_consumer();
  };
  ```

Figure 3.8 Using an event channel.

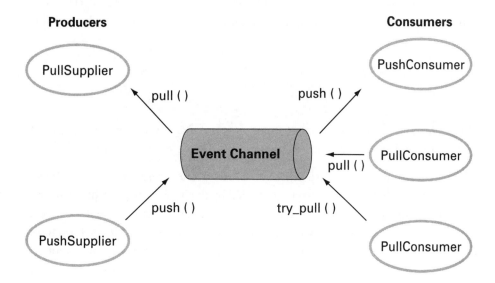

- *PushConsumer*. The PushConsumer interface allows the client to receive events asynchronously from the channel. To do this, the application must implement the PushConsumer interface. This is a bit more complicated because the developer must now create an object to handle asynchronous requests, which often must use some multithreading mechanism.

```
interface PushConsumer {
    void push (in any data) raises(Disconnected);
    void disconnect_push_consumer();
};
```

- *PullSupplier*. A PullSupplier implements the PullSupplier interface, allowing the event channel to request events when it is ready to receive them. The try_pull() method allows a nonblocking call to be made that returns immediately with an indication of whether an event was available.

```
interface PullSupplier {
    any pull () raises(Disconnected);
    any try_pull (out boolean has_event)
        raises(Disconnected);
    void disconnect_pull_supplier();
};
```

- *PushSupplier.* The `PushSupplier` interface is implemented by the event channel and allows an application to send events to the channel when necessary.
  Again, this is the simplest supplier interface to use, but it may not be useful in
  all situations.

```
interface PushSupplier {
    void disconnect_push_supplier();
};
```

CORBA defines other interfaces for creating and managing event channels, but
they are not discussed here. Future chapters will discuss them in more detail.

Finally, though the CORBA specification clearly defines these interfaces, it offers no
guarantees about the quality of service provided by the implementation of the interface. Event channels are a form of asynchronous messaging, but they do not explicitly
offer guaranteed message delivery or communication optimizations. It is left up to the
ORB vendor to determine what will be offered by each particular implementation.

Multiway, Anonymous Communication

An event channel can supply multiple consumers. As illustrated in Figure 3.9,
the event channel supplies events to both the `Chart` and the `Portfolio` objects. The
event channel independently communicates with the `Chart` object and with
the `Portfolio` object in either push or pull styles.

The event channel makes the communication anonymous. The `Stock` object is
unaware of the consumers. Structuring a distributed application around anonymous
event communication makes it easily extensible. The portfolio functionality was
added to the application in Figure 3.9 without modifying the stock object. The
stock object continues to supply events, unaware of the consumers.

An event channel can also consume events from multiple suppliers. For example,
multiple stocks can independently supply events to the same event channel; all consumers receive events from all suppliers.

When there are multiple suppliers, the suppliers of an event are anonymous. If the
consumers need to distinguish the multiple suppliers, they can do so in event data.

Scoping Events

An event channel provides a scope for events. There is no need for unrelated application domains to share an event channel. By definition, the consumers of one event
channel will not receive the events supplied by another.

Figure 3.9 An event channel with multiple consumers.

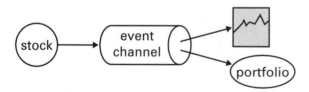

In practice, we have found scoping events by supplier to be an effective technique for organizing event communication.

Filtering Events

Even within the scope of a single event channel, not all consumers want to consume all events. In the stock example, the `Chart` object wants to consume all changes in a stock's price, but suppose the `Portfolio` object wants to consume stock price changes only when the price of a stock reaches a certain price. This can be achieved with a special event channel called a filter. A *filter* is a specialized event channel that consumes events from another event channel but supplies only those events that satisfy some condition. The filter simply discards events that do not satisfy the condition.

In Figure 3.10, only stock prices that are above (or below) a certain price are forwarded to the `Portfolio` object; the filter discards those that are not.

Filters are usually lightweight event channels that just evaluate the event data. A typical implementation of a push-style filter supports only a single consumer and makes no attempt to store and retry the event notification if it has difficulties communicating with its consumer. The filter itself simply fails. The event channel that supplies events to the filter detects the failure and attempts to supply the event to the filter later.

Filters are best configured to be near the event channels they are filtering. This reduces communication costs when the filter consumes but then discards an event.

Property Service

Sometimes there is a need to add attributes to an already existing object. Consider a document being sent to a print queue. Ideally we would like to attach a priority to each document so that more important documents would be printed first. This priority is not an inherent feature of the document object. It is useful

Figure 3.10 An event channel that filters events for its consumers.

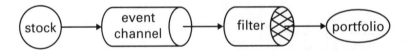

in some situations but not in others, and it is not a part of the object's type. Rather than modify the document object to have it support a priority attribute, there ought to be some way of attaching it when necessary. The Property service allows a developer to attach different "properties" to an object to suit various application needs.

The idea of a Property service may seem strange for an object-oriented environment. Why not just inherit the original object's class and add the needed attributes? Sometimes it is not always possible to do this. What if the object had been developed by a third party? Remember that IDL inheritance is interface inheritance, and the implementation will not always be readily available. The developer would have to reimplement the original object's functionality as well as any new functionality, not a desirable task by any means.

A *property* is simply a name-value pair that associates a name with a user-defined value. The name is simply a string that allows clients to access the property value. The property value can be anything the programmer desires. It is represented by the any IDL type. An object can handle properties in a number of ways. One is for it to support the PropertySet interface. This interface provides methods for setting and getting properties of an object. By implementing this interface, an object allows itself to be treated as a PropertySet object. The property service specification does not explicitly define any other method of supporting properties. It is left up to the implementor to choose an appropriate method.

Property sets are created by using the create_propertyset operation defined by the PropertySetFactory interface. Once a property set is created, a property is defined using the define_property operation. The is_property_defined operation tests for the existence of a particular property. The get_property operation returns the data associated with the key. All properties in a property set can be retrieved using the get_pairs operation. Finally, property sets support a destroy operation to destroy the property set and all of its properties.

Relationship Service

CORBA clients use object references to request the services of other objects. When a CORBA client is itself an object, it may store the object reference in its private state. From an object modeling point of view, the objects are related. For some applications, this relationship needs to be "formalized" in a standard way. Rather than storing the object reference directly in its state, it can use the Relationship service.

The Relationship service supports the creation and manipulation of one-to-one, one-to-many, and many-to-many *n*-ary relationships between typed objects. The Relationship service enforces type, cardinality, and referential integrity constraints on relationships. The relationships can be navigated and enumerated.

"Formalizing" a relationship between two objects has certain benefits over the direct storage of an object reference:

- Relationships are multidirectional; object references are "one-way."
  - When objects are in a relationship, the relationship can be navigated to locate all related objects. Object references can be navigated in only a single direction.

- Relationships can be manipulated by third parties.
  - Because relationships are represented externally in a standard way by the Relationship service, programs outside of the objects can create, navigate, and destroy relationships between objects. Because object references are part of an object's encapsulated state, external programs cannot manipulate them in a standard way.

- Relationships can be extended with attributes and operations; object references cannot be extended.

Often, when modeling an application as a collection of objects and their relationships, the relationships themselves have attributes and behavior. For example, the number of shares of stock owned by a portfolio is not an attribute of either the portfolio or the stock. Instead, it is an attribute of the relationship between the portfolio and the stock. Because the relationship is itself an object, it can be extended with this information.

The Relationship service supports the explicit representation of relationships between distributed objects. The service defines three interfaces: `Role`, `Relationship`, and `Node`.

Figure 3.11 illustrates an ownership relationship between `Portfolio` objects and `Stock` objects. It indicates that portfolio #1 owns 50 shares of IBM and 100 shares of SUNW, and portfolio #2 owns 250 shares of SUNW. We will use this figure to explain the `Role`, `Relationship`, and `Node` interfaces.

The Relationship Interface

The Relationship service implements objects that support the Relationship interface. In Figure 3.11, the diamonds are relationship objects. The Relationship interface defines an attribute `named_roles` and a `destroy` operation. The `named_roles` attribute indicates the roles of the related objects in the relationship. In Figure 3.11, the `named_roles` attribute of a diamond provide the "owner" and "ownedby" roles.

The `destroy` operation destroys the relationship. (Relationships are created using the `create_relationship` operation defined by the `RelationshipFactory` interface.)

The Role Interface

`Role` objects represent an object in a relationship. Connected roles represent relationships. In Figure 3.11, the small circles are the "owner" roles for the portfolio objects and the "ownedby" roles for the stock objects.

The `get_relationships` operation enumerates all of the relationships in which the role participates. In Figure 3.11, `get_relationships` on portfolio #1's role would return relationships O1 and O2.

Figure 3.11 Portfolio objects and stock objects in an ownership relationship using the Relationship service.

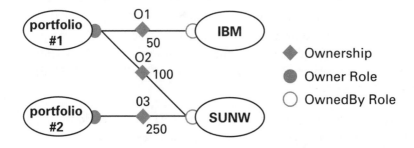

The `get_other_related_object` operation navigates a relationship and returns an object reference for the other object in the relationship. In Figure 3.11, the `get_other_related_object` operation executed at portfolio #1's owned role would return SUNW, given the identifier for O2; similarly, the `get_other_related_object` operation executed at IBM's owned role would return portfolio #1.

The Node Interface

Related objects that participate in multiple relationships are represented by multiple roles: one for each role the object plays in each relationship. Related objects support the `Node` interface in order to differentiate roles from related objects.

In Figure 3.11, the Stock and Portfolio objects all support the `Node` interface. The `Node` interface enables a client to traverse a graph of related objects in a standard way. In particular, the `Node` interface defines a `roles_of_node` operation and an attribute for related objects to reveal their roles.

Traversing a graph of nodes is done using the `Traversal` interface. Using a combination of these two interfaces, operations such as copy can be safely performed on compound objects.

Lifecycle Service

The Lifecycle service provides an interface for managing an object throughout its lifetime, from initial creation until its final destruction. It defines standard conventions for copying, moving, and removing objects. Creation is generally implementation dependent. Attempts by the OMG to define concrete standards for object creation would likely have limited the number of choices available to ORB developers, thereby reducing CORBA's generality.

However, the Lifecycle service clearly defines the `copy`, `move`, and `remove` methods. Standard mechanisms and data types for specifying source and destination and any other criteria required by these operations are provided. By creating well-defined, object-independent interfaces for these operations, clients can easily manipulate objects without knowing the details of their individual types. Objects inherit from the `lifecycle` interface and provide their own implementations of these methods.

Chapter Summary

This chapter has provided a brief glimpse of the OMG's standardization efforts. Those efforts are expressed in the conceptual architecture of the OMA. The first concrete component of the OMA to be developed was the CORBA specification. This forms the foundation of all the other components necessary to create the component-based architectures that represent the OMG's vision of the future.

We also took a look at some of those other components, specifically CORBAServices, which represent low-level services necessary for seamless distributed object interaction. Quite a few of these have already been defined, and even more are currently in process. Once these become widely available, CORBA development will be even easier as programmers start to leverage the development efforts of their peers.

Higher-level components, such as the CORBAFacilities and the various industry-specific domain technologies, are still in the process of being defined; implementations of these are still a long way off. CORBA, however, still offers an environment for the development of distributed applications that is matched by few others in terms of interoperability and component reuse. Developers can construct business objects and make them available to an amazingly wide variety of users on different platforms with different environments. Perhaps the best example of the flexibility of CORBA architectures is that business objects developed prior to the rise of the Internet can now be accessed from a Web browser with no modification, or at least with very little additional development. Harnessing this power and flexibility is what the rest of this book is all about.

4

Distributed Architecture Concepts

If you are a software developer, your primary goal in reading this book is probably to get your hands into the machinery of building real, useful applications as quickly as possible. In fact, once you get started, you may be surprised at how Java IDL and CORBA simplify the complexities of network programming on multiple, incompatible platforms.

If you are also experienced in using object-oriented techniques, or if your responsibilities include software management, you know that a rigorous approach to architectural matters is a critical success factor.

In this chapter, we will discuss the impact of CORBA and Java on some important design areas of distributed systems. If you are impatient to start hacking, by all means forge on. But come back to these pages later—you may need to convince your manager of the virtues of CORBA before you actually get to write some code!

Our goal is to introduce some system-level ideas for using the tools discussed in the remainder of the book. In the first part of the chapter, we will focus on systems integration and requirements issues. In the second part, we will discuss some design concepts that are specific to object-based distributed applications.

Distributed Systems Integration

Let's spend a moment here to talk about what object orientation means for distributed systems.

Distributed OO

The basic tenets of OO (encapsulation, information hiding, inheritance, and so on) can be thought of as a way of controlling the *relationships* between software entities. Anyone who has worked extensively with older, so-called "procedural" development methods, where such control is generally lacking, knows that it can be very difficult to determine all the side effects that even small changes may introduce. This is a major factor in the high maintenance cost of software.

The same ideas are relevant to networked applications. In fact, the standard client/server model can be considered an extension of the procedural model, with servers representing "data" and clients representing "procedures." To pursue this analogy, just as the "tight coupling" of data structures and functional code leads to software instability, clients are likely to fail if they are too sensitive to architecture implementation details. For example, moving servers from one network location to another is a frequent cause of such failures.

Object orientation addresses these issues at the language level by enforcing the separation of an entity's interface from its implementation. CORBA extends this principle to the network itself; by defining interfaces in IDL and delegating all knowledge of the underlying implementations to the Object Request Broker, we can hide locations, platforms, internal data formats, languages, and so on. This can greatly simplify the management of distributed applications and enable us to design architectures based on *components*.

Components and Standards

The idea of building systems from components is familiar in everyday life. Consider how easily nontechnical users can replace components of their home stereo systems: Plug in a new unit from any manufacturer, and it works! It would be difficult to find a more convincing example of the value of separating interfaces from implementations. Industry-wide agreement about the interface standards themselves, however, is required to make this a practical reality.

Compared to many other engineering domains, the software industry is still at an early stage of standards definition. Consider the difficulty of integrating a complex piece of software—a transaction-processing monitor, for example—into a banking system. Typically, companies expend significant resources in choosing such a product because they know that once it has been adopted, backing out is a practical impossibility. However, if the banking industry (in OMA jargon, a "vertical" domain) unites to promote conformance with the CORBA Object Transaction Service, then replacing one TP monitor with another could become as straightforward as replacing your home CD player!

The OMG's Object Management Architecture and Domain Technical Committee play an important role in the process of establishing a software component marketplace.

Organizational Issues

Systems integration and standards are not merely technological issues but organizational ones as well. What approach should be taken to introduce an object-oriented way of thinking about systems?

CORBA Represents a Strategy for System Lifecycle Management

Many organizations will be interested in CORBA and Java as ways to export services to their intranets and to the public Internet, thus treating them as a kind of development framework for distributed, object-based applications. This is certainly a valid approach to the introduction of object-oriented methodology, but it is also a somewhat restrictive one if we consider the enormous potential of these interoperability technologies for large-scale system management.

Drawing on another example from the financial industry, many firms have accounting systems that have grown up over decades as a chaotic mixture of purchased and locally developed applications. A great deal of effort is expended in "gluing" these systems together to achieve some measure of interoperability. CORBA offers an opportunity to rationalize this process by expressing the infrastructure in a system-independent manner with the OMG's Interface Definition Language. This makes it possible to integrate new systems or to migrate existing ones to new platforms without the interruptions in service so common today.

Interface Definition Language is thus the linchpin of a software management strategy based on distributed OO:

> *Migration to CORBA should be approached with technology independence in mind. A primary goal of the migration should be the creation of an effective software architecture. The software architecture (specified in OMG IDL)*

should be designed to provide functionality in a cost-effective manner. This can be achieved by selectively hiding, exposing, and abstracting the complexities of the subsystems. The software architecture should isolate the subsystems from each other and provide overall product independence so that subsystems can be replaced readily. [...] If this technology-independent approach is taken, the opportunity cost of using CORBA will be a net benefit, regardless of the success or failure of the CORBA standard.[1]

Finally, establishing a comprehensive system lifecycle strategy requires the cooperation of all the business and technical sectors involved. Just as correct object models for software depend on an understanding between end users and developers, object models for an organization's information infrastructure cannot be effective without a high degree of consensus across the organization. Interface definitions represent contracts between users and suppliers, and violating them can be very costly.

Standards Policies Are Critical Success Factors

Many companies interested in applying the solutions we are discussing are finding their way into the OMG's Domain Technical Committee, both as a venue for making valuable technology contacts and because they are becoming aware that there is strength in numbers. Some will find that to participate in a standards-based marketplace they need to revise their own internal standards policies.

Comprehensive software standards are difficult to enforce for a variety of reasons:

• The adoption of new products and technologies is frequently driven by overriding, short-term business goals, especially when a competitive advantage is perceived.

• Local development areas often have a great deal of autonomy in defining their own policies.

• Vendor support for industry standards is limited.

These points reflect the idea that standards policies must encompass not only products and tools brought inhouse, but also local development and administrative protocols. In fact, the software we develop ourselves can represent just as much of a proprietary lock-in as an exclusive dependency on Vendor X.

As we have mentioned, CORBA can help to address this situation. However, like any other new technology, it can raise the environment's level of complexity. Hence, the need for standards and thoughtful planning.

CORBA Systems Architecture

In this section we will discuss a number of areas of design that are relevant to CORBA-based systems.

Limits of Location Transparency

As we discussed earlier, location transparency is one of the important benefits of CORBA-based architectures. Objects may reside on the network or on the local host—even in the process space of the client application itself. Delegating knowledge about the physical disposition of objects to the ORB makes it possible to alter their distribution with minimal disruption to users.

Unfortunately, it does not follow that developers and administrators can remain blissfully ignorant of where services are actually located. Although location transparency may apply to access semantics, assuming invariance of all parameters, such as reliability and performance, would not be wise.

These issues are addressed in a Sun Microsystems Laboratories White Paper, "A Note on Distributed Computing."[2] The authors issue a rather apocalyptic warning about the danger of ignoring the implications of location.

> *Much of the current work in distributed, object-oriented systems is based on the assumption that objects form a single ontological class. This class consists of all entities that can be fully described by the specification of the set of interfaces supported by the object and the semantics of the operations in these interfaces. ...*

> *It is the thesis of this note that this unified view of objects is mistaken. There are fundamental differences between the interactions of distributed objects and the interactions of nondistributed objects. Further, work in distributed object-oriented systems that is based on a model that ignores or denies these differences is doomed to failure, and could easily lead to an industry-wide rejection of the notion of distributed object-based systems.*[3]

The authors discuss several architecture areas they feel are critically sensitive to location:

- *Latency.* There are four to five orders of magnitude of difference between local and remote invocations.

- *Memory access.* The invalidity of memory addresses across remote address spaces imposes some knowledge of location and a corresponding difference in coding.

- *Failure.* On a local machine, failure may be total, and it is in any case detectable, for example, by the operating system. In distributed computing, one of many components may fail, and the nature of the failure (network link or CPU) may not be determinable. Consistency of state after such a failure cannot be guaranteed.

- *Concurrency.* Support for concurrency is required for distributed objects. Guaranteeing the mobility of objects may require all of them to be burdened with "the weight of concurrency semantics."

The authors recognize that the first two problems are subject to amelioration over time by advances in technology.[4]

> *While unlikely, it is at least logically possible that the differences in latency and memory access between local computing and distributed computing could be masked. It is not clear that such a masking could be done in such a way that the local computing paradigm could be used to produce distributed applications, but it might still be possible to allow some new programming technique to be used for both activities. Such a masking does not even seem to be logically possible, however, in the case of partial failure and concurrency. These aspects appear to be different in kind in the case of distributed and local computing.[5]*

The conclusion is that it is necessary to accept the existence of some irreconcilable differences between local and distributed computing, and to be "conscious of those differences at all stages of the design and implementation of distributed applications."

Analysis and Design

The previous discussion indicates only a few of the open questions of analysis and design in the rapidly evolving CORBA universe. The OMG's Analysis and Design Task Force is seeking to address some of the principal issues through the definition of an Object Analysis and Design facility. The RFP (Request for Proposal)[6] issued by the Task Force states the following:

> *The OA&D facility defines the interfaces and semantics needed to support the creation and manipulation of a core set of OA&D models, that define the structure, meaning, and behavior of object applications within the OMG Object Management Architecture. These models may be*

> - *static models (also known as structural models, e.g., class models, type models, instance models)*

- *dynamic models (also known as behavioral models, e.g., state transition models, object interaction models, object dataflow models)*

- *usage models (e.g., use-case models)*

- *architectural models (also known as system composition models, e.g., subsystem models, modules-component models, process maps)*

or other models of value during analysis and design.

The OA&D facility will play a key role in achieving semantic interoperability between OA&D tools, such that users of these tools may be ensured that models created by one tool are meaningful to another tool. The use of a common OA&D facility will help ensure that a core set of OA&D models can be interchanged between OA&D tools without semantic loss. Users of a conforming tool will have confidence that they can import/export models from/to other conforming tools.

In this book we can give only a passing glance at some of the issues of object modeling specific to the CORBA environment, but the following ideas may be helpful to those just starting out.

First of all, it is useful to keep in mind that IDL interfaces map most closely to a service-level view of a system. This differs in some respects from both its logical and physical views. "The logical view of a system serves to describe the existence and meaning of the key abstractions and mechanisms that form the problem space or that define the system's architecture. The physical model of a system describes the concrete software and hardware composition of the system's context or implementation."[7]

For example, assume that an `Account` interface provides users with access to operations on their savings accounts. Now consider an administrative interface that returns, as a result, the set of all current accounts. It is unlikely to be practical to return tens of thousands of object references, each to an allocated `Account` object! Thus, the IDL `Account` interface does not necessarily map directly to business objects specified in the analysis model. And, of course, it tells us nothing at all about the physical entities that implement the user's operations.

Indeed, are the implementations even objects? Only the implementor should know (or care). IDL's language independence is one of its great strengths, but we pay for it by not being able to specify a language-specific entity, say a C++

`Account` object, as the return type of an operation. For a rigorous OO practitioner, the public data of an IDL `struct` definitely represents a compromise with reality.

Thus, the position of IDL in the spectrum that extends from analysis to design and implementation models is, at the very least, a topic for discussion. This suggests that the IDL definitions now derived from object models by some CASE tools may be more useful as a starting point for design work than as actual production code.

Finally, we agree with Martin Fowler that models are not right or wrong, they are more or less useful.[8]

Design Patterns

The complexity of multi-tiered, object-based software demands a reasoned approach to design. The approach we take will affect the "granularity" of system components, and this is a critical parameter for reusability. The "middle" tier of a well-designed distributed object system can be likened to a "cloud" of objects that can link dynamically with one another to create different forms of collaboration. Such a structure cannot be created *ad hoc*.

As we saw in the first part of this chapter, extending OO programming concepts to the broader area of distributed systems can provide useful insights into some critical problems of software management. This extension can be applied to questions of design and implementation as well.

In recent years the study of "design patterns" for software has become an important area of OO research, and modeling the distribution of responsibilities within networks of collaborating objects is one of its central goals. Earlier we pointed out how the search for more rigorous software methodologies led to the adoption of ideas from engineering domains. Likewise, design patterns originate in the codification of architectural ideas common to many epochs and cultures.[9] These practical examples of reusing solutions that have proven to work well in the past have much to offer software designers, who frequently find themselves "reinventing the wheel."

Discovering and classifying valid design patterns requires a great deal of effort, but it is invariably a source of valuable ideas. Some of the concepts in the following sections are related to patterns you will encounter as you explore the design of CORBA architectures.

Citing Fowler again, "Patterns are a starting point, not a destination."[10]

Factories

Suppose an interface Account defines a service that allows a user to deposit and withdraw sums and to determine the current balance, and that this interface is implemented by a server accessible to the network through the ORB. How can we support the requirement that an unspecified number of users be able to perform inquiries at any time?

If the server creates a single Account instance, only one user will be supported. We might try other schemes, such as instantiating multiple Account objects or starting multiple servers, but there is still the possibility of a mismatch, with either wasted system resources or users blocked while waiting for an Account to free up. Furthermore, how are we to advertise the references to these objects? We might use the Naming service, but clients are now burdened with the task of searching the namespace for a free Account. If we think about how people use real-world bank accounts, this is not a very sensible design![11]

We need a way to create Account objects on demand: an Account factory. In general, factory objects implement interfaces for creating other objects. Here is a simple Factory solution for our Account problem expressed in IDL:

```
// Account.idl
interface Account {
    readonly attribute double Balance;
    void deposit( in double Amount );
    void withdraw( in double Amount );
};
interface AccountManager {
    Account newAccount( in string Name,
                                in string AccountID );
};
```

The AccountManager interface defines a factory for Account objects. Only one AccountManager object needs to be created by the server. Given a reference to this object, the client invokes the newAccount() method with his or her name and ID and receives a reference to a new Account instance.

Inheritance and Composition

Inheritance and composition are the most common techniques used in designing object models, and anyone engaging in serious OO development must understand them thoroughly.

In brief:

- *Inheritance* bases the implementation of one class on that of another.

- *Composition* creates new functionality by assembling objects with well-defined interfaces and reciprocally opaque implementations.

The choice of which technique to use in a specific case requires a good understanding of the implicit trade-offs.

> *Inheritance and composition each have their advantages and disadvantages. Class inheritance is defined statically at compile-time and is straightforward to use, since it's supported directly by the programming language....*
>
> *But class inheritance has some disadvantages, too. First, you can't change the implementations inherited from parent classes at run-time, because inheritance is defined at compile-time. Second, and generally worse, parent classes often define at least part of their subclasses' physical representation.... The implementation of a subclass becomes so bound up with the implementation of its parent class that any change in the parent's implementation will force the subclass to change.*
>
> *Implementation dependencies can cause problems when you're trying to reuse a subclass. Should any aspect of the inherited implementation not be appropriate for new problem domains, the parent class must be rewritten or replaced by something more appropriate....*
>
> *Object composition is defined dynamically at run-time through objects acquiring references to other objects.... Any object can be replaced at run-time by another as long as it has the same type....*
>
> *Favoring object composition over class inheritance helps you keep each class encapsulated and focused on one task.*[12]

The matter has special significance for CORBA developers. Inheritance is used extensively in the generation of skeleton (that is, server-side) code from IDL definitions, in order to invoke the actual implementation objects as instances of the interface classes. However, this can be problematical when we are "wrapping" legacy APIs. In some cases, the code may already use inheritance, and the imposition of multiple inheritance may be undesirable. Indeed, we may not have access to the source code at all. In such cases, composition by delegation may be the best solution.

"Delegation is a way of making composition as powerful for reuse as inheritance. In delegation, *two* objects are involved in handling a request: a receiving object delegates operations to its **delegate**. This is analogous to subclasses deferring requests to parent classes." [13]

In other words, delegation involves mapping invocations of one object's methods to those of another, to which the delegator holds a reference.

The OMG's CORBA specification discusses in some detail the implications of inheritance and delegation for server-side mapping.

18.3.1 Using C++ Inheritance for Interface Implementation

Implementation classes can be derived from a generated base class based on the OMG IDL interface definition. The generated base classes are known as skeleton classes, and the derived classes are known as implementation classes. Each operation of the interface has a corresponding virtual member function declared in the skeleton class. The signature of the member function is identical to that of the generated client stub class. The implementation class provides implementations for these member functions. The BOA invokes the methods via calls to the skeleton class's virtual functions....

18.3.2 Using Delegation for Interface Implementation

Inheritance is not always the best solution for implementing interfaces. Using inheritance from the OMG IDL-generated classes forces a C++ inheritance hierarchy on the implementor. Sometimes, the overhead of such inheritance is too high. For example, implementing OMG IDL interfaces with existing legacy code might be impossible if inheritance from some global class was enforced.

In some cases delegation can be used to good effect to solve this problem. Rather than inheriting from some global class, the implementation can be coded in any way at all, and some wrapper classes will delegate upcalls to that implementation. This section describes how this can be achieved in a type-safe manner using C++ templates.... [14]

Several ORB implementations offer the choice of using either or both methods for server-side code generation.

Chapter Summary

In this chapter, we have focused on the "big picture": systems integration, standards, design patterns, and more. Even though object-oriented design and programming has been around long enough to have achieved consensus in a number of areas, there is ample room here for innovative contributions.

Indeed, the successful application of object orientation to distributed systems design requires a high order of skill in an unusually broad range of disciplines, from requirements analysis to object modeling and implementation. Organizational issues come into play as well, as experts in this domain are frequently called on to evaluate not only the readiness of new technologies for "prime time," but also the preparedness of the institutions that wish to deploy them.

As you explore the inner workings of CORBA and Java, keep in mind that while bricklayers and carpenters are essential, it is the architects who are remembered by history.

Endnotes

1 T. J. Mowbray and R. Zahavi, *The Essential CORBA* (New York: Wiley, 1995), 164–5.

2 J. Waldo, et al., www.sunlabs.com/techrep/1994.

3 Ibid., p. 2.

4 ORB technology and Java Remote Method Invocation (RMI) eliminate this problem through the exclusive use of object references.

5 Ibid., p. 7.

6 "Object Analysis & Design RFP-1," OMG document ad/96-05-01.

7 G. Booch, *Object-Oriented Analysis and Design* (Redwood City, CA: Benjamin/Cummings, 1994), p. 175.

8 M. Fowler, *Analysis Patterns* (Menlo Park, CA: Addison-Wesley, 1997), 2.

9 See E. Gamma, R. Helm, R. Johnson, and J. Vlissides, *Design Patterns* (Reading, MA: Addison-Wesley, 1995).

10 Fowler, *Analysis Patterns*, p. 13.

11 Note that all of the solutions we have mentioned—and rejected—may be perfectly appropriate in other situations.

12 Gamma, *Design Patterns*, p. 19.

13 Ibid., p. 20.

14 Common Object Request Broker: Architecture and Specification, Section 18.

5

Getting to Know
Java IDL

Java IDL is a reference implementation in Java of an Object Request Broker (ORB) that is compliant with the OMG-approved Java mapping for IDL. It is designed to provide interoperable CORBA support, including ubiquitous thin client Web access to other IIOP-compliant Common Object Request Broker Architecture (CORBA) services, for Java applications.

Java IDL is designed to work with the Web model of zero-install clients that are downloaded from the network into a browser. Because the runtime is implemented completely in Java, it can be packaged and downloaded with any applets that depend on it onto any platform that supports Java. These downloaded applets can then communicate directly with IIOP-compliant enterprise services, thus providing ubiquitous access at low cost. In some cases, the runtime support may already be integrated directly into the Java platform.

Although Java IDL was specifically designed to support the downloaded applet model, it works equally well for applications—Java clients and servers running stand-alone.

This book describes an Early Access release of Java IDL that supports the new OMG-standardized Java language mapping for IDL. For the latest information about Java IDL, see http://java.sun.com/products/jdk/idl/, or look for information about the Java Enterprise API on the JavaSoft Web site.

This chapter begins with a discussion of the newly standardized Java language mapping for IDL, including the Java IDL infrastructure. We then describe the application bootstrapping process and the namespace structure that supports it. Some of the main components of the runtime and transport are described with the help of some representative parts of their API. We briefly describe the application-level API and give some excerpts of client and server initialization code. We then discuss some issues specific to Java, and in particular to its downloaded applet model, and describe some mechanisms used to work with or around them.

The Java Language Mapping and API

Java IDL is the OMG standards-based distributed object framework from JavaSoft. Like the OMG CORBA standard on which it is based, Java IDL's design center focuses on language and environment independence. CORBA's support for multi-language interoperability is based on its use of IDL, the OMG Interface Definition Language, to unambiguously define the interfaces of exported object services in a form independent of any particular programming language. A consequence of this approach is that in order for a new programming language to be added to the CORBA infrastructure, it is first necessary to define a detailed language mapping between that language and IDL. Such a mapping must enable an unambiguous translation of any valid IDL specification into that native programming language, and it must also provide a compliant mapping for that language of all basic CORBA APIs.

The Java language mapping (see Appendix A) used in Java IDL has been standardized by the OMG. The submission was a joint effort of Sun Microsystems and several other ORB vendors. Because Java's portability and the flexibility of its downloaded applet model create requirements for the portability of object implementations as well as interoperability between objects implemented using ORBs from various vendors, the Java language mapping for IDL goes beyond existing IDL language mappings in the scope of its specification. The full specification is available from the OMG at www.omg.org.

Java IDL consists of several major parts: a Java version of the standard CORBA API, a portable stub API, an ORB runtime that supports the Internet Inter-ORB

Protocol, an *idltojava* compiler, and an object Naming service. Java IDL requires JDK 1.0.2 or better.

The CORBA API

Java IDL implements the standard Java version of the CORBA API from the OMG. This API is described in the CORBA specification in a language-neutral way using IDL. This IDL is written using OMG stylistic conventions that are substantially different from typical Java programming conventions. In particular, object method names are written using underscores rather than mixed case; the low-level runtime CORBA exceptions have class names that are all uppercase; application-level exceptions, known as UserExceptions, do not have class names that end in *Exception*; and, because much of the API is described in IDL, individual API elements often map to multiple Java interfaces or classes. The end result can be a somewhat jarring experience for a Java developer new to CORBA. Don't be intimidated by the large number of classes that are included with Java IDL. Most of them support dynamic typing and interface reflection. The actual number of CORBA classes used by a developer in a typical application will be quite small. Many applications will use only the ORB class, application-specific CORBA objects described in IDL, and the object Naming service described later in this chapter.

Because the Java version of the CORBA API is an implementation of an evolving framework defined by a large standards organization, the OMG, the API is packaged under the `org.omg` namespace. The core CORBA API is defined in an IDL module named `CORBA`. The Java version of this API is therefore in the `org.omg.CORBA` package. The same holds true for other parts of the Java IDL API. The IDL specification for the object Naming service defined in the `CosNaming` IDL module, for example, is contained under the `org.omg.CosNaming` Java package.

The `org.omg.CORBA` package consists of the following major groups of classes and interfaces: `ORB`, `Object`, exceptions, primitive holders, dynamic typing, Dynamic Invocation Interface (DII), and interface reflection.

The ORB class represents an Object Request Broker. All CORBA objects created in Java are associated with an ORB instance. Once created and initialized, an ORB instance can be used to obtain initial CORBA object references and can be used to implement CORBA objects in Java by associating suitable Java objects with the ORB. Additional object references can be obtained as return or *out* values from calls on CORBA objects, and they will be associated with the ORB of the object being called.

Every Java CORBA object implements the `org.omg.CORBA.Object` interface. The `Object` interface defines several methods common to all Java CORBA objects, much like the way in which all Java objects inherit from java.lang.Object. Having an object implement the `CORBA Object` interface, however, is not enough to make it a full CORBA object. For instance, if you implement an object and don't register it with an ORB, then any calls on the methods in `org.omg.CORBA.Object` may fail and result in a `BAD_OPERATION` exception being thrown.

CORBA defines a set of low-level runtime exceptions that can be thrown as a result of almost any method call on a Java CORBA object. All of these system exceptions inherit from `org.omg.CORBA.SystemException`, and their names are all uppercase, as defined in the CORBA specification. The `SystemException` class inherits from `java.lang.RuntimeException`, and so all Java IDL system exceptions are *unchecked* Java exceptions. They can be thrown by any CORBA method, even if they aren't explicitly declared in that method's Java throws clause. Application-level exceptions may be defined in IDL; they are derived from the `org.omg.CORBA.UserException` class and are normal Java exceptions.

Java IDL implements the standard CORBA container class `org.omg .CORBA.Any`, which can contain any IDL-defined datatype. The actual type contained within an instance of the `Any` class is described by an `org.omg.CORBA .TypeCode` object. The `TypeCode` class provides several methods that give full access to the CORBA type described by a particular `TypeCode` instance. The `TypeCode` for each primitive or IDL-defined CORBA data type is available at runtime, along with type-specific methods for manipulating the contents of `Any` objects.

The CORBA Dynamic Invocation Interfaces (DII) allow methods to be called on CORBA objects whose interfaces are discovered at runtime rather than statically at compile time. DII is supported by several classes, including Request, NamedValue, and NVList. This facility allows applications the flexibility to interoperate, at some cost to performance and transparency, with objects whose types cannot be predicted in advance.

Many of the classes and interfaces in the `org.omg.CORBA` package make up the CORBA Interface Repository API. This API allows the full CORBA type information of a CORBA object to be discovered at runtime. CORBA type information consists of the IDL interface inheritance, all IDL operations that the object supports, and the parameters of each operation. In this way, CORBA provides a

language-independent network datatype equivalent of the JDK 1.1 `java.lang`
`.reflect` reflection API.

Stubs and Skeletons

As with most RPC systems, Java IDL's location transparency is provided by *stubs*,
local proxy objects that implement the same interface as the desired remote object.
They are automatically generated from IDL specifications that define the interfaces
to the remote services. The stub compiler used by Java IDL is *idltojava*. Of course,
developers program to the Java interfaces generated by the IDL compiler, not to the
stub classes. If the Java object that implements an IDL interface is remote, the ORB
will automatically create an instance of the appropriate stub class that implements
that IDL interface. In addition to stubs, skeleton classes may optionally be generated for use in implementing CORBA server objects. Like stubs, skeletons implement the operation-specific argument marshalling and unmarshalling for a CORBA
invocation.

Perhaps the single most important example of the Java language mapping's
extensions beyond more traditional IDL language mappings is in the area of the
stub and skeleton implementations. This was not covered in traditional language
mappings because it was assumed that the stubs and skeletons could be considered
to be coupled with the specifics of the implementation of a particular vendor's
ORB. However, with the downloaded applet model, CORBA applets can be truly
portable only if stubs and skeletons can run on any vendor's ORB. This means that
stub and skeleton implementations must be able to rely on access to certain APIs
that were not formerly included in the language-mapping specifications. The specification of these APIs enables binary compatibility between stubs and skeletons from
arbitrary vendors and compliant ORBs.

The *idltojava* compiler takes IDL input and generates Java stubs and skeletons that
support the IDL Java language mapping described in Appendix A. For Java IDL, *idltojava* is available on Solaris, Windows 95, and Windows NT. The Java stubs and
skeletons generated by the compiler are then included in the usual Java compilation
of the desired Java application (client or server).

The Object Request Broker

The central interface in the ORB core is the ORB itself. The ORB is the programmer interface to the Object Request Broker. The ORB runtime provides the general
infrastructure to support object location and remote connections. Together with the

generated stubs and skeletons, it enables the transparent access to heterogeneous remote objects that characterizes the CORBA architecture.

Some of the most relevant methods of the ORB API are described in Figure 5.1.

Figure 5.1 Excerpts from class org.omg.CORBA.ORB.

```java
import java.util.Properties;

  public class ORB {

  // Return the ORB singleton object. This method always returns
  // the same ORB which is an instance of the class described by
  // the org.omg.CORBA.ORBSingletonClass system property. When
  // called in an applet environment, the returned ORB can only
  // be used as a factory for TypeCodes. The resulting TypeCodes
  // can be safely shared between untrusted applets.
  public static ORB init();

  // ORB constructors for applets and applications
  public static ORB init(Applet app, Properties props);
  public static ORB init(String args[], Properties props);

  // Objects created by the user become ORB objects
  // after connect is called.
  public abstract void connect(org.omg.CORBA.Object obj);

  // To stop an ORB object from receiving remote invocations
  // disconnect needs to be called.
  public abstract void disconnect(org.omg.CORBA.Object obj);

  // Locate references to initial services
  public abstract String[] list_initial_services();

  // Resolve one of the initial CORBA references by name
  public abstract org.omg.CORBA.Object
    resolve_initial_references(String object_name)
    throws ORBPackage.InvalidName;

  // Convert a CORBA object reference to a string
  public abstract String object_to_string(org.omg.CORBA.Object obj);

  // Restore a stringified CORBA object reference
  public abstract org.omg.CORBA.Object string_to_object(String str);

    [....]
}
```

The static ORB initialization methods differentiate between applets and applications. The arguments provide state to the ORB for initialization and later use.

The list_initial_services() and resolve_initial_references() methods are used for bootstrapping and are discussed in more detail in the *Bootstrapping* section. The object_to_string() and string_to_object() methods are used for archival and linearization purposes. They provide the means to convert a CORBA object reference to a string and to later restore it to its original state with all of its type information preserved. Because the format of object references is standardized, this translation works across different CORBA 2.0-compliant ORB implementations.

Holders and Helpers

Although this chapter does not specifically delve into the details of the Java mapping specification, it is nevertheless useful to describe two categories of support classes that will appear in a number of the examples throughout the remainder of the book.

IDL supports three types of parameters: **in**, **out**, and **inout**. As the names indicate, **in** parameters are transmitted only from client to server, **out** parameters are transmitted only from server to client, and **inout** parameters are transmitted in both directions. Because Java's parameter-passing semantics do not support **out** or **inout** parameters directly, the mapping required the introduction of *holder* classes to support these parameter-passing modes. The underlying system includes predefined holder classes for basic IDL data types, with new ones being generated by *idltojava* for all user-defined types. A holder includes a public data member that holds its value, and a pair of constructors: one taking no arguments and one taking an initial value.

```
package org.omg.CORBA;
public class LongHolder {
  public long value;
  public LongHolder () { }
  public LongHolder (long initial)  {value = initial;}
}
```

For all user-defined IDL types, *idltojava* generates a class of the same name that represents the type as well as a *helper* class that contains static methods for manipulating the type. In addition to the basic manipulation methods (*Any* insert and extract, typecode access, etc.) that appear on all *helper* classes, *helper* classes for interfaces also include a static narrow() method, used to convert a more general superclass such as Object to the particular type on which the method is invoked.

Initializing Java IDL Applications

Although the focus of the CORBA specification is interoperability, it does not currently specify the bootstrapping process in sufficient detail to ensure portability at that level. The details of how one connects to an ORB to get the object reference to an initial Naming context are left ambiguous, leading to vendor-specific implementations that do not interoperate.

To address this problem, Sun Microsystems has developed a proposal for an Interoperable Naming Service (INS) in cooperation with other ORB vendors. This proposal covers the details of the bootstrapping protocol, as well as some common initial namespace contexts and common Naming conventions. This proposal is still in draft form and has not yet been officially standardized by the OMG, but as several key vendors are planning to implement key components of the proposal it is likely to be useful even prior to formal standardization. Java IDL implements the bootstrapping protocol, and the designated bootstrapping port (900) has been reserved with the Internet Assigned Numbers Authority (IANA). The proposal draft can currently be found at www.sun.com/solaris/neo/wp-naming-svc.

COS Naming

Perhaps the most important service for a distributed application is Naming. The OMG defines the COS Naming service as one of its Common Object Services, and a transient version of this service is implemented as part of Java IDL.

The COS Naming service divides the namespace into a number of contexts. Contexts are roughly comparable to directories (or folders), and much like directories, they may be arbitrarily nested. Names are composed of an ordered series of name components. The last component is the name of the designated object, which is comparable to a file in its position as a leaf node in the Naming hierarchy. The intermediate components are an ordered list of contexts that are used to navigate the namespace. Names may be added to and deleted from the namespace via the bind(), unbind(), and rebind() methods; objects are located via the resolve() method (see Figure 5.2).

Access to the COS namespace is generally provided at initialization time, where a reference to an initial Naming context is provided as one of the CORBA Initial Services, as described in the next section.

Figure 5.2 Excerpts from org.omg.CosNaming.NamingContext.

```
package org.omg.CosNaming;
import org.omg.CosNaming.NamingContextPackage.*

public interface NamingContext {

  // bind an object reference to a named location in a NamingContext

  public abstract void bind(NameComponent n[],
                                 org.omg.CORBA.Object obj)
  throws NotFound, CannotProceed, InvalidName, AlreadyBound;

  // bind a NamingContext to a named location in another context

  public abstract void bind_context(NameComponent n[],
                                    NamingContext nc)
  throws NotFound, CannotProceed, InvalidName, AlreadyBound;

  // bind a new object reference to an existing named location

  public abstract void rebind(NameComponent n[],
                                 org.omg.CORBA.Object obj)
  throws NotFound, CannotProceed, InvalidName;

  // bind a new context object reference to an existing named location

  public abstract void rebind_context(NameComponent n[],
                                      NamingContext nc)
  throws NotFound, CannotProceed, InvalidName;

  // resolve a named location into the corresponding object reference

  public abstract org.omg.CORBA.Object resolve(NameComponent n[])
  throws NotFound, CannotProceed, InvalidName;

  // unbind (remove) the named object reference from the namespace

  public abstract void unbind(NameComponent n[])
  throws NotFound, CannotProceed, InvalidName;
}
```

Bootstrapping

In steady state, using CORBA is extremely transparent to the programmer. Clients have already located the remote objects that they wish to interact with and stored them in local variables for easy reference. Remote method invocation simply involves an apparently local method invocation on that object, and the stubs, skeletons, and ORB runtime take care of almost everything else. To reach such a steady state, however, it is necessary to gain access to an initial ORB runtime object that, in turn, needs to be able to locate and connect to the remote ORB runtime objects responsible for the designated remote objects.

Bootstrapping is the process of connecting a client to a CORBA object from which it can locate the servers it wants to access. Typically this will be a root COS Naming context running on a designated CORBA host.

The CORBA 2.0 specification defines a bootstrapping process based on two methods on the ORB: `list_initial_services` and `resolve_initial_references` (see Figure 5.1). `list_initial_services()` returns an array of Java strings containing the names of the available initial services, which generally include a reference to an initial COS Naming context. `resolve_initial_references()` takes one of these names and returns a CORBA object reference for the CORBA object it represents. Once the returned object is narrowed to the appropriate type, it is ready to be used by the application.

Java IDL implements the bootstrapping API described in the Interoperable Naming Service proposal as an integrated part of the COS Naming server. Eventually, most ORBs will support the bootstrap API by default. The proposal specifies a default port on which the bootstrap server listens (port 900) and a very simple IIOP-based interface for requesting a list of initial object references.

Client Setup

Clients need add only minimal Java IDL-specific code to their Java programs to access CORBA objects. Figure 5.3 illustrates the necessary steps.

Inside the application class, it is first necessary to initialize the ORB, as shown in the example code. Once the ORB is initialized, a client can access the ORB initial services to locate a root Naming Context and use it to locate the desired service (in this case, "Example"). The service, once located, is returned as a generic CORBA object reference, which must then be narrowed to the appropriate type (in this case, Example) using the ExampleHelper class.

Once this initialization has been completed, the example variable may be used throughout the remainder of the application as a normal Java variable. Method invocations on the object reference held by that variable appear to be local but will, in fact, be converted into method invocations on the appropriate remote object. Of course, in reality, these CORBA objects may not be local so applications should be

Figure 5.3 Java IDL client initialization.

```
package ExampleModule; // Contains classes specified in the IDL module

import org.omg.CORBA.*;
import org.omg.CosNaming.*;

public class ExampleClient
{
    public static void main(String args[])
    {
        try{
            // create and initialize the ORB
            ORB orb = ORB.init(args, null);

            // get the root naming context
            org.omg.CORBA.Object objRef =
                orb.resolve_initial_references("NameService");
            NamingContext ncRef = NamingContextHelper.narrow(objRef);

            // resolve the Object Reference in Naming
            NameComponent nc = new NameComponent("Example", "");
            NameComponent path[] = {nc};
            Example exampleRef = ExampleHelper.narrow(ncRef.resolve(path));
        } catch (java.lang.Exception e) {
            System.out.println ("Failure resolving object: " + e);
        }


        // invoke on 'example' as a normal Java object...

        [ ... ]
    }
}
```

prepared to catch and recover from any exceptions thrown when access to a remote object fails unexpectedly.

Server Support

The CORBA architecture includes support for both persistent and transient objects. A *transient object* exists for no longer than the lifetime of its process. A *persistent object* exists beyond the lifetime of a particular process, and an object reference for a persistent object is guaranteed to remain valid over time. The server-side ORB maintains persistent information about the server object implementation and its state, although the responsibility for maintaining persistent data remains with the developer. This information allows the ORB to activate such a persistent object server in response to an incoming request even if it happens to be inactive at the time the request arrives.

Java IDL currently supports only transient objects. The original CORBA API for persistent objects, known as the BOA (Basic Object Adapter), was not specified in sufficient detail to ensure interoperability. The BOA has now been deprecated by the OMG in favor of a new Portable Object Adapter (POA) API.

Java IDL Transient Object API

The Java IDL transient object API is the easiest way to implement a CORBA object. The next few subsections describe how to create an object using the transient object API.

The Servant Base Class

A server developer implements an IDL interface by providing a programming language class called a *servant*. The servant implements the operations in the IDL interface. A server is a program that implements one or more IDL interfaces; that is, it provides one or more servants.

For each IDL interface X, a class named _XImplBase will be generated by *idlto-java*.

```
public abstract class _XImplBase implements X {

}
```

_XImplBase is declared to implement the interface X, but, in fact, it does not itself actually provide implementations for X's methods. The developer must subclass from it and implement all of the methods in an X servant class.

The Servant Class

For each object implementation, the developer must write a servant class. Instances of the servant class implement potential CORBA objects. Each servant class implements an IDL interface. To implement an interface named X using the Java IDL transient object API, the servant class must extend an _XImplBase class. The servant class must implement the methods corresponding to the operations and attributes of the IDL interface, as defined by the Java mapping specification for IDL interfaces. Providing these methods is sufficient to satisfy all abstract methods defined by _XImplBase.

Creating a CORBA Object

To use the newly implemented object, just create a new instance of the servant class. Initially, the object is just an ordinary Java object and can be used as such. The easiest way to create a CORBA identity for the new servant instance is to pass the object as a parameter to calls on other CORBA objects. If the object that is called is outside the local Java Virtual Machine (VM), the passed servant instance will automatically be turned into a full CORBA object. To directly associate the servant with an ORB instance and give it a CORBA identity immediately, you can call the connect() method on that ORB (see Figure 5.1). Even after a servant is connected to an ORB and becomes a CORBA object, local calls on the object will continue to go directly to the servant. Only remote calls will be processed by the ORB. To disassociate the CORBA identity of a servant use the disconnect() method on the same ORB to which that object was originally connected.

Because a reference to the servant object will become a CORBA object reference automatically if it is ever passed to a remote client, developers can implement objects that are as efficient as regular Java objects when used locally but can be distributed across a network when needed.

The Portable Object Adapter

The role of an object adapter is to create CORBA object references that correspond to objects that a server wishes to make available to CORBA clients. An object adapter is a server-side API only. When a client makes a request, the adapter notifies the developer's server code that a request has come in for that particular object reference. In theory, there could be multiple object adapters available for use by a server. Adapters could be specialized to different problem domains or oriented towards supporting certain kinds of object data persistence. The scheme described earlier in the chapter for implementing transient CORBA objects in Java is actually a very simplified object adapter built into the Java ORB class.

The Portable Object Adapter, or POA, is a new OMG standard API for implementing CORBA objects in any language with an IDL mapping. The POA can be used to implement objects using a wide range of different styles or policies including both transient objects and persistent objects. The POA is a general-purpose adapter that has a flexible set of policies that guide its behavior.

It is specified in IDL, which is mapped into a specific language using the normal rules for mapping IDL. In addition, a few features are specified specifically for each language. At the time of writing, the Java mapping of the POA has not been completed and has thus not yet been included in the Java IDL implementation. As a result, the Java code examples in this section may undergo a few minor changes, but most of this section will remain accurate. The complete POA specification is available from the OMG Web site, www.omg.org. The current version is also available as ftp://ftp.omg.org/pub/docs/orbos/97-04-14.pdf.

An ORB that supports implementing objects via the POA API will return an instance of org.omg.PortableServer.POA when its resolve_initial_references() method is called with the name "RootPOA." The root POA can be used directly to implement CORBA objects or it can be used to create named child POA instances, which are then themselves used to implement objects.

The entire POA IDL specification is contained inside a PortableServer IDL module. All standard OMG IDL specifications are defined to be mapped under the org.omg Java package prefix, so the POA code lives under the org.omg.PortableServer package.

The following code example shows a subset of methods from the POA interface related to creating new child POA instances.

```
package org.omg.PortableServer;

public interface POA ...
{
    // POA readonly attributes.
    POA the_parent();
    POAManager the_POAManager();

    POA create_POA(String name, POAManager manager,
                   org.omg.CORBA.Policy[] policies)
    throws AdapterAlreadyExists, InvalidPolicy;
}
```

POA Policies

Every POA instance follows a set of policies established when it was created. The root POA has a standard set of policies appropriate for implementing simple transient objects. Developers can create new POA instances that follow different policies.

The root POA implements the following policies: ORB_CTRL_MODEL, TRANSIENT, UNIQUE_ID, SYSTEM_ID, RETAIN, USE_ACTIVE_OBJECT_MAP_ONLY, and IMPLICIT_ACTIVATION. This means that a separate thread may be used to handle each incoming request to the servant, that object references are transient and invalid after the server exits, that each servant can implement only one object reference (and therefore one object id), and that the object id is chosen automatically by the POA and kept in an active object map.

The following table shows each of the different policy types and the range of policy options.

Policy Type	Policy Options
Thread	ORB_CTRL_MODEL, SINGLE_THREAD_MODEL
Lifespan	TRANSIENT, PERSISTENT
Object Id Uniqueness	UNIQUE_ID, MULTIPLE_ID
Object Id Assignment	USER_ID, SYSTEM_ID
Implicit Activation	IMPLICIT_ACTIVATION, NO_IMPLICIT_ACTIVATION
Servant Retention	RETAIN, NON_RETAIN
Request Processing	USE_ACTIVE_OBJECT_MAP_ONLY, USE_DEFAULT_SERVANT, USE_SERVANT_MANAGER

Creating a CORBA Object

To create a CORBA object with POA you need three items: a POA instance, an interface repository id, and an object id. The interface id determines the most-derived IDL interface that the object represents. The object id is used to determine which object is being called when a request comes into the ORB. Every distinct CORBA object reference created by a particular POA instance has its own unique object id. The developer has total control over each of these. Different styles of object implementation need different kinds of flexibility.

For simple transient objects, the root POA can be used and it can determine the interface id from the IDL compiler-generated servant base class. It will also automatically choose the object id because it uses the SYSTEM_ID policy. This means you need only create an instance of the servant and call the POA servant_to_reference() method to create the CORBA object reference.

Sometimes it is useful for the developer to assign the object id. For instance, each entry in an existing computerized personal calendar database may already be assigned a unique id by the underlying implementation. To create CORBA object references that represent this existing database, each calendar entry can be its own CORBA object and the existing database id can be used as the object id. A POA object id is just a sequence of octets (in other words, a byte array in Java).

The following methods in the POA interface can be used to create new CORBA object identities. The actual behavior of these methods is subject to the policy configuration of the actual POA instance that is used.

```
package org.omg.PortableServer;

public interface POA ...
{
    // Use following 2 methods with RETAIN policy. Obtain object reference
    // through servant_to_reference() or id_to_reference() methods
    byte[]
    activate_object(Servant p_servant)
    throws ServantAlreadyActive, WrongPolicy;

    void
    activate_object_with_id(byte[]id, Servant servant)
    throws ServantAlreadyActive, ObjectAlreadyActive, WrongPolicy;

    // Requires SYSTEM_ID policy.
    org.omg.CORBA.Object
    create_reference(String interface_id)
    throws WrongPolicy;

    org.omg.CORBA.Object
    create_reference_with_id(byte[] oid, String interface_id)
    throws WrongPolicy;

    // Useful with root POA for transient objects
    org.omg.CORBA.Object
    servant_to_reference(Servant servant)
    throws ServantNotActive, WrongPolicy;
}
```

Servant Managers and the Active Object Map

Other than creating new object references, the primary task of the POA is to process incoming requests from clients. To do this it must find the servant that provides the runtime behavior for the target object reference. The way in which it does this is controlled by POA policies.

Using typical policies, the POA takes the object id from the target and looks for a servant in its *active object map*. If the map does not contain a servant for that object id then the POA will check to see if a servant manager has been registered. If so, it calls the servant manager passing it the object id and asking it to return a servant. By implementing and registering a servant manager, a developer can directly control the association of object ids with servants. By choosing to use an active object map, the developer can cause the POA to cache the results of the servant lookup.

It is also possible to choose POA policies that use a single *default servant* for all objects or for any objects not explicitly activated by the server.

Persistent Objects

Persistent objects are objects whose lifespan is independent of the server that created them. If a client makes a request on a persistent object and its server has exited, an ORB agent will cause the object's server to be restarted automatically. The newly started server must recreate any POA instances it has used to create its object references. These can be recreated during startup or the server can implement and register an *Adapter Activator*, which will be called to recreate the POA instances as required for incoming client requests. It is up to each POA implementation to provide administrative tools for configuring ORB agents so they may start persistent servers when needed.

The POA Manager

Every POA instance is associated with a POA Manager that controls its request processing state. By default, each POA has its own unique manager, but POAs can also be associated at creation time with an existing manager. Newly created managers are in the *holding* state. The POAs controlled by the manager will begin processing requests when their manager's activate() method is called. POA Managers can also be set to discard incoming requests or can be deactivated as part of server shutdown.

Servants and Servant Base Classes

Just like the Java IDL transient object API, the POA also specifies a standard servant base class that will be generated for each IDL interface. The POA servant base class contains abstract method declarations for each of the IDL interface's methods. The object developer writes a servant class to implement an object. The servant class inherits from the servant base class and provides implementations for each of the IDL operations in the interface.

The POA methods shown here support looking up the associations between servants, object ids, and object references for objects implemented with a particular POA instance.

```
package org.omg.PortableServer;

public interface POA ...
{
  // Methods for obtaining servants, references and object ids
  byte[]
  servant_to_id(Servant p_servant)
  throws ServantNotActive, WrongPolicy;

  org.omg.CORBA.Object
  servant_to_reference(Servant p_servant)
  throws ServantNotActive, WrongPolicy;

  Servant
  reference_to_servant(org.omg.CORBA.Object reference)
  throws ObjectNotActive, WrongAdapter, WrongPolicy;

  byte[]
  reference_to_id(org.omg.CORBA.Object reference)
  throws WrongAdapter, WrongPolicy;

  Servant
  id_to_servant(byte[] oid)
  throws ObjectNotActive, WrongPolicy;

  org.omg.CORBA.Object
  id_to_reference(byte[] oid)
  throws ObjectNotActive, WrongPolicy;
}
```

Java IDL Infrastructure

In this section, we'll take a look at how the Java IDL implementation is structured
to maintain portability across ORB implementations. The interfaces described in
the following subsections are not used by developers, but they help to understand
the infrastructure underlying the developer API.

The Portable Stub API

The portable stub API is part of the OMG Java IDL mapping standard. It is
designed to maintain a separation between the classes generated by an IDL compiler and the underlying ORB implementation. This allows ORBs that implement
different network protocols, different qualities of service, and other features to be
used with the same application and stub and skeleton classes. It also means that

applets can be written so that they can be downloaded into any Web browser that contains an embedded ORB implementation, even if that ORB implementation is different from the one for which the applet was originally developed. As long as the ORB in the browser supports the OMG Java IDL mapping standard, your applet can use the bundled ORB without having to download the ORB implementation classes with your applet. You can still download your own ORB implementation and use it instead, if desired.

To make this work, the classes generated by the IDL compiler depend on the portable stub API in the org.omg.CORBA.portable Java package to interface with the underlying ORB. This means that an interface that was previously private, the one used by generated stubs and skeletons to access the ORB internals, must now be standardized across different vendors' ORB implementations. Note that the portability of the Stub API is independent of object implementation details on the server, and thus has no specific relation to the POA or any other object adapter.

There are four primary classes defined there: the ObjectImpl class, the Delegate class, and the input and output streaming classes. Note that this API is typically used by generated stubs, not by developers.

ObjectImpl

Every stub and skeleton generated by an IDL compiler for Java will extend the ObjectImpl class (see Figure 5.4) defined in the org.omg.CORBA.portable package. The ObjectImpl class contains a single instance variable called a *delegate*. The methods defined by the CORBA Object interface are implemented by forwarding the invocations to the delegate object, which is described in the following section. Figure 5.5 illustrates the inheritance relationship for the stubs of an interface X.

Delegate

The delegate contains the ORB-specific state and implementation for the object reference. The separation of the type-specific information in the stub and the ORB-specific information in the delegate allows the same delegate implementation to be used for any IDL interface. In addition, this separation also allows the same stub to be used with different ORB implementations. Each ORB implements delegate classes by extending the common Delegate base class (see Figure 5.6).

Figure 5.4 ObjectImpl API.

```
public abstract class ObjectImpl implements org.omg.CORBA.Object {
  private Delegate _delegate;
  public Delegate _get_delegate() {
    if (_delegate == null)
      throw new org.omg.CORBA.BAD_OPERATION();
    return _delegate;
  }
  public org.omg.CORBA.InterfaceDef _get_interface() {
    return _get_delegate().get_interface(this);
  }
  public boolean _is_a(String repository_id) {
    return _get_delegate().is_a(this, repository_id);
  }
  [...]
}
```

Input and Output Streams

The other part of enabling IDL compiler-generated classes to be ORB independent is handling the streaming or marshalling of IDL data types. IDL data types are converted into protocol-specific formats using instances of the InputStream and

Figure 5.5 Inheritance for object stubs.

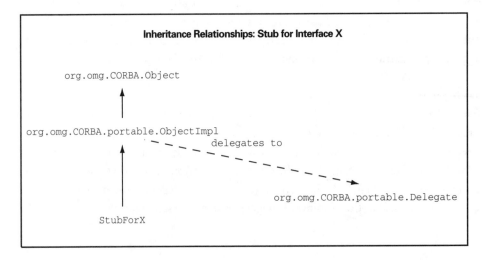

Figure 5.6 Delegate API.

```
public abstract class Delegate {
  public abstract org.omg.CORBA.InterfaceDef
  get_interface(org.omg.CORBA.Object self);

  public abstract boolean
  is_a(org.omg.CORBA.Object self, String repository_id);

  public abstract boolean
  is_equivalent(org.omg.CORBA.Object self, org.omg.CORBA.Object rhs);
  [...]
}
```

OutputStream classes (see Figure 5.7). These are abstract classes that each ORB implementation must subclass to implement specific data-encoding formats such as the one used for IIOP. Simple types are marshalled directly while composite types such as IDL structs are marshalled as combinations of the primitive ones.

Figure 5.7 InputStream and OutputStream API.

```
public abstract class InputStream {
  // simple type unmarshalling
  public abstract byte read_octet();
  public abstract short read_short();

  // array type unmarshalling
  public abstract void read_octet_array(byte[] value, int offset,
    int length);
  [...]
}
public abstract class OutputStream {
  // simple type marshalling
  public abstract void write_short(int arg);
  public abstract void write_string(String arg);

  // array type marshalling
  public abstract void write_char_array(char[] arg, int offset,
    int length);
  // object marshalling
  public abstract void write_Object(org.omg.CORBA.Object value);
  [...]
}
```

Living Inside Firewalls (HTTP Tunneling)

Many companies protect their internal data by surrounding their internal networks with *firewalls*. In general, firewalls work by requiring that all external communication pass through a single secure gateway. Some firewalls restrict only incoming communication; others restrict outgoing communication to connections initiated by a small set of known programs or protocols, such as browsers, mail programs, ftp, and Telnet programs; others completely restrict both incoming and outgoing communication.

There is no workaround for this problem in the first release of Java IDL, although some ORB vendors provide strategies such as HTTP tunneling or special firewall modules. A real fix will require firewall vendors to properly support IIOP.

Applet Issues

Downloaded applets represent arbitrary active content running on a user's private machine. This provides a great deal of flexibility, but it also enables a number of potential security attacks. Unlike other types of active content such as ActiveX, Java restricts applets to an applet *sandbox* from which their access to system resources such as disk, memory, and the network is carefully controlled.

Prior to the JDK 1.1 release, applets were effectively prevented from most external accesses. They were not allowed access to the local disk or to underlying operating system calls, they were not allowed to listen for incoming connections, and they were prevented from opening outgoing connections to any host other than the one from which they were downloaded.

These restrictions are great for security, but they severely restrict the functionality of distributed programs. The JDK 1.1 and later provide support for relaxing these restrictions based on certificates and digital signatures.

Digitally Signed Applets

The restrictions imposed on applets are based on the assumption that because they are downloaded they are inherently not trusted. As the state of the art in distributed security and authentication improves, this assumption can gradually be relaxed.

The JDK 1.1 release supports digitally signed applets. An applet can be tagged with a particular digital signature, or a set of digital signatures, and applet security

:ional based on the acceptance of particular digital
 worse than trusting the software that comes on a

ig on functionality rather than performance, perfor-
of the basic model of the Java Virtual Machine and

ince has been a problem has been applet download
P protocol requires a new TCP connection for each
l the default Java class-loading protocol requests a
ise the Java compiler allows only a single Java class
cause "good" Java coding technique encourages large
:ombination of features ensures problematic down-
t of any reasonable size.

ause most of these conditions are in the process of
, the HTTP protocol has evolved toward permitting
tion, Java archive files enable the large number of
small data transfers involved in current applet downloads to be replaced by a small
number of much larger data transfers. This will significantly reduce the download
time.

JDK 1.1 and Netscape 4.0 already support Java archive files. These are referred
to as *JAR* files and consist of a collection of Java classes (and other data such as
image files) in optionally compressed Zip format along with some meta information. A list of archive files may be designated via the keyword ARCHIVE within an
HTML Java APPLET tag followed by a comma-separated list of archive filenames.
The named archive files will be searched for in the location defined by the already
existing applet CODEBASE keyword.

Another performance issue has to do with Java's being an interpreted language. Its portability depends on the fact that the Java source code is compiled
into architecture-neutral bytecodes rather than architecture-specific executables.
Interpretation provides a great deal of flexibility, but it necessarily adds some
performance overhead.

One solution to this problem is *JustInTime* (JIT) compilers. These compilers are built into the Java VM runtime and translate the Java bytecodes into native processor instructions on the fly. For smaller, short-lived applications, the overhead of running a JIT compiler may not be beneficial; however, for larger, longer-lived applications it can significantly improve the overall performance.

Chapter Summary

Java IDL provides support for Java applications to participate fully in the world of three-tier enterprise distributed systems. Java itself contributes an easy, lightweight entry into Web-based computing with its zero-administration thin client model. Together, these complementary technologies provide businesses with a way to extend their heterogeneous enterprise systems, complete with legacy data, to include widespread client access over the Web.

Java IDL's architecture and implementation are compliant with the new OMG Java language mapping, which goes beyond the language mappings of more traditional languages to provide a portable binary interface between applications, their IDL compiler-generated stubs, and ORB implementations.

Now that we have a basic under   ire and some of the key APIs, the following chap   ts and servers of increasing complexity to illustrat   truction of distributed enterprise applications.

A Basic Java IDL
Applet and Server

Now that you're acquainted with some of the concepts of Java IDL, let's see how we apply those concepts to create a simple Java IDL applet. The primary purpose of this applet is to demonstrate basic Java IDL programming techniques, not to write a really complex applet (later examples will do that). We'll start with something that could be written as a single-tier applet in pure Java. In time-honored tradition, we'll start with a variation on "Hello World!"

Figure 6.1 shows a somewhat interactive "Hello World!" applet running. There are three areas to the applet's user interface: The upper-left region displays a message; the upper-right area has a Choice menu with a Label; and at the bottom is a text entry field. We can change the color in which the message is displayed by choosing different colors from the Choice menu, and we can change the text of the message by entering new text in the field at the bottom.

This is certainly simple enough to implement in plain Java, so let's look at how to do that; then we'll see how to use Java IDL to turn it into a client/server application.

Figure 6.1 A running "Hello World!" applet.

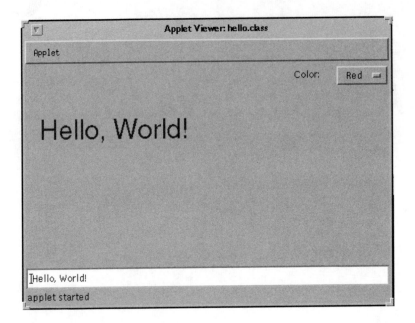

The Java Applet

Here's one possible implementation of the applet:

We'll define two classes called `Hello` and `myCanvas`. `Hello` is a subclass of the Java-supplied class `java.applet.Applet`; it is responsible for laying out and initializing the various GUI elements. `myCanvas` is a subclass of `java.awt.Canvas`. It is a display area that will exhibit the text in the selected color. Following is a simple block diagram of the classes and their responsibilities.

Let's look at the code a piece at a time.

```
import java.awt.*;
import java.awt.event*;

public class Hello extends java.applet.Applet
                    implements ItemListener, ActionListener
{

    TextField  canvasText;
    Label      colorLabel;
```

Figure 6.2 GUI elements and their responsibilities.

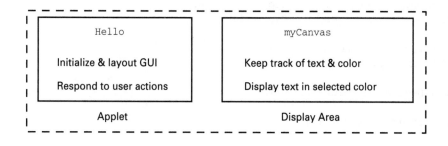

```
Choice      colorChoice;
myCanvas    HelloCanvas;
Panel       colorPanel;
```

We import all the classes in the packages `java.awt` and `java.awt.event` as a convenience; we'll be using a number of these classes, and by importing them, we won't have to give the full package name each time we use one. Next, we define our class `Hello` and declare some instance variables of that class; these variables are the different pieces of our GUI. The classes `TextField`, `Label`, `Choice`, and `Panel` are all Java-supplied classes (part of `java.awt`); we will define the class `myCanvas` later. Note that we have defined `Hello` to implement two `Listener` interfaces; this will allow us to enable the applet to handle events generated in the GUI elements.

```
/**
 * init
 * Set up the initial graphical interface and set the various
 * objects (choice button, textfield) with default values
 */
public void init() {

  setLayout(new BorderLayout(10,10));

  colorPanel = new Panel();
  colorLabel = new Label("Color: ");
  colorChoice = new Choice();
  colorChoice.addItem("Red");
  colorChoice.addItem("Green");
  colorChoice.addItem("Blue");
  colorPanel.add(colorLabel);
  colorPanel.add(colorChoice);
```

```
    colorChoice.addItemListener(this);

    HelloCanvas = new myCanvas("Hello World!", "Red");
    canvasText = new TextField("Hello World!");

    add("East", colorPanel);
    add("South", canvasText);

    canvasText.addActionListener(this);

    add("Center", HelloCanvas);
}
```

Java defines the notion of a layout manager to manage screen real estate. We choose a built-in layout manager called BorderLayout. Our init() method initializes the elements of the GUI and adds them to the layout. colorChoice is a Choice menu with the three items "Red," "Green," and "Blue"; colorPanel consists of colorChoice and a Label with the text "Color:"; HelloCanvas is initialized with the text "Hello World!" and the color "Red"; and the text entry field canvasText also has an initial text of "Hello World!". We have registered the applet as a listener for selected events taking place in colorChoice and canvasText. The results of executing this method and then displaying the applet are illustrated in Figure 6.1. For more information on laying out Java GUI items and java.awt in general, see Chapter 2, "Java Fundamentals."

```
public void itemStateChanged(ItemEvent e)
    {
        if(e.getSource() == colorChoice)
        {
          // Set the new color
          HelloCanvas.setDisplayColor((String)e.getItem());
          HelloCanvas.repaint();
        }
    }

public void actionPerformed(ActionEvent e)
    {
        if(e.getSource() == canvasText)
        {
            // Set the new string to display
            HelloCanvas.setDisplayText(canvasText.getText());
            HelloCanvas.repaint();
        }
    }
```

These methods receive events when the user does something with our GUI elements. If the user has chosen a color, then `colorChoice` will fire off an `ItemEvent`. Because we have registered the applet with `colorChoice` as an `ItemListener`, the applet's `itemStateChanged()` method will be called. This in turn calls `HelloCanvas'` `setDisplayColor()` method. If the user has entered new text, then the applet's `actionPerformed()` method will call `HelloCanvas'` `setDisplayText()` method. In either case, the canvas is repainted.

Next, we look at the `myCanvas` class:

```
class myCanvas extends Canvas
{
  private int width=200;
  private int height=200;

  private String displayText;
  private String displayColor;

  public myCanvas(String t, String c)
  {
    setBounds(new Rectangle(5, 5, width, height));
    setDisplayText(t);
    setDisplayColor (c);
  }

  public void setDisplayText(String t)
  {
    displayText = t;
  }

  public void setDisplayColor(String c)
  {
    displayColor = c;
  }
```

`myCanvas` is a subclass of `java.awt.Canvas`. It has two `String` instance variables that hold the text and the color to be displayed and a public constructor that takes two `String` input parameters, one for text and one for color. The constructor calls two methods that set the object's instance variable to the values of the input parameters.

```
  public String getDisplayText() {

    return displayText;
  }
```

```
public Color getDisplayColor() {

  Color returnColor = Color.lightGray;

  if (displayColor.equals("Red"))
    returnColor = Color.red;
  else if (displayColor.equals("Green"))
    returnColor = Color.green;
  else if (displayColor.equals("Blue"))
    returnColor = Color.blue;

  return returnColor;
}
```

The next two methods retrieve the text and color instance variables. getDisplayText() simply returns the string stored in the variable displayText with no changes, but getDisplayColor() examines the string in displayColor and then returns a Color object whose value depends on the string.

```
/**
 * paint
 * Use the current display values (text, color) to display
 * the new canvas picture
 */
public void paint(Graphics g) {

  g.setColor(Color.lightGray);
  g.fillRect(0, 0, width, height);
  g.setColor(getDisplayColor());
  g.setFont(new Font("Helvetica", Font.PLAIN ,36));
  g.drawString(getDisplayText(), 20, (height/2));
}
```

The final method of myCanvas displays the text in the appropriate color. It uses the two *get* methods to retrieve the correct values and then calls methods defined by the java.awt.Graphics class to do the actual displaying.

That's all the code we need for the Java-only version of our "Hello World!" applet. What follows is a listing of the entire applet.

```
import java.awt.*;
import java.awt.event.*;

public class Hello extends java.applet.Applet
                   implements ItemListener, ActionListener
{
```

```java
    TextField  canvasText;
    Label      colorLabel;
    Choice     colorChoice;
    myCanvas   HelloCanvas;
    Panel      colorPanel;

/**
 * init
 * Set up the initial graphical interface and set the various
 * objects (choice button, textfield) with default
 * values.
 */
  public void init()
  {
     setLayout(new BorderLayout(10,10));

     colorPanel = new Panel();

     colorLabel = new Label("Color: ");
     colorChoice = new Choice();
     colorChoice.addItem("Red");
     colorChoice.addItem("Green");
     colorChoice.addItem("Blue");
     colorPanel.add(colorLabel);
     colorPanel.add(colorChoice);

     colorChoice.addItemListener(this);

     HelloCanvas = new myCanvas("Hello World!", "Red");
     canvasText = new TextField("Hello World!");

     canvasText.addActionListener(this);

     add("East", colorPanel);
     add("South", canvasText);
     add("Center", HelloCanvas);

  }


  public void itemStateChanged(ItemEvent e)
  {
      if(e.getSource() == colorChoice)
      {
          // Set the new color
      HelloCanvas.setDisplayColor((String)e.getItem());
      HelloCanvas.repaint();
```

```
            }
    }

    public void actionPerformed(ActionEvent e)
    {
        if(e.getSource() == canvasText)
        {
          // Set the new string to display
            HelloCanvas.setDisplayText(canvasText.getText());
            HelloCanvas.repaint();
        }
    }


}
class myCanvas extends Canvas {

    private int width=200;
    private int height=200;

    private String displayText;
    private String displayColor;

    public myCanvas(String t, String c) {

      setBounds(new Rectangle(5,5,width,height));
      setDisplayText(t);
      setDisplayColor (c);
    }

    public void setDisplayText(String t) {

      displayText = t;
    }

    public void setDisplayColor(String c) {

      displayColor = c;
    }

    public String  getDisplayText() {

      return displayText;
    }

    public Color getDisplayColor() {

      Color returnColor = Color.lightGray;
```

```
    if (displayColor.equals("Red"))
      returnColor = Color.red;
    else if (displayColor.equals("Green"))
      returnColor = Color.green;
    else if (displayColor.equals("Blue"))
      returnColor = Color.blue;

    return returnColor;
  }

/**
 * paint
 * Use the current display values (text, color) to display
 * the new canvas picture
 */
  public void paint(Graphics g) {
    g.setColor(Color.lightGray);
    g.fillRect(0, 0, width, height);
    g.setColor(getDisplayColor());
    g.setFont(new Font("Helvetica", Font.PLAIN, 36));
    g.drawString(getDisplayText(), 20, (height/2));
  }
}
```

Setting Up for Java IDL

Now that we've seen how to write an interactive "Hello World!" applet in Java, let's turn it into a CORBA client/server application using Java IDL. Because the main purpose of the applet is to display a string, the server piece of our application ought to hold and return the string, and the client ought to retrieve the string from the server and display it. We'll be using CORBA's Interface Definition Language (IDL) to define the interface of the server.

The IDL looks like this:

```
module Hello
{
  interface HelloWorld
  {
   void setHello(in string HelloString);
   void getHello(out string HelloString);
  };
};
```

As you can see, it's very straightforward; we define an interface named HelloWorld within a module named Hello. This interface has two methods, one for setting the string, setHello(), that takes a string as an input parameter, and one for returning the string, getHello(), that takes a string as an output parameter. (We could have defined getHello() to return a string instead, but this definition helps illustrate how IDL output parameters are mapped.)

To use an object defined by this IDL in a program written in Java, we need to compile the IDL into Java code. This generates Java stub classes that let our client access the server object. For more on how CORBA clients and servers communicate, see Chapter 3, "Introduction to CORBA."

The Java IDL Applet

We are now ready to turn our Java applet into one that uses Java IDL. The essential steps for doing that are these:

- Establish a connection to the server ORB.

- Ask the ORB for a reference to the HelloWorld server object.

- Use the reference to make calls on the server object.

In order to accomplish these steps, we'll have to make changes to both the Hello and myCanvas classes.

The changes to the applet class are as follows (**boldface** type indicates new or modified code):

- Add a new instance variable to hold a reference to the server:

```
Hello.HelloWorld helloObj;
```

  - Note the multilevel Hello.HelloWorld type for this variable. This convention will be explained in the *Mapped Classes* section that follows.

- Make changes to init():

  - Establish a connection to the ORB. This is done by initializing a new ORB object.

```
ORB orb = ORB.init(this, null);
```

- Use the ORB's Name Service to find the server, which is named "Hello", and return a reference to it.

```
org.omg.CORBA.Object obj =
    orb.resolve_initial_references("NameService");
NamingContext ncRef = NamingContextHelper.narrow(obj);

// resolve the Object Reference in Naming
NameComponent nc = new NameComponent("Hello", "");
NameComponent path[] = {nc};
helloObj = Hello.HelloWorldHelper.narrow(ncRef.resolve(path));
```

- Pass `helloObj` to the `myCanvas` constructor.

```
HelloCanvas = new myCanvas(helloObj, "Red");
```

- Obtain the string from `helloObj` and use it to initialize the text entry field. The `stringHolder` object is an instance of the Holder objects described in the *Holders and Helpers* section of Chapter 5.

```
helloObj.getHello(stringHolder);
canvasText = new TextField(stringHolder.value);
```

- Make changes to `actionPerformed()`.
  - If new text is entered, change the string in the server.

```
helloObj.setHello(canvasText.getText());
```

There are some other minor code additions, such as importing new packages, defining the `stringHolder` object used to get the string from the server (the `StringHolder` class, along with other new classes used by Java IDL will be discussed in detail in the next section), and handling any exceptions that can potentially be raised by most of the calls involving the ORB or the server object. You will see those things in the listing that follows.

The changes to `myCanvas` essentially convert references to the `displayText` variable to references or calls to the server object. Here they are:

- Substitute a reference to a `HelloWorld` server object for the `displayText` instance variable.

```
private Hello.HelloWorld helloObj;
```

- Make changes to the constructor:

- Take a `HelloWorld` object as an input parameter.

  ```
  public myCanvas(Hello.HelloWorld obj, String c)
  ```

- Call a new method to set the `helloObj` instance variable.

  ```
  setHelloObj(obj);
  ```

- Make changes to `getDisplayText()`:
  - Retrieve the text from the server and return that.

    ```
    helloObj.getHello(stringHolder);

    return stringHolder.value;
    ```

- Use a new method to set `helloObj`, replacing `setDisplayText()`.

  ```
  public void setHelloObj(Hello.HelloWorld obj)
  {
      helloObj = obj;
  }
  ```

Similar to the changes just made to the `Hello` class, the changes to `myCanvas` also include exception handling and other minor tasks. These are shown in the code listing that follows.

Here's all the code for the Java IDL version of the "Hello World!" applet:

```
import java.awt.*;
import java.awt.event.*;
import org.omg.CosNaming.*;
import org.omg.CosNaming.NamingContextPackage.*;
import org.omg.CORBA.*;


public class HelloJoe extends java.applet.Applet
                      implements ItemListener, ActionListener
{
    TextField   canvasText;
    Label       colorLabel;
    Choice      colorChoice;
    myCanvas    HelloCanvas;
    Panel       colorPanel;

    Hello.HelloWorld helloObj;
```

```
public void init()
{
   org.omg.CORBA.StringHolder stringHolder =
      new org.omg.CORBA.StringHolder("");

   try
   {
      ORB orb = ORB.init(this, null);

      // get the root naming context
         org.omg.CORBA.Object obj =
               orb.resolve_initial_references("NameService");
         NamingContext ncRef = NamingContextHelper.narrow(obj);

         // resolve the Object Reference in Naming
         NameComponent nc = new NameComponent("Hello", "");
         NameComponent path[] = {nc};
         helloObj = Hello.HelloWorldHelper.narrow(ncRef.resolve(path));

   }
   catch (Exception e)
   {
      System.out.println ("caught Exception "
                             + e.toString());
      throw new Error ("find/narrow failed!");
   }


   setLayout(new BorderLayout(10,10));

   colorPanel = new Panel();

   colorLabel = new Label("Color: ");
   colorChoice = new Choice();
   colorChoice.addItem("Red");
   colorChoice.addItem("Green");
   colorChoice.addItem("Blue");
   colorPanel.add(colorLabel);
   colorPanel.add(colorChoice);

   colorChoice.addItemListener(this);



   HelloCanvas = new myCanvas(helloObj, "Red");
   try
```

```
          {
            helloObj.getHello(stringHolder);
          }
          catch (Exception e)
          {
              System.out.println ("caught Exception "
                                    + e.toString());
              throw new Error ("getHello failed");
          }

          canvasText = new TextField(stringHolder.value);

          canvasText.addActionListener(this);


          add("East", colorPanel);
          add("South", canvasText);
          add("Center", HelloCanvas);
      }



      public void itemStateChanged(ItemEvent e)
      {
          if(e.getSource() == colorChoice)
          {
              // Set the new color
          HelloCanvas.setDisplayColor((String)e.getItem());
          HelloCanvas.repaint();
          }
      }

      public void actionPerformed(ActionEvent e)
      {
          if(e.getSource() == canvasText)
          {
            // Set the new string to display
            try
            {
              helloObj.setHello(canvasText.getText());
            }
            catch (Exception ex)
            {
              System.out.println ("Exception "
                                    + ex.toString());
              throw new Error ("setHello() failed!");
            }
```

```
            HelloCanvas.repaint();
        }
    }
}


class myCanvas extends Canvas
{
    private int width=200;
    private int height=200;

    private Hello.HelloWorld helloObj;
    private String displayColor;


    public myCanvas(Hello.HelloWorld obj, String c)
    {
        setBounds(new Rectangle(5,5,width,height));
        setHelloObj(obj);
        setDisplayColor(c);
    }

    public void setHelloObj(Hello.HelloWorld obj)
    {
        helloObj = obj;
    }

    public void setDisplayColor(String c)
    {
        displayColor = c;
    }


    public String getDisplayText()
    {
        org.omg.CORBA.StringHolder stringHolder = new
            org.omg.CORBA.StringHolder("");
        try
        {
            helloObj.getHello(stringHolder);
        }
        catch (Exception e)
        {
            System.out.println ("caught Exception "
                                    + e.toString());
            throw new Error ("getHello failed");
```

```
        }

    return stringHolder.value;
    }

  public Color getDisplayColor()
  {
      Color returnColor = Color.lightGray;

      if (displayColor.equals("Red"))
      returnColor = Color.red;
      else if (displayColor.equals("Green"))
      returnColor = Color.green;
      else if (displayColor.equals("Blue"))
      returnColor = Color.blue;

      return returnColor;
    }

/**
 * paint
 * Use the current display values (text, color) to display
 * the new canvas picture
 */
  public void paint(Graphics g) {
    g.setColor(Color.lightGray);
    g.fillRect(0, 0, width, height);
    g.setColor(getDisplayColor());
    g.setFont(new Font("Helvetica", Font.PLAIN, 36));
    g.drawString(getDisplayText(), 20, (height/2));
  }
}
```

The Java IDL Applet—A Closer Look at the Classes

In the example just shown, we saw references to some new classes, some of them provided in the Java IDL packages, others generated by the IDL compiler. Let's spend some time going over these classes in more detail.

Java IDL Classes

The Java IDL classes used in the applet are `org.omg.CORBA.Object`, `org.omg.CORBA.StringHolder`, `org.omg.CORBA.ORB`,

org.omg.CosNaming.NamingContext, and org.omg.CosNaming
.NameComponent.

- org.omg.CORBA.Object

  This is a reference to a generic CORBA object; it is the top of the hierarchy for all CORBA object references, and it must be downcast (narrowed) to a particular type of reference before the methods for that type can be used.

- org.omg.CORBA.StringHolder

  This is a class that holds strings; the string is contained in a public data member called *value*. Objects of this class are used as parameters to methods whose IDL definition includes an **out** or **inout** parameter of type string, as does getHello() in our example (see the earlier section, *Setting Up for Java IDL*).

- org.omg.CORBA.ORB

  This class represents an ORB implementation. We use its static init() method to establish a connection to the ORB instance, from which the applet obtains server object references, and its resolve_initial_refer-ences() method to retrieve a NamingContext object, described next.

- org.omg.CosNaming.NamingContext

  This class provides methods for placing and finding object references in a Naming context tree. We use its resolve() method in our example to return a reference to the HelloWorld server.

- org.omg.CosNaming.NameComponent

  This class encapsulates a string and is required by NamingContext methods.

  For more on Java IDL classes, see Chapter 5.

Mapped Classes

When you map IDL that looks like

```
module X
{
      interface Y
      { ...
      }
}
```

to Java, a mapping of the form

```
module -> package
interface -> classes
```

takes place. In our "Hello World!" example, we had

```
module Hello
{
        interface HelloWorld
        { ...
        }
}.
```

This leads to the creation of classes whose names start with `Hello.HelloWorld`. A number of such classes are created by the mapping, but our client code deals with only two: `Hello.HelloWorld` and `Hello.HelloWorldHelper` (we'll see another such class when we look at implementing a server).

- `Hello.HelloWorld`

    This is actually a Java interface rather than a class. The Java interface has operations that correspond to each declaration in the IDL interface. Thus, the Java `Hello.HelloWorld` interface declares methods

    ```
    void setHello(String)
    void getHello(StringHolder),
    ```

    corresponding to the method declarations

    ```
    void setHello(in String)
    void getHello(out String)
    ```

    in the IDL.

    Note: Because `Hello.HelloWorld` is an interface, there must be some class that implements it. There indeed is a class, invisible to the programmer, called `Hello.HelloWorldStub`. The stub does not perform the actual operations on the server, but rather marshalls and unmarshalls the method parameters; the ORB then transports these to the remote server object, which executes the actual methods.

- `Hello.HelloWorldHelper`

    In addition to methods used internally by Java IDL, helper classes also have a `narrow()` method, described later.

In a development environment, the Java IDL programmer may be given the generated classes, or he or she may be given the IDL and then may generate the mapped classes using the *idltojava* compiler.

The Fundamental Java IDL Idiom

One Java IDL idiom that should be especially noted is the resolve() ... narrow() idiom; it is the primary means by which references to ORB objects are accessed in Java IDL applets. In our example code, we had the lines:

```
NameComponent nc = new NameComponent("Hello", "");
NameComponent path[] = {nc};
helloObj = Hello.HelloWorldHelper.narrow(ncRef.resolve(path));
```

The first two lines set up a construct analogous to a pathname. The third line uses the `NamingContext`'s `resolve()` method to locate a particular ORB object identified by the name "Hello." The `resolve()` method, however, returns an object of the generic type `org.omg.CORBA.Object`; `resolve()` doesn't know what type of object it is finding. To use the methods specific to `Hello.HelloWorld`, we need somehow to convert the type of the returned object to the proper interface type.

We use the static `narrow()` method of `Hello.HelloWorldHelper` to create an object of the proper type. The Helper classes generated for IDL-defined interfaces all have such a static method. We should use these methods, rather than the Java-supplied `instanceof` operator and casting, to ensure that correct Java and CORBA semantics are maintained.

In Java IDL code, these lines typically reside within a `try` block. If the object cannot be found or cannot be properly narrowed, an exception will be thrown. In our example, when the exception is caught, an error message is output. In a more realistic example, more sophisticated exception handling would probably be done.

Implications of a Client/Server Implementation

An important thing to note is that the functionality of a Java IDL applet is *distributed*. Our original Java-only applet was entirely local; changing the text in one browser or applet viewer had no effect on what was seen in another. In our new implementation, all clients get their text from the same server; if one client updates the text, any other client will see that new text when it is repainted, say, by changing the color or covering and then uncovering the client's window.

Enhancing the Java IDL Applet Using an IDL Attribute

Now that we've got a basic Java IDL applet, let's see what it would take to move more functionality to the server. In addition to the server's keeping track of the text to be displayed, let's have it keep track of the color as well.

First, we have to add the notion of a color attribute to the IDL:

```
module Hello
{
  interface HelloWorld
  {
      void setHello(in string HelloString);
      void getHello(out string HelloString);
      attribute string color;
  };
};
```

Here, we've used the CORBA notion of an attribute. We could have added another pair of explicit setters and getters, but this helps to illustrate how attributes are mapped in Java.

Very few changes have to be made to either of our classes; indeed, there are some simplifications.

The changes to the applet class are as follows:

- Make changes to `init()`.

  Only one change needs to be made to this method; only one parameter is passed to the constructor for `myCanvas` because that constructor is simplified.

  ```
  HelloCanvas = new myCanvas(helloObj);
  ```

- Make changes to `itemStateChanged()`.

  Again, only one change is made here. Because the color is now stored by the server, we update it when the user chooses a new color.

  ```
  helloObj.color((String)e.getItem());
  ```

The changes to `myCanvas` reflect the fact that both color and text are obtained from the server.

- Eliminate the `displayColor` instance variable.

- Simplify the constructor, taking only one parameter and setting only one instance variable.

```
public myCanvas(Hello.HelloWorld obj)
{
setBounds(new Rectangle(5,5,width,height));
setHelloObj(obj);
}
```

- Eliminate the `setColor()` method.

- Change `getDisplayColor()` to get the color from the server, rather than the instance variable.

```
String displayColor;
displayColor = helloObj.color();
```

And that's all there is! We've actually eliminated more than we've added.

There are two things to note here: the technical details of how attributes are mapped and the ease with which Java applets can be turned into Java IDL applets.

Mapping Attributes

Notice that in the IDL we have the single line

```
attribute string color;
```

This doesn't tell us how we access that attribute in our code; such implementation details are specified in the mappings from IDL to various languages. In Java, we have the following mapping:

```
                    setter: void  x(XObject)
attribute x ->
                    getter: XObject  x()
```

In the case of our color attribute, this becomes

```
void color(String) and String color()
```

These methods are called in, respectively, `HelloJoe.itemStateChanged()` and `myCanvas.getDisplayColor()`.

Porting to Java IDL

One of the nice things about Java IDL is that, if you have a Java applet that you'd like to convert to it, there is no drawn-out porting process. Essentially, by instantiating ORB and `NamingContext` objects, you enable the Java IDL facilities. As you find portions of your applet that are better suited to a server than a client, you can define (or modify) the IDL for the server, compile the IDL to Java, and generally make a very few modifications. (Of course, someone has to write the server code as well. We'll discuss how to do this later in the chapter.)

Here's the complete listing for our revised Java IDL applet:

```java
import java.awt.*;
import java.awt.event.*;
import org.omg.CosNaming.*;
import org.omg.CosNaming.NamingContextPackage.*;
import org.omg.CORBA.*;

public class HelloJoe extends java.applet.Applet
                        implements ItemListener, ActionListener
{
    TextField   canvasText;
    Label       colorLabel;
    Choice      colorChoice;
    myCanvas    HelloCanvas;
    Panel       colorPanel;

    Hello.HelloWorld helloObj;
    public void init()
    {
        org.omg.CORBA.StringHolder stringHolder = new
          org.omg.CORBA.StringHolder("");

        try
        {

            ORB orb = ORB.init(this, null);

            // get the root naming context
            org.omg.CORBA.Object obj =
                    orb.resolve_initial_references("NameService");
            NamingContext ncRef = NamingContextHelper.narrow(obj);

            // resolve the Object Reference in Naming
```

```
            NameComponent nc = new NameComponent("Hello", "");
            NameComponent path[] = {nc};
            helloObj = Hello.HelloWorldHelper.narrow(ncRef.resolve(path));


}
catch (Exception e)
{
    System.out.println ("Exception "
                            + e.toString());
    throw new Error ("find/narrow failed!");
}


setLayout(new BorderLayout(10,10));

colorPanel = new Panel();

colorLabel = new Label("Color: ");
colorChoice = new Choice();
colorChoice.addItem("Red");
colorChoice.addItem("Green");
colorChoice.addItem("Blue");
colorPanel.add(colorLabel);
colorPanel.add(colorChoice);


colorChoice.addItemListener(this);

HelloCanvas = new myCanvas(helloObj);
try
{
   helloObj.getHello(stringHolder);
}
catch (Exception e)
{
    System.out.println ("Exception "
                            + e.toString());
    throw new Error ("getHello failed");
}

canvasText = new TextField(stringHolder.value);

canvasText.addActionListener(this);


add("East", colorPanel);
```

```
        add("South", canvasText);
        add("Center", HelloCanvas);
    }


    public void itemStateChanged(ItemEvent e)
    {
        if(e.getSource() == colorChoice)
        {
            // Set the new color
            try
            {
                helloObj.color((String)e.getItem());
            }
            catch (Exception ex)
            {
                System.out.println ("Exception "
                                    + ex.toString());
                throw new Error ("setcolor() failed!");
            }
            HelloCanvas.repaint();
        }
    }


    public void actionPerformed(ActionEvent e)
    {
        if(e.getSource() == canvasText)
        {
            // Set the new string to display
            try
            {
                helloObj.setHello(canvasText.getText());
            }
            catch (Exception ex)
            {
                System.out.println ("Exception "
                                    + ex.toString());
                throw new Error ("setHello() failed!");
            }
            HelloCanvas.repaint();
        }
    }

}

class myCanvas extends Canvas
```

```
{
  private int width=200;
  private int height=200;

  private Hello.HelloWorld helloObj;

  public myCanvas(Hello.HelloWorld obj)
  {
    setBounds(new Rectangle(5,5,width,height));
    setHelloObj(obj);
  }

  public void setHelloObj(Hello.HelloWorld obj)
  {
    helloObj = obj;
  }

  public String getDisplayText()
  {
    org.omg.CORBA.StringHolder stringHolder = new
        org.omg.CORBA.StringHolder("");
    try
    {
        helloObj.getHello(stringHolder);
    }
    catch (Exception e)
    {
        System.out.println ("Exception "
                              + e.toString());
        throw new Error ("getHello failed");
    }

    return stringHolder.value;
  }


  public Color getDisplayColor()
  {
      Color returnColor = Color.lightGray;
      String displayColor;
      try
      {
          displayColor = helloObj.color();
      }

      catch (Exception e)
      {
```

```
        System.out.println ("Exception "
                            + e.toString());
        throw new Error ("getcolor() failed!");
    }

    if (displayColor.equals( new String("Red")))
        returnColor = Color.red;
    else if (displayColor.equals( new String("Green")))
        returnColor = Color.green;
    else if (displayColor.equals( new String("Blue")))
        returnColor = Color.blue;

    return returnColor;
  }


/**
 * paint
 * Use the current display values (text, color) to display
 * the new canvas picture
 */
  public void paint(Graphics g) {
     g.setColor(Color.lightGray);
     g.fillRect(0,0,width,height);
     g.setColor(getDisplayColor());
     g.setFont(new Font("Helvetica",Font.PLAIN,36));
     g.drawString(getDisplayText(), 20, (height/2));
  }
}
```

Implementing the HelloWorld Object Server

Now that we know how to write a basic Java IDL client, let's take a look at how to implement a simple server. We will show in detail how to implement the HelloWorld service used in our HelloWorld applet. We'll show this implementation in Java, using Java IDL, but remember that, since we're using CORBA, the server could be written in an entirely different language, such as C++ or Smalltalk.

First, let's remember the final form of the IDL used by our HelloWorld applet:

```
module Hello
{
  interface HelloWorld
  {

    void setHello(in string HelloString);
```

```
    void getHello(out string HelloString);

    attribute string color;
  };
};
```

We will implement this service with a Java class called
`Hello.HelloWorldServer` (recall that the IDL module `Hello` maps to the Java
package `Hello`). Let's look at the code for this class.

HelloWorldServer.java

Our `HelloWorldServer` class extends a base class generated for us by the *idltojava* compiler called `_HelloWorldImplBase`:

```
public class HelloWorldServer extends _HelloWorldImplBase
```

`_HelloWorldImplBase` is an abstract base class that plays a roughly analogous
role on the server side to that of `HelloWorldStub` on the client side. Note that
both `HelloWorldStub` and `_HelloWorldImplBase` are generated for us by the
idltojava facility; we never deal with `HelloWorldStub` directly at all (we needn't
even know it exists), and our sole interaction with `_HelloWorldImplBase` is in
the extends clause in the code just shown.

Our `HelloWorldServer` class has the following data members:

```
private String helloString = "Hello World";
private String colorString = "Red";
```

These data members contain strings that will be used by the methods that implement our setters and getters.

Unlike the applet client, the server has a `main()` method. This method first sets
up a connection to the ORB in exactly the same manner as the client:

```
public static void main(String[] argv)

        // create and initialize the ORB
        ORB orb = ORB.init(argv, null);
```

Because `main()` is a static method, it can be called even though there is no
instance of the `HelloWorldServer` class. We therefore create such an instance in
the `main()` method (this is a common practice in Java applications) and register it
with the ORB.

```
HelloWorldServer server   = new HelloWorldServer();
orb.connect(server);
```

Next, we get the root naming context for this ORB object, just as we did with the client (the code is identical). Unlike what we did with the client, however, we use the Naming Context to register our server under the name "Hello" (or *bind* the server object to that name); the client, you will recall, used the Naming Context to find the server.

```
// get the root naming context
    org.omg.CORBA.Object obj =
    orb.resolve_initial_references("NameService");
    NamingContext ncRef = NamingContextHelper.narrow(obj);

// bind the Object Reference in Naming
    NameComponent nc = new NameComponent("Hello", "");
    NameComponent path[] = {nc};
    ncRef.rebind(path, server);
```

The last bit of code in `main()` invokes an object called `Wait`, whose sole purpose is to keep the server running.

```
// Keep main from exiting.
Wait.Wait();
```

The other methods of our server are simple Java implementations of the `get` and `set` methods we have promised to implement in the IDL interface. Remember that the methods for getting and setting the attribute *color* are implemented by overloaded `color()` methods. The complete code for the server, including the `Wait` class, is listed here:

```
package Hello;

import org.omg.CosNaming.*;
import org.omg.CosNaming.NamingContextPackage.*;
import org.omg.CORBA.*;
public class HelloWorldServer   extends _HelloWorldImplBase
{
  public static void main(String[] argv)
  {
    try
    {
      // create and initialize the ORB

      ORB orb = ORB.init(argv, null);
```

```java
        /// create servant and register it with the ORB
        HelloWorldServer server  = new HelloWorldServer();
        orb.connect(server);

        // get the root naming context
            org.omg.CORBA.Object obj =
            orb.resolve_initial_references("NameService");
            NamingContext ncRef = NamingContextHelper.narrow(obj);

        // bind the Object Reference in Naming
            NameComponent nc = new NameComponent("Hello", "");
            NameComponent path[] = {nc};
            ncRef.rebind(path, server);
        // Keep main from exiting.
        Wait.Wait();
    }
    catch (Exception e)
    {
        System.err.println("HelloWorldServer.main caught error " + e);
    }

}


    public synchronized void setHello(String inString)
    {
        helloString = inString;
    }

    public synchronized void getHello(StringHolder outString)
    {
        outString.value = helloString;
    }


    public synchronized void color(String inString)
    {
        colorString = inString;
    }

    public synchronized String color()
    {
        return  colorString;
    }

public HelloWorldServer() { }
```

```
      private String helloString = "Hello World";
      private String colorString = "Red";


}
class Wait {
   public static void Wait() {
      try {
         java.lang.Object sync = new java.lang.Object();
         synchronized (sync) {
         sync.wait();
         }
      } catch (Exception e) {
         System.err.println("Wait.Wait internal error " + e);
         System.exit(1);
      }
   }
}
```

Chapter Summary

These are the major points of this chapter:

- A Java IDL applet is a CORBA client written entirely in Java.

- The interface for the server to which the Java IDL client connects is written in IDL.

- Java stub and skeleton classes are generated from the IDL using the *idltojava* compiler, which implements the Java language mapping for IDL.

- Java IDL client programmers require no knowledge of how servers are implemented; they just need the IDL for the server or the generated Java classes.

- Java IDL client or server programmers need not be concerned with the code in these generated classes. The only files the programmer had to write in our example were HelloWorldClient.java (client) and HelloWorldServer.java (server).

- Java IDL programming is just Java programming using a few new classes and objects.

Internet Polling

Now that you've seen a simple Java IDL example in the previous chapter, it is time to illustrate more of the elegance of the Java IDL technology for real-world Internet and intranet programming. This chapter guides you through the requirements, design, and implementation of an Internet polling application that allows you to survey, in real time, the opinion of the Internet population. Through the use of a three-tier CORBA-based architecture, we illustrate how using high-level CORBA objects allows easy mapping of problem domain abstractions to networked objects. You can focus on the design of a solution without worrying about low-level network computing issues.

Introduction

Internet polling runs surveys over the Internet. This style of instant surveying fits well into the Internet phenomena that is becoming more widespread and lively. The Internet community offers interesting challenges given that it encompasses a wide variety of computer hardware and software. Thanks to the Java IDL technology, anyone with a Java-enabled Web browser and a connection to the Internet can participate in sophisticated surveys, regardless of their computing environment.

When we first began, we thought of several different examples to showcase the range of Internet/intranet solutions offered by the Java IDL technology. We chose polling as the problem domain for our sample application because it is interesting in the context of the Internet and because it is also very easy to understand. It presents the Java IDL technology in a real-world application that anyone reading this book can deploy within his or her own organization and eventually customize and expand according to his or her own requirements.

The sample Internet polling GUI application discussed in this chapter is based on a core set of polling services that are referred to as the "InterPoll" services. These services embody the middle tier of our architecture, encapsulating the logic associated with running surveys over the Internet.

Before discussing the design of these services, let's have a brief look at the particular GUI we have decided to implement using these services. GUI clients can be implemented in several different ways. In fact, it was a design requirement that the InterPoll services be flexible enough to have many different kinds of front-end clients. For this chapter, we are using an InterPoll GUI that solicits opinions about the 1996 U.S. Presidential Election. We call this GUI *Election '96.*

If you were to sit at your computer and access our Web site for Internet polling, you would go through the user experience presented in Figure 7.2.

- **Poll Selection.** InterPoll can offer a selection of different polls. The example poll we have implemented is Election '96. The published URL leads users to a page ("Polls" in Figure 7.2) that is composed of simple HTML links that

Figure 7.1 Using the Internet for global real-time opinion polls.

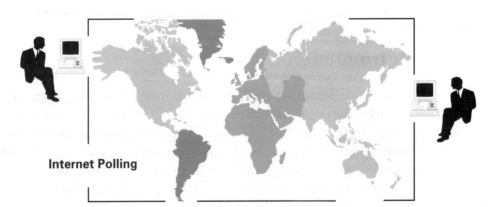

Internet Polling

download Java IDL applets that use InterPoll services. Offering more than one poll per polling application not only shows GUI and commercial flexibility, but also illustrates how each individual poll can reuse large parts of the common InterPoll services.

- **Login** (**Authentication**). You identify yourself to the system by giving a unique user ID and a password. First-time users are then directed to the Registration page.

- **Registration.** The registration process allows the InterPoll system to collect demographic information for each participant. All of this information is stored and can be used by any of the polls offered at our Web site. The demographic information collected for a poll is used to analyze poll results. For example, in the Election '96 poll, you can request to see the votes of all women between the ages of 20 and 40.

  Once registered, you are ready to vote using the polling page.

- **Polling.** In the Election '96 poll, you enter your vote on several questions. As you do, you see real-time status updates of everyone's answers to the polling questions, either on a map or as a bar chart. Also, you can analyze the polling results according to your own chosen demographic selection criteria.

Requirements

We had several meetings to help clearly define the elements of Internet polling. This iterative process led us to the system presented in Figure 7.3. The important value

Figure 7.2 Election '96 graphical user interface.

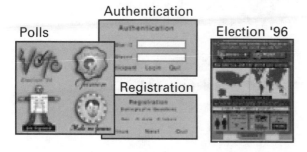

in the requirements analysis step is not only in defining the key elements, but also in determining how and why they interact with each other.

We agreed that the central concept of the system was that of a poll. A poll is simply a collection of questions that a polling participant answers. It was important to us that the system support the ability to present the poll in visually interesting ways. A question can always be a standard, boring piece of text. But why limit yourself when you have the world as your audience? Getting attention on the Internet is a competitive business. The more life on the screen, the more successful your poll. Therefore, we decided that all polling questions would be full-blown Java classes. With Java's dynamic binding capabilities, poll designers can continuously reinvent the art of polling people. For the polling questions in Election '96, we combined pictures with the text and realistic button behaviors.

After defining how polls, questions, and participants interact, other important pieces of the architecture quickly became obvious. Answers to poll questions are collected by a Collector service that acts as a wrapper around our third-tier data storage solution. The data store can be anything from flat files to relational or object-oriented databases. In turn, answers are used by Analysis services to analyze the poll results in a multitude of ways.

We also wanted to be able to provide real-time feedback as people answered questions. This feedback could be presented to participants through the GUI or as

Figure 7.3 Conceptual model of the InterPoll system design.

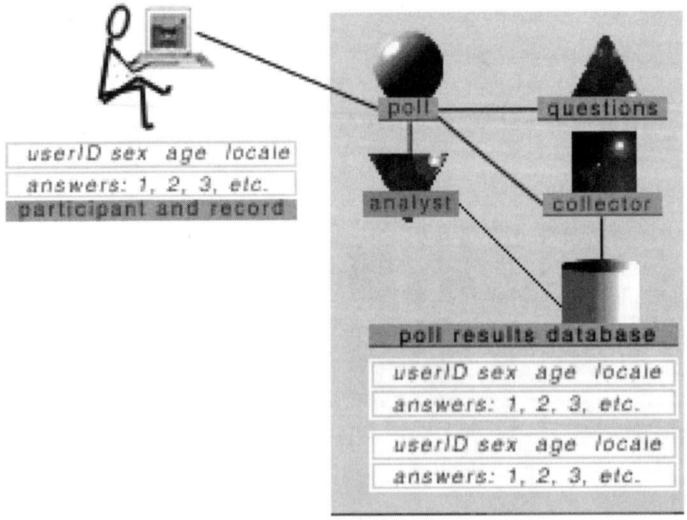

input to other computer programs. For the GUI, the presentation could be any variety of display formats.

Finally, by introducing demographic information to the polling concepts, the process becomes even more interesting. As mentioned before, in our Election '96 poll, each participant registers gender, age, and location information. Selection of different demographics allows participants to analyze, in real time, subsets of the global polling data. As different combinations of this demographic information are requested, the map or bar chart on the polling page updates, showing the resulting filtered statistics.

System Architecture

The Internet polling application can be used by a polling participant in one corner of the world, while the polling information is being collected and analyzed on an entirely different machine a continent away. All that is needed is an Internet connection. An InterPoll client performs this by transparently invoking operations on remote network services through well-defined IDL (Interface Definition Language) interfaces.

Internet polling has been designed as a three-tier client/server system. It consists of the client tier's GUI presentation layer, which is seen by the users; the middle tier's set of network services; and the third tier's data storage solution. This is illustrated in Figure 7.4.

By dividing the system into three pieces, we can develop an application that can easily adjust to change across all three tiers.

- The GUI client tier is subject to several different types of change. Polls, by their nature, are topical; there can be several different GUI clients for a poll's services. Also, each GUI changes as the implementation matures. The Election '96 GUI grew from a simple set of buttons to a sophisticated presentation. As long as the services defined in the IDL do not change, the GUI designer can define and refine as many client GUIs as necessary without being affected by the developers working on the middle tier's CORBA services or the back-end database.

- For the middle tier of network services, transparent change is reciprocal. While the front-end GUI designers are reusing the IDL for InterPoll's network services,

Figure 7.4 Internet polling system architecture.

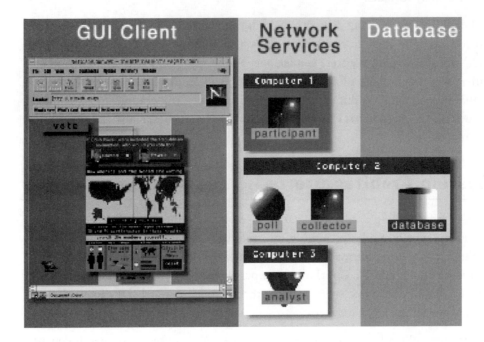

CORBA server developers can alter existing services or introduce new functionality for the existing IDL. If a network services IDL file changes, however, then both the client and the middle-tier services are affected.

- In the third tier, if additional databases or changes in the way data is stored do not alter the IDL, then only the middle-tier services are affected.

The Middle-Tier Network Services

Our goal in designing the InterPoll services was to come up with a set of robust network services that would provide a foundation for any Internet polling.

Figure 7.5 shows a class diagram of the InterPoll set of network objects that are accessible to user client applications. There are five core classes in InterPoll: Poll, Question, Participant, Collector, and Analyst.

A Poll is built from a set of Questions and has exactly one Collector associated with it for the collection of polling data. At any given time, any number of Analysts can be associated with the poll for the analysis of polling results. Analyst objects are created on demand by the GUI client applications. Participant objects represent the people who are actually participating in a poll. There is a many-to-many relationship between participants and polls. Remember, Participant registration information is shared among the polls at the polling Web site.

Please note that this chapter discusses the InterPoll "public" interfaces; that is, interfaces that are "safe" and openly accessible to client applications. The internal or "private" IDL interfaces add operations that are accessible only to InterPoll system developers and administrators. For more information about the internal IDL interfaces, see Chapter 8.

Poll

The Poll object is at the heart of the InterPoll set of network services. It encapsulates all information related to a specific poll. The public interface of the Poll object, shown here in IDL, allows a client application to get the basic information associated with that poll as well as the object references of the Questions composing the poll.

Figure 7.5 Class diagram of InterPoll network services/objects.

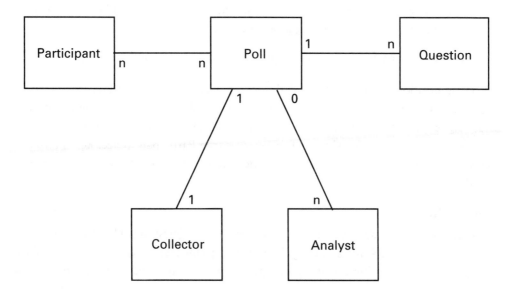

```
struct PollBaseInfo {
    string name;
    string description;
    StringSeq question_names;
    short number_demographic_questions;
};

interface Poll {
    void get_info(out long id,
                      out PollBaseInfo info);
    QuestionSeq get_questions(out long n_demog_q);
};
typedef sequence<Poll> PollSeq;
```

A poll designer creates a Poll object with the following information:

- A unique name that is registered in the public InterPoll Naming context of the Naming service

- A short textual description of the poll

- A list of the names of the demographic and poll questions composing that poll

    Demographic questions are not an intrinsic part of the poll, but answers to these questions are used for more interesting analysis of poll results. The distinction between demographic questions and poll questions is made by having demographic questions listed first and by letting the poll know the exact number of demographic questions it contains.

- The number of demographic questions contained in the poll

Upon creation, a unique identification number generated by the PollFactory is returned. This unique ID is also registered in the public InterPoll Naming context. This ID is useful for compact identification of Poll objects when they need to be represented in other objects' state. For example, the Participant object keeps a reference to all polls in which the user has participated. For more information about the PollFactory, see Chapter 8.

Question

The first step in the design of a poll is the creation of Questions. Questions are specific both to demographic and to polling results. Demographic questions are used to get personal information about a participant. They are included in our definition of a poll because they can be used to present analyses of poll answers across demo-graphic categories.

```
struct QuestionBaseInfo {
    string name;
    string description;
    string java_question_class;
    short n_elements;
    short value_range;
    StringSeq initParameters;
};

interface Question {
    void get_info(out long id, out QuestionBaseInfo info);
};

typedef sequence<Question> QuestionSeq;
```

One important design issue for the Question object is how to represent the answer to a question. We wanted our design to be able to support a wide range of possible answers for any one question, but at the same time, we also wanted to make it as compact as possible for performance reasons. This is handled through two attributes in the Question object

- n_elements. Number of elements contained in the answer to that question.

- value_range. Range of values that each element of the answer can take.

Using this scheme, the answer to a question can be represented in a compact array of short integers, where the length of the array and the range of values the elements of this array can take are specific to each question. Some examples follow:

- Among these five candidates, who will you vote for?

    n_elements = 1   value_range = 5

    The answer to this question is an array of a single element, whose value is the index of the candidate selected (0–4).

- Among this list of 10 countries, check the ones you have visited.

    n_elements = 10   value_range = 2

    The answer to this question is an array of 10 elements, whose values (0–1) tell whether the country has been visited or not.

- Among this list of 20 movies, rate your top 5 movies.

  n_elements = 5   value_range = 20

  The answer to this question is an array of five elements, ordered from the first to last selection, and whose values (0–19) are the index of the movies selected in the list.

Another interesting aspect of the InterPoll Question object is that Questions are designed as Java classes that run in the client application (field `java_question_class` in the `QuestionBaseInfo` IDL structure). Having dynamic binding of objects in Java is a key benefit that allows us to design Question classes with lots of creativity. These Java Question classes can be seen as templates that are rendered for a specific Question according to the initialization parameters associated with them.

Now that we've covered the main components of a Question object, let's summarize the information required for their creation:

- A unique name that is registered in the public InterPoll Naming context of the Naming service

- A short textual description of the Question

- An answer format defined by the number of elements making up the answer and the range of values allowed for these answer elements

- A name for the Java class that renders the Question in the client GUI application

- Initialization parameters for the Question's Java class

Upon creation, a unique identification number generated by the QuestionFactory is returned. This unique ID is also registered in the public InterPoll Naming context. This ID is useful for compact identification of Question objects when they need to be represented in other objects' state. For example, the Participant object keeps a reference to the demographic questions it has already answered.

Collector

The Collector is the middleware service responsible for collecting polling records. It acts as an intermediary between the client applications and the data store, hiding the details of the actual storage solution used.

There is a polling record for each one of the participants who enters a poll. These records contain the participant's user ID and all the answers given by that user to the poll's questions.

Three structures define the format of a record handled by the Collector:

```
struct RecordIn {
    long user_id;
    Answers ans;
};

struct RecordSystem {
    long time_stamp;
};

struct RecordOut {
    RecordIn rec_in;
    RecordSystem rec_system;
};
typedef sequence<RecordOut> RecordOutSeq;
```

`RecordIn` defines the structure of the poll record when submitted by a client application. It consists of a unique user ID, followed by the answers of the participant to the poll (an array of shorts). `RecordSystem` consists of the additional system information the Collector appends to each poll record. It currently consists of a time stamp of when the poll record was created. Finally, `RecordOut` is the structure returned by the system on all queries for poll records. It includes the information contained in both the `RecordIn` and `RecordSystem` structures.

The Collector's interface is private. A client application can access the Collector only indirectly through the following operations of the Participant interface:

```
RecordOut get_record(in long pollId) raises(IpollException);
void set_record(in long pollId, in Answers ans)
  raises(IpollException);
```

Because a reference to a Participant object can be obtained only through proper authentication, access to the database is secure. The Collector's private interface is described in Chapter 8.

Analyst

The Analyst is responsible for analyzing the data contained in polling records and for returning results of interest to client applications.

Because polling data can be analyzed in many ways, there is no generic interface to an Analyst object. Rather, each Analyst interface is a specialized case that analyzes poll data in its own specific way. It is up to the client application to request the type of Analyst(s) in which it is interested.

Client applications obtain a reference to an Analyst object through the following operation in the Participant interface:

```
Object get_analyst(in long pollId, in string analystType)
                                    raises(IpollException);
```

It is important to note that the return value is of type `Object` because the Participant must support all possible Analyst types. It is up to the client to narrow the returned object to the proper type.

The IDL module `AnalystTpcMcpl`, shown in the following code, was developed to support simple analysis of data related to political surveys. Results can be compiled only for a single question at a time. That is, in this implementation, no correlation can be made among answers to different questions. The results are expressed as follows:

- *Totals Per Choice (Tpc)*. Reports the number of people who selected each choice available in the question.

- *Majority Choice Per Location (Mcpl)*. Each poll participant is associated with a location. This returns the candidate with the majority of votes at each location.

```
module AnalystTpcMcpl{
      const short VOTE_MAX_CHOICES = 6;
      const short VOTE_N_LOCATIONS = 70;

      typedef long TotalsPerChoice[VOTE_MAX_CHOICES];
      typedef ipoll::Answer MajorityChoicePerLocation[VOTE_N_LOCATIONS];

      struct Selection {
            short question_number;
            ipoll::Answer sex;
            ipoll::Answer age_begin;
            ipoll::Answer age_end;
            long time_begin;
            long time_end;
```

```
        };

        struct Results {
            long total_records;
            long selected_records;
            long noAnswer_records;
            TotalsPerChoice tpc;
            MajorityChoicePerLocation mcpl;
        }

        interface ResultsCallback {
            oneway void results_update(in Results res);
        };

        interface Analyst {
            Results get_results(in Selection select)
                                    raises(ipoll::IpollException);
            unsigned long register_callback(
                    in ResultsCallback cb,
                    in Selection select) raises(ipoll::IpollException);

            void update_callback(
                    in unsigned long cbId,
                    in Selection select) raises(ipoll::IpollException);

            void unregister_callback(
                    in unsigned long cbId) raises(ipoll::IpollException);
        };
    };
```

To be able to offer the `AnalystTpcMcpl` Analyst to its client applications, a poll must conform to the following requirements:

- Questions can have only a single element for their answer.

- There is a maximum of VOTE_MAX_CHOICES choices per poll question.

- The poll must have the following questions specified as its first three demographic questions:

  1. Gender of the participant (n_answers = 1, value_range = 2)

  2. Age of the participant (n_answers = 1, value_range = up to 255)

  3. Location of the participant (n_answers = 1, value_range = VOTE_N_LOCATIONS)

When calling the Analyst object to get results, the client application specifies via the `Selection` structure the selection criteria to be applied on the poll records. This prunes the set of records to be considered for the computation of the results.

The `Selection` structure contains the following information:

- The question for which the results will be computed

- The gender to be used for filtering

- The age bracket

- The time period when the record was originally submitted

The `No_Answer` constant may be used to specify that no selection should be performed on a specific selection criterion. The exception is `question_number`, which must always be specified.

The `Results` structure returned by the `get_results()` operation contains the following information:

- Total number of records in the Collector's database

- Total number of records selected after applying the `Selection` criteria

- Total number of records selected that have a `No_Answer` (that is, that cannot be compiled in the results)

- Totals per choice

- Majority choice per location

The Analyst also supports automatic updates to client applications whenever new data is collected in the poll's Collector database or existing records are modified. All a client application has to do to receive these asynchronous notifications is create a Callback object with the `ResultsCallback` interface and register it with the Analyst. The `results_update(in Result res)` operation is called by the Analyst object on all registered `ResultsCallback` objects whenever changes occur in the polling database.

Participant

Participants are the InterPoll users. While we were designing the Internet Polling application, we felt it was important to support user registration and authentication, allowing participants to see previous answers to a poll as well as having the capability of changing their answers.

Also, because Participant objects are shared among different polls, the registration information does not have to be reentered when a participant enters more than one poll at a specific site.

The design and implementation of the Participant and ParticipantFactory objects were extremely simple because they were leveraged off commercial CORBA components supporting the registered user paradigm that is common in WWW applications. Users are registered and then later authenticated with a name and a password. These classes are shown in the class diagram in Figure 7.6.

When InterPoll's ParticipantFactory is registered in the system, it first contacts the UserManagerAdminFactory to create a new UserManager/UserManagerAdmin pair of objects (the public/private pair of interfaces of the UserManager abstraction). The ParticipantFactory is then created and registered as the "User factory" of the newly created UserManager. It is this UserManager object that is finally registered in the Naming service as the Manager supporting the registration/authentication of InterPoll participants.

On the client side, an InterPoll client application asks the user to provide name and password information. If the user is not yet registered, the client calls the operation `register_user()` on the UserManager to create a new User object. If the user is already registered, then operation `authenticate_user()` is called to find the existing User object of that Participant.

It is the ParticipantFactory that creates a new Participant object. The UserManager provides the factory with one argument, the User object it created to hold the information associated with the newly registered user. That User object is then defined as the delegate of the Participant object created by the ParticipantFactory.

Two types of "personal" information are stored with each Participant. First, there is the demographics information, which is used in polls for the analysis of poll data. Second, there is other user personal information not otherwise covered by the demographics information. For each poll a participant participates in, a `recordId` key of the record associated with that participant in that poll Collector's database is kept.

Figure 7.6 Class diagram for InterPoll user management and authentication.

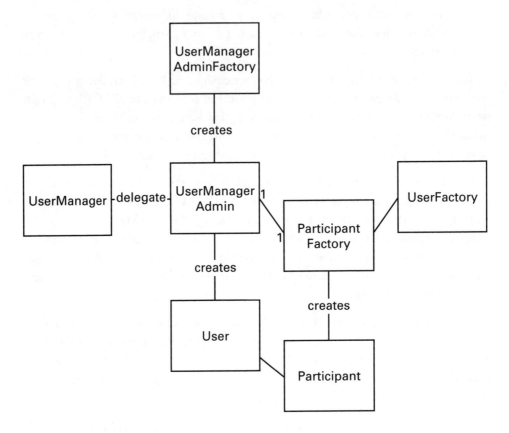

The Participant interface and associated structures are listed here.

```
struct ParticipantDemographic {
    long questionId;
    Answer ans;
};
typedef sequence<ParticipantDemographic> ParticipantDemographicSeq;

struct ParticipantProfile {
    string email;
};

struct PollEntered {
    long pollId;
```

```
        long recordId;
    };
    typedef sequence<PollEntered> PollEnteredSeq;

    interface Participant : App::User {
        attribute ParticipantDemographicSeq demographics;
        attribute ParticipantProfile profile;
        RecordOut get_record(in long pollId);
                                raises(IpollException);
        void set_record(in long pollId, in Answers ans)
                                raises(IpollException);
        Object get_analyst(in long pollId, in string analystType)
                                raises(IpollException)
    };

    interface ParticipantFactory : App::UserFactory {};
```

As shown in the previous code sample, Participant inherits from App::User and is created with a pointer to the User delegate to which it delegates all "registration"-related operations.

ParticipantFactory inherits from App::UserFactory. It is registered with UserManagerAdmin as the factory to be used for the creation of new users. The `create_User(in User delegate)` operation is called by UserManagerAdmin whenever a new user needs to be created. The delegate argument identifies the delegate to associate with the newly created Participant.

The Participant object has a pair of operations to get/set the polling record of that participant for a specific poll. If these operations are called on a poll in which the user has not yet participated, a new record is created automatically.

Finally, the `get_analyst()` operation of the Participant object provides a reference to an Analyst object for the analysis of poll data.

The First Tier: GUI Client

The InterPoll set of network services, described in the previous sections, supports a wide range of first-tier GUI clients. In this section, we describe the design and implementation of Election '96, a first-tier GUI client application for a political poll.

In designing Election '96, we had two primary goals in mind. First, the front-end client had to be architected so that GUI functionality would be encapsulated in a well-defined set of classes. Initially we developed a very simple GUI implementation while giving our primary focus to the core issues of implementing a Java IDL front-end application. We later added a more sophisticated implementation of the GUI. All that changed between these two versions is the look and feel implemented in the GUI classes.

Our second goal dealt with the core implementation issues. We needed to encapsulate all client access to the network services within a single "model" class called `InterPollModel`. There are many benefits to this approach:

- A model class offers a higher-level interface for first-tier developers, meeting their needs more specifically.

- The details of network programming are isolated. Only the programmer who implements the model class needs to be knowledgeable about the IDL interfaces to the InterPoll middle-tier network services, IDL-to-Java mapping, and the Java IDL API.

- Because the first and middle tiers are often implemented independently and at different rates, the client tier needs to be tested independently of the middle tier. To accommodate this, the interface defined by `InterPollModel` is implemented in two classes:

  - `InterPollModelLocal` simulates access to remote services via "fake" sample local data for testing.

  - `InterPollModelRemote` accesses the true remote network services.

Switching the test network services is simply a matter of instantiating `InterPollModelRemote` rather than `InterPollModelLocal`. Nothing else in the source code needs to be modified.

Architecture

In the Introduction section of this chapter, Figure 7.2 presents Election '96, our sample InterPoll client application. Election '96 has been modeled after the PAC (Process-Abstraction-Control) architectural pattern. This architecture, presented in Figure 7.7, features a hierarchy of cooperating agents, where each agent is responsible for a specific aspect of the application's functionality.

Communication between the agents is not performed directly. Rather, it is handled indirectly through a simple publish and subscribe mechanism that promotes loose coupling of the agents. Changes to individual agents, or extensions of the application with new agents, have minimal impact on the whole system.

Figure 7.7 Architecture of Election '96 poll.

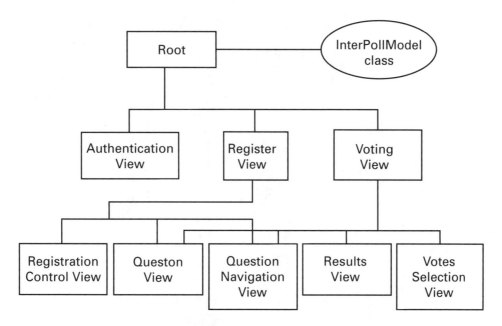

Our top-level PAC agent, the Root class, controls the state of the application and activates the second-level view that corresponds to the current state. In Election '96, an Internet polling session consists of three major states: User Authentication (login), User Registration, and Voting (polling).

Similarly, each one of the second-level agents controls a set of lower-level agents. Through this decomposition of the application, we aim at defining a clean implementation where the granularity of the bottom-level agents is at a level that promotes their reuse.

The whole logic of the application is centered around the set of events that the application supports. These application events are published and, in turn, consumed by the agents composing the application. Figure 7.8 is a state transition diagram showing a view of the dynamic model of the application. It shows the different states and events that shape the behavior of our client application.

In the following sections, we take a closer look at how the client application interacts with the InterPoll model and how this model has been implemented to interface with the real InterPoll network services.

Figure 7.8 InterPoll runtime state transition diagram.

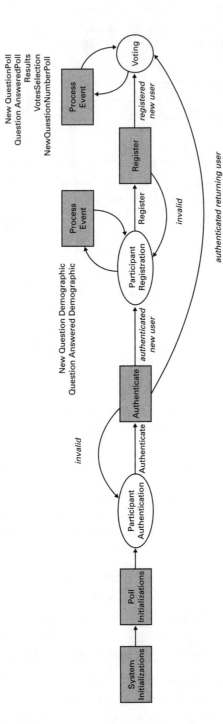

System Initializations

System initializations are controlled by the top Root class. An important part of this process is to create an instance of the InterPollModelRemote class. In the rest of this chapter, we refer to that class as the *model*.

```
model = new InterPollModelRemote(eventMgr, orbInitialHost)
```

There are two arguments required for the creation of the model. The first argument, eventMgr, refers to the publish and subscribe object responsible for the propagation of events among the set of loosely coupled components making up the application. Every agent in the hierarchy is therefore instantiated with this argument.

The second argument, orbInitialHost, identifies the ORB initial host where the initial services of an InterPoll site can be found. If running the client as an applet, this is by default the host from which the applet was downloaded. If running the client as an application, this host is retrieved from a command-line argument.

The constructor for InterPollModelRemote is shown here.

```
public InterPollModelRemote(AppEventMgr eventMgr,String orbInitialHost)
    throws java.lang.Exception {
        org.omg.CORBA.Object obj;

        // Set the properties for the ORB
1       java.util.Properties props = new java.util.Properties();
2       props.put("org.omg.CORBA.ORBInitialHost", orbInitialHost);

        try {
            // create and initialize the ORB
            String[] args = {};
3           _orb = org.omg.CORBA.ORB.init(args, props);

                // Get the root naming context
4           obj = _orb.resolve_initial_references("NameService");
5           _rootNC = org.omg.CosNaming.NamingContextHelper.narrow(obj);

            // Get the naming context for Interpoll objects
6           org.omg.CosNaming.NameComponent[] rootComponents = {
7               new org.omg.CosNaming.NameComponent("host", ""),
8               new org.omg.CosNaming.NameComponent("resources", ""),
9               new org.omg.CosNaming.NameComponent("interpoll", "")};
10          obj = _rootNC.resolve(rootComponents);
11          _interpollNC =
12              org.omg.CosNaming.NamingContextHelper.narrow(obj);
```

```
                    // Initialize ParticipantManager
13                  org.omg.CosNaming.NameComponent[] pmComponents = {
14                      new org.omg.CosNaming.NameComponent("host", ""),
15                      new org.omg.CosNaming.NameComponent("resources", ""),
16                      new org.omg.CosNaming.NameComponent("factories", ""),
17                      new org.omg.CosNaming.NameComponent("ParticipantManager", "")};
18                  obj = _rootNC.resolve(pmComponents);
19                  _participantMgr =
20                      sunw.neo.netc.App.UserManagerHelper.narrow(obj);
                } catch (java.lang.Exception ex) {
                    throw new java.lang.Exception("Initialization error: " + ex);
                }

                    // Subscribe to events of interest for the model
                    _eventMgr = eventMgr;
21                  _eventMgr.subscribe("QuestionAnsweredDemographic", this);
22                  _eventMgr.subscribe("QuestionAnsweredPoll", this);
23                  _eventMgr.subscribe("NewQuestionNumberPoll", this);
24                  _eventMgr.subscribe("VotesSelection", this);
                }
```

There are three major steps in the initialization of the model: create an ORB object, get the initial references to CORBA objects, and subscribe to events in which the model has interest.

Before our client application can invoke any operation on a CORBA object, it must first create an instance of an ORB. Doing so introduces the application to the ORB and gives it access to important operations that are defined on the ORB object. Properties of the ORB can be specified at creation time. This is done in lines 1–2 where a java.util.Properties object is used to specify the host where the initial services can be found (this initial host was provided as the second argument of the constructor). The ORB is then instantiated in line 3.

To get initial references to CORBA objects, we must first set up our access to the Naming service. We do this through the CORBA CosNaming interfaces. In lines 4–5, we resolve the initial reference to the root Naming context of our initial host. In lines 6–9, we build an array of name components that hold the path to the InterPoll base Naming context. Finally, we resolve that Naming context in line 10, narrow it to its proper type, and save it in a variable (lines 11–12) so future references to InterPoll objects can be resolved according to this base Naming context.

Retrieving the object reference to the ParticipantManager follows the same pattern: build an array of name components (lines 13–17), resolve and narrow (lines 18–20).

All methods in the implementation of the model catch exceptions that can be thrown by the code they execute. They convert them into `java.lang.Exception` with the message of the exception set to as best a description as the model can make. In designing the client application, we found that we did not need to differentiate between the different types of exceptions that could occur in the model. Rather, getting a proper description of the error condition was all that was required because all error-handling routines in the client simply consist of displaying the message associated with the occurring error condition.

Starting at line 21, we see the model subscribing to the application events in which it is interested. The next sections of this chapter discuss how these events are generated and how the model handles them.

Poll Initializations

Once the model is instantiated, the system enters the Poll Initialization phase, where we first activate the poll selected by the Participant and then initialize the Questions associated with that poll.

Poll Activation

The client application invokes the `activatePoll()` method of the model to activate the poll on which it will be operating. The source of that method is shown here:

```
public ipoll.PollBaseInfo activatePoll(String pollName)
    throws java.lang.Exception {
      org.omg.CORBA.Object obj;

      try {
          // Get the object reference to that poll
1         org.omg.CosNaming.NameComponent[] nameComponents = {
2             new org.omg.CosNaming.NameComponent("polls", ""),
3             new org.omg.CosNaming.NameComponent(pollName, "")};
4         obj = _interpollNC.resolve(nameComponents);
5         _poll = ipoll.PollHelper.narrow(obj);

          // Get information for the poll
6         org.omg.CORBA.IntHolder idHolder =
7             new org.omg.CORBA.IntHolder();
8         ipoll.PollBaseInfoHolder infoHolder =
9             new ipoll.PollBaseInfoHolder();
10        _poll.get_info(idHolder, infoHolder);

          // reset the poll's state
11        _pollId = idHolder.value;
```

```
12        resetPollState();

13        return infoHolder.value;
     } catch (java.lang.Exception ex) {
         throw new java.lang.Exception(
             "Error activating the poll " + pollName + ": " + ex);
     }
}
```

The method takes as an argument the name of the poll to be activated. This is the name that has been registered in the Naming service of the polling site when that poll was created.

In lines 1–3, the model builds the array of name components identifying the path to the binding in the Name service where the object reference for that poll can be found. That path is relative to the InterPoll root naming context, _interpollNC, that we previously initialized in the model's constructor. The "resolve then narrow" pair of operations is performed in lines 4–5.

The next thing we do is get the information associated with that poll. It is important to note that because Java supports only call-by-value semantics, holders are required for CORBA operations that take out or inout arguments. This is the case for id and pollBaseInfo of the get_info() operation of the Poll object. We therefore create holders for these values in lines 6–9. The get_info() operation is invoked in line 10.

Finally, we reset the internal state of the model that is affected by the activation of a new poll (lines 11–12), and return the poll's base information (line 13).

Questions Initialization

The client needs one more piece of information to complete the poll initialization phase: the set of Questions associated with that poll. The client gets this set by calling the getQuestions() method on the model.

```
public ipoll.QuestionBaseInfo[] getQuestions() throws java.lang.Exception {
    ipoll.Question[] questions;
    ipoll.QuestionBaseInfo[] questionsInfo;

    try {
        org.omg.CORBA.IntHolder nDemogQuestionsHolder =
            new org.omg.CORBA.IntHolder();
1       questions = _poll.get_questions(nDemogQuestionsHolder);
```

```
2        _nPollQuestions = questions.length;
3        _nDemogQuestions = nDemogQuestionsHolder.value;

4        _answers = new short[_nPollQuestions];

5        questionsInfo = new ipoll.QuestionBaseInfo[_nPollQuestions];
6        for (int i=0; i<_nPollQuestions; i++) {
7            org.omg.CORBA.IntHolder id = new org.omg.CORBA.IntHolder();
8            ipoll.QuestionBaseInfoHolder infoHolder =
9                new ipoll.QuestionBaseInfoHolder();
10           questions[i].get_info(id, infoHolder);
11           questionsInfo[i] = infoHolder.value;
12       }
13       return questionsInfo;
      } catch (java.lang.Exception ex) {
          throw new java.lang.Exception(
              "Error getting the poll questions: " + ex);
      }
}
```

The getQuestions() method retrieves from the middle-tier Question objects the information associated with each question composing the currently active poll.

The model first invokes in line 1 the get_questions() operation on the Poll object. From the list of object references returned, the model can set the total number of questions in the poll (line 2). From the output argument, it sets the number of demographic questions defined for that poll (line 3).

The model keeps a cache of the answers of the Participant for the poll. It is initialized to the proper size in line 4.

Finally, for each one of the Questions in the poll, the model invokes the get_info() operation to fill in the ipoll.QuestionBaseInfo array returned to the client program. This is done in lines 5–13.

Participant Authentication

Once the poll initialization phase is completed, the client application enters the "authentication" (login) phase. This is handled by the AuthenticationView class. The participant simply needs to enter a user name and a password, then specify whether this is a new account that needs to be created (new user) or an account that already exists (login). An Authentication event is then published with the ParticipantInfo structure as an argument. The Root class subscribes to that event and invokes the `authenticate()` method of the model to perform the authentication.

```
public short[] authenticate(ParticipantInfo pi)
   throws java.lang.Exception {
1    org.omg.CORBA.Any authenticateInfo = _orb.create_any();
2    authenticateInfo.insert_string(pi.id + "\n" + pi.passwd + "\n");

     try {
         sunw.neo.netc.App.User user;
         if (pi.userType == ParticipantInfo.OldUser) {
3            user = _participantMgr.authenticate_user(authenticateInfo);
         } else {
4            user = _participantMgr.register_user(authenticateInfo);
         }
5        _participant = ipoll.ParticipantHelper.narrow(user);

6        ipoll.RecordOut record = _participant.get_record(_pollId);
7        _answers = record.rec_in.ans;
8        resetParticipantState();

9        return _answers;
     } catch (java.lang.Exception ex) {
         throw new java.lang.Exception(
             "CORBA error on participant authentication: " + ex);
     }
}
```

There is one argument to the method, a `ParticipantInfo` object that provides the model with all the information required for proper authentication: name, password, and whether this is a new user or one previously registered.

Authentication is performed in InterPoll via the set of User services. The simplest way to communicate authentication information to the `UserManager` abstraction is through an `Any` structure containing the name and password of the user as standard strings. This is done in lines 1–2.

If this is an old user, the model calls the `authenticate_user()` operation on the `ParticipantManager` (line 3). Otherwise, it calls the `register_user()` operation (line 4). Both these methods return an object reference to a `User` object, which is then narrowed (line 5) to a `Participant` object and saved as an instance variable of the model.

The model then needs to initialize the answers of the participant to their proper values. The model keeps a cache of these answers for future updates to the database. By calling the operation `get_record()` on the `Participant` object (line 6), we get a full record of the participation to that poll. It is important to note that when calling `get_record()` on a poll not yet entered by the participant, a new record is automatically created in the database, with all answers initialized to the IDL-defined `No_Answer` value.

The cache of the answers of the participant for the poll is updated in line 7, and in line 8 we reset the rest of the internal state of the model that is affected by the activation of a new participant. The method returns the participant's current answers to that poll (line 9). This is used by the `Root` class to initialize the registration and voting views with the proper answers.

Analyst Activation

Once a participant has been properly authenticated, the model is ready to initialize the analyst that will be used in the polling phase to get real-time updates of the polling results. Multiple types of analysts can be supported by a poll. In the case of Election '96, `AnalystTpcMcpl` (Totals Per Choice_Majority Choice Per Location) is the only type supported. The following code shows how the analyst is initialized in the model:

```
void activateAnalystTpcMcpl() throws java.lang.Exception {
    try {
        org.omg.CORBA.Object obj =
1               _participant.get_analyst(_pollId, "TpcMcpl");
            _analyst = ipoll.analystTpcMcpl.AnalystHelper.narrow(obj);
2           _orb.connect(this);
    } catch (java.lang.Exception ex) {
        throw new java.lang.Exception(
            "Error activating the analyst: " + ex);
    }
}
```

The model invokes the `get_analyst()` operation of the Participant object in line 1 to get a reference to an `Analyst` object. The model then creates an instance of a transient CORBA servant object that we will use as a callback mechanism to get real-time updates from the Analyst once we enter the polling phase. This is done in line 2. This transient callback object is, in fact, the model itself because the

`InterPollModelRemote` class extends the servant base for the
`ResultsCallback` IDL interface.

```
public class InterPollModelRemote
    extends ipoll.analystTpcMcpl._ResultsCallbackImplBase
    implements InterPollModel {
  ...
}
```

Participant Registration

For a participant who has never entered a poll at the current InterPoll site, authentication is followed by a registration phase. In that phase, the participant is asked to answer the demographic questions associated with the active poll. This is handled by the `RegistrationView` class, which is the aggregate of three lower-level agents: `QuestionView`, `QuestionNavigationView`, and `RegistrationControlView`.

`QuestionView` and `QuestionNavigationView` are used in both the registration and the voting phases. It is their responsibility to know the context in which they are used so they can generate the proper event when an action is performed on them. These views are therefore instantiated with one argument, `context`, which tells whether the view is used in the context of the registration phase (value of context is "Demographic"), or in the context of the voting phase (value of context is "Poll").

QuestionView

`QuestionView` is responsible for rendering a demographic/poll question in the client application. It simply runs the Java code associated with a question. Whenever the participant changes his or her answer to the question, an `ActionEvent` is generated and handled as follows by the question.

```
public class Question implements ActionListener {
  ...
    protected void actionPerformed(ActionEvent e) {
        ...
        _eventMgr.publish("QuestionAnswered"+_context, this);
    }
  ...
}
```

This method publishes event `QuestionAnswered`*Type*, where *Type* is "Demographic" in the context of a participant's registration. The model subscribes to the QuestionAnsweredDemographic event. Its handler for that event is shown here:

```
public void questionAnsweredDemographic(ipoll.client.Question q)
   throws java.lang.Exception {
     int[] qAnswers = q.getAnswers();
     _answers[q.getIndex()] = (short)qAnswers[0];
}
```

This method simply updates the answers cache maintained in the model at the index of the specific question just answered.

QuestionNavigationView

QuestionNavigationView is responsible for displaying GUI elements that allow the participant to navigate among the questions within the current context. An action of the participant in the QuestionNavigationView generates a NewQuestion*Type* event. The argument accompanying that event is an integer specifying the new question number to be processed or a special negative value (defined in the Question class) that specifies to move either to the next or to the previous question. QuestionView subscribes to the NewQuestionDemographic event, and the handler for that event simply displays the question requested.

RegistrationControlView

Finally, RegistrationControlView displays a GUI element to allow the participant to signify the completion of the registration phase. When completion is requested, RegistrationControlView publishes the Registration event. Root subscribes to the Registration event. When it receives that event, it invokes method register() on the model (shown in the code following). That method simply invokes the set_record() operation on the Participant object. Upon successful registration, the participant may then proceed to the polling phase.

```
public void register() throws java.lang.Exception {
     try {
         _participant.set_record(_pollId, _answers);
     } catch (java.lang.Exception ex) {
         throw new java.lang.Exception(
             "Error on participant registration: " + ex);
     }
}
```

With respect to demographic questions, an update to the polling database therefore occurs only when the participant is done answering all questions and triggers the "register" action. This is different from polling questions, where updates to the database are performed as soon as the answer to a poll question changes. More on this in the next section.

Voting

Once a participant has been properly authenticated/registered, he or she enters the Voting (polling) phase. This phase is controlled by the VotingView class, which is the aggregate of four lower-level agents: QuestionNavigationView, QuestionView, ResultsView, and VotesSelectionView.

The four logical parts of the VotingView consist of the following:

- A navigation view to navigate from question to question

- A question view where the questions of the poll are shown one at a time

- A results view to monitor the poll results of the currently displayed question in real time

- A selection view to specify the set of records we are interested in for the analysis of poll data

QuestionNavigationView

QuestionNavigationView was previously discussed in the *Participant Registration* section. We know that QuestionNavigationView generates a NewQuestionPoll event whenever a new question needs to be displayed in the QuestionView. Just as was the case in the registration phase, QuestionView subscribes to that event. Upon reception of that event, QuestionView computes the index of the new question to be displayed (because the argument may simply specify a directive relative to the current question: previous or next), displays it, and generates a NewQuestionNumberPoll event whose argument specifies the exact number of the question currently displayed. The model subscribes to that event. This is necessary so that the state of our callback registered with the analyst can be updated as soon as a new question needs to be displayed. An extra layer of event generation is required when a NewQuestion event occurs because the knowledge of the exact question being displayed is encapsulated in QuestionView. The following source code shows the processing done in the model for a NewQuestionNumberPoll event.

```
public void appEvent(String event, Object arg) {
    ...
    else if (event.equals("NewQuestionNumberPoll")) {
1       gotoQuestion(((Integer)event.arg).intValue());
    }...
    ...
}


public void gotoQuestion(int questionId) throws java.lang.Exception {
    if (questionId ==  Question.NewQuestionNone) {
2       unregisterCallback();
    } else {
            _questionId = questionId;
            _vsi.question_number = questionId;
3       updateCallback();
    }
}


public synchronized void updateCallback() throws java.lang.Exception {
    try {
        if( _callbackId < 0 ) {
4           _callbackId = _analyst.register_callback(this, _vsi);
        } else {
5           _analyst.update_callback(_callbackId, _vsi);
        }
6       getResults();
    } catch(java.lang.Exception ex) {
        throw new java.lang.Exception(
            "Failed to update analyst callback object: " + ex);
    }
}


public void getResults()throws java.lang.Exception {
    try {
7       ipoll.analystTpcMcpl.Results results = _analyst.get_results(_vsi);
        _eventMgr.publish("Results", results);
    } catch (java.lang.Exception ex) {
        throw new java.lang.Exception(
            "Failed to get results from the analyst: " + ex);
    }
}
```

When a `NewQuestionNumberPoll` event is received, the method `gotoQuestion()` is invoked (line 1). The argument tells which question is currently displayed in the `QuestionView`. Assuming that `questionId` does not have the value NewQuestionNone, a call is made to update the callback (line 3). In the updateCallback() method we simply invoke the register_callback() operation on the analyst if this is the first time we register our callback (callbackId < 0, line 4), or we invoke the update_callback() operation with our callback ID number if we were previously registered (line 5). By registering the callback (which, in fact, is the model itself) with the analyst, the model receives automatic result updates for the currently displayed question.

A call is made to the getResults() method (line 6) to get an immediate result update on that new question. This is necessary because the callback will come only when the results change in the polling database, which may take some time if there is no activity on the poll. We get the results in line 7 by invoking the operation get_results() on the analyst. As soon as we get these results, we publish a Results event to be processed by the ResultsView.

It is important to note that whenever the participant quits the voting phase, the deactivation of the VotingView generates a NewQuestion event with the argument set to the NewQuestionNone value. This special value is used by the model to unregister the callback because it is no longer required (line 2). Whenever the view is reactivated, another NewQuestion event is generated, this time with the argument set to 0 (so question 0 is displayed).

QuestionView

From the *Participant Registration* section, we know that QuestionView generates a QuestionAnsweredPoll event whenever the answer to a poll question changes. The model subscribes to that event and handles it as follows:

```
public void questionAnsweredPoll(ipoll.client.QuestionAnswered q)
    throws java.lang.Exception {
1    int[] qAnswers = q.getAnswers();
2    _answers[q.getIndex()] = (short)qAnswers[0];
3    _participant.set_record(_pollId, _answers);
}
```

Just as was the case for the QuestionAnsweredDemographic event, the model first simply updates the answers array for the participant (lines 1–2). But it does not stop there, as was the case for the demographic questions. It also invokes the set_record() method on the participant object to update the polling record associated with that participant immediately. This way, real-time updates are sent to registered applications as soon as a new answer is entered by a participant.

ResultsView

When poll results change in the polling database, the Analyst calls the opera-tion `results_update()` on its registered callbacks. Upon receiving the up-date, the model simply generates the `Results` event to be processed by the `ResultsView`. `ResultsView` displays the results in one of two ways, either as a bar chart or as a map.

```
public synchronized void result_update(ipoll.analystTpcMcpl.Results res) {
    _eventMgr.publish("Results", res);
}
```

VotesSelectionView

`VotesSelectionView`'s responsibility consists in getting from the participant the criteria to apply at the Analyst for the selection of the polling records used for the computation of polling results.

Whenever a selection criteria changes, `VotesSelectionView` generates a `VotesSelection` event. The model subscribes to that event and handles it as follows:

```
public void votesSelection(ipoll.analystTpcMcpl.Selection vsi) {
    _vsi = vsi;
    _vsi.question_number = _questionId; // Selection view does not know
                                        // about current questionId
    try {
        updateCallback();
    } catch (java.lang.Exception ex) {
        System.err.println("Error on callback update: " + ex);
    }
}
```

The model sets its `Selection` instance variable and calls the `updateCallback()` routine so that future automatic result updates take into account these new selection criteria.

Chapter Summary

In this chapter, we've shown how a real-world Internet application can be built using Java IDL. Through the presentation of the InterPoll set of network services, we stressed the fact that the careful design of these shared services is key to the suc-cess of three-tier CORBA-based applications. Once IDL interfaces are well defined, tapping into the power of your organization's intranet, or even of the world's biggest computer, the Internet, is no more difficult than programming standard, single address-space applications.

8

InterPoll Shared Services

Chapter 7 presented the public IDL interfaces for the InterPoll set of network services. This chapter expands InterPoll's network services to include the unpublished private IDL interfaces developed for InterPoll.

Public versus Private IDL Interfaces

The public interfaces described in Chapter 7 have certain common characteristics. These interfaces are publicly available to any InterPoll client application. An IDL interface is public if object references of its instances are openly accessible to client applications. Usually, this is done via the Naming service or as a result of calling a method on another public object.

Public interfaces support "safe" operations—operations that, even if used by malicious programmers, do not have harmful effects on the system.

The InterPoll system defines private interfaces as well. Private interfaces are used when operations need to be sensitive to security issues and could have detrimental effects on the system if used inappropriately. These interfaces are therefore restricted to administrative programs and trusted object implementations. In InterPoll, private object references are kept in files on a secure host.

In the following sections, we introduce the two types of private interfaces used for the InterPoll network services: Factory and Admin.

Factory Interface

In a distributed environment, a remote object cannot be created simply by invoking the creation operator of a specific programming language, for example, invoking new on a C++ or Java class constructor. When using CORBA, remote objects are typically created through Factory objects, which are responsible for allocating instances of these network objects, obtaining their object references, and registering them with the CORBA infrastructure.

In the InterPoll services, each of the five core object abstractions has an associated factory. Each one of these factories has an IDL operation of the form:

```
create_objectname(creation-parameters)
```

Factory interfaces are all private in InterPoll. Creation of objects is therefore possible only through administrative programs (available to poll designers for the creation of Questions and Polls), or trusted object implementations ("Admin" objects are used for the creation of Collector, Analyst, and Participant objects).

If a newly created object implements a public interface, its object reference is made accessible to client applications either through the Naming service or through methods on other accessible objects. Let's see how this is handled in InterPoll.

- Poll and Question objects are registered in the InterPoll public Naming context under the object's name (an attribute of the creation operation) and under a unique ID generated by the factory. This ID is useful for compact identification of Question and Poll objects when they need to be represented in other objects' state. For example, the Participant object keeps a reference to all polls in which the user has participated, as well as a reference to the demographic questions the user has already answered.

- A Participant object can be accessed by a client application only if the user associated with that Participant object can be authenticated. The Participant interface is therefore public, but only to a properly authenticated user.

- A reference to an Analyst object is obtained by invoking the get_analyst() operation on the Participant object.

- Collector has a private interface only. It is accessed indirectly via a Participant object, yielding authenticated access to its operations.

Admin Interface

Administrative interfaces support operations that are "unsafe," for example, destroying an object or adding a record to the vote database.

The Admin interface is derived from the public interface and adds administrative operations to it. The implementation of the public interface simply delegates all its operations to the Admin object, so that, in fact, the real implementation of the object resides only in the Admin object.

When InterPoll factories create an object that supports both Public and Admin interfaces, they do the following:

- Create the Admin object

- Create the Public object

- Assign the Admin object to be the delegate of the Public object

- Register the Public object in the public InterPoll naming context

- Register the Admin object in the file system of a secure host

Admin interfaces support the following two operations:

```
get_objectname()
```

where objectname is the name of the public peer

```
destroy()
```

Operation get_objectname() returns the object reference of the publicly accessible object. The destroy() operation handles the destruction of both the Admin object and its associated public counterpart.

PollAdmin and PollAdminFactory

The Admin and Factory interfaces of the Poll abstraction are shown here.

```
interface PollAdmin : Poll {
    CollectorAdmin get_collector()
                        raises(IpollException);
    Object get_analyst(in string analystType)
                        raises(IpollException);
    Poll get_poll();
    void destroy();
};
```

```
interface PollAdminFactory {
    PollAdmin create_PollAdmin(in PollBaseInfo info)
                raises(IpollException);
};
```

The Admin interface gives direct access to the Collector object responsible for collecting the vote records for that poll. It also supports the management of Analyst objects that client applications use for real-time analysis of the poll results. In the public interface discussed in Chapter 7, access to the Collector and the Analyst is possible only through the Participant object, allowing client applications to operate on Collector and Analyst only on behalf of an authenticated participant.

QuestionAdmin and QuestionAdminFactory

The Admin and Factory interfaces of the Question abstraction are shown here.

```
interface QuestionAdmin : Question {
    Question get_question();
    void destroy();
};

interface QuestionAdminFactory {
    QuestionAdmin create_QuestionAdmin(in QuestionBaseInfo info)
                raises(IpollException);
};
```

ParticipantFactory

Participant does not have an Admin interface. The public interface, however, is accessible only to a properly authenticated user.

With respect to its factory, we saw in Chapter 7 that the creation of Participant objects is simply delegated to the UserManager service.

```
interface ParticipantFactory : App::UserFactory {};
```

CollectorAdmin and CollectorAdminFactory

The Admin and Factory interfaces of the Collector abstraction are shown here.

```
interface CollectorAdmin {
    long append_record(in long user_id, in Answers ans)
                                raises(IpollException);
    void update_record(in long rec_id, in Answers ans)
                                raises(IpollException);
    RecordOut get_user_record(in long record_id)
```

```
                                        raises(IpollException);
    RecordOut get_user_record_from_user_id(
        in long user_id, out long record_id)
                                        raises(IpollException);
    RecordOutSeq get_records(in long index, in long cnt)
                                        raises(IpollException);
    void destroy() raises(IpollException);
};

interface CollectorAdminFactory {
    CollectorAdmin create_CollectorAdmin(in string name)
                raises(IpollException);
};
```

The Collector abstraction does not have a public interface, only an administrative one. As discussed in Chapter 7, it can be accessed by a client application only through the Participant interface, allowing only authenticated users to access its operations.

For each new record appended in its database, the Collector generates a unique record ID that the trusted application is required to use to get or update the participant's voting record. Operation get_user_record_from_user_id() is provided to retrieve the record ID associated with a specific user ID when the record ID is not available.

Operation get_records() is used by administrative programs to get a list of all the records in the database.

A name uniquely identifying the Collector is provided as an argument to the CollectorFactory creation operation.

AnalystAdmin and AnalystAdminFactory
The Admin and Factory interfaces of the Analyst abstraction are shown here.

```
interface AnalystAdmin {
    void process_callbacks();
    ipoll::StringSeq active_callbacks();
    unsigned long get_callback_update_interval();
    void set_callback_update_interval(in unsigned long interval);
    Analyst get_analyst();
    void destroy();
};

interface AnalystAdminFactory {
    AnalystAdmin create_AnalystAdmin()
                raises(ipoll::IpollException);
};
```

The Admin interface supports administrative operations to request the immediate processing of the callbacks, to obtain a list of the currently active callbacks, and get/set the current update interval (update interval is in seconds). A value of zero means that callbacks are called as soon as results are updated. If the value is not zero, the callback updates are processed at the rate specified in the update_interval value.

Chapter Summary

The InterPoll public and private IDL interfaces are both simple and powerful. Each CORBA IDL interface clearly presents its services using a standard notation. From the simplicity of IDL interfaces comes the power to let an arbitrary number of clients reuse and share the InterPoll services now and into the future.

9

The Network Pricing System: Building a
Distributed Financial Services Application with Java IDL

In this chapter and its companion, Chapter 10, we will develop a sample application that illustrates a number of issues typically encountered in the design of distributed object applications. This application is based on a common problem in the financial services industry: distributing streams of financial data to multiple clients in real time. While the architecture is general enough to support streams of any data, this system provides stock price information. In this chapter, we will present the overall design of the system and the implementation of a Java/Java IDL client for the data feed. In Chapter 10, we'll present the implementation of the server objects.

Requirements

We know that our system will be delivering streams of stock price data to multiple clients, but we need a little more detail before we can start designing the system. In this section, we'll discuss the requirements for our application.

Data Distribution

Our system is designed to distribute stock pricing information to individual investors rather than institutional clients. Therefore, we need a system that will reach as many people as possible, reliably and cost-effectively. Because we are distributing information that customers will access from their computers, we have two choices. We can have them dial in using a modem, or we can distribute the data via the Internet. Using the direct dial-in option means that we have to maintain a fairly large modem pool and the phone lines to access them. The Internet is a far better option. The Internet allows us to reach the widest possible audience using networks that are already in place.

Software Distribution

A data feed by itself is pretty useless to the individual investor. We also need to provide some kind of application that allows our clients to access the data feed. This means that we need to send the software to any clients that sign up. Because we are already using the Internet for distribution of our data, why not use it for distribution of our software? This approach greatly simplifies and reduces the cost of distribution. Currently, the most elegant way to distribute software over the Internet is by using Java. Applets can be distributed and updated from a central location as desired. Moreover, we don't need to write a separate application for every possible type of client machine. With Java we get that for free. Therefore, another requirement of our application is that the client-side software be written in Java and distributed over the Internet.

Open Interface

Because our primary business is data distribution and not software development, we would like to provide a well-defined and open interface to the data feed to allow third-party developers to create applications that use the data feed functionality. Example applications include technical analysis software, option pricing software, and various personal finance programs. CORBA provides an ideal mechanism for specifying and distributing such an interface. An IDL interface to our data feed allows anyone to create a CORBA-compliant application that can use our data feed. They don't need specialized training from us or detailed knowledge of our servers and their implementation. Any CORBA developer can use it. By providing a standards-based interface to our data, we make the development of third-party software easier and cheaper.

Access Control

Controlling access to the data is another important requirement. Because this is a commercial service, we want to be able to bill clients for using the service. We therefore need to verify that users are legitimate clients before granting them access to the data. We need to implement some kind of security that will ensure that access to the data can be strictly controlled.

Performance

Because we will be using the Internet as the distribution channel for our service, we need to consider its performance. The universe of stocks for which data is available is potentially very large. In offering a service such as ours, we would like to have as much coverage as possible if our service is to be attractive to our clients. We don't, however, want to indiscriminately ship large amounts of data across the network. Most of our clients will be accessing our system over a modem connection, and these connections do not handle large volumes of data very well. Also remember that an Internet connection rarely involves just the two machines at its endpoints. Our data will almost certainly be routed through countless machines between the server and the client's PC. The more data we send, the more load we put on these intermediate machines and the network itself. We would like to minimize this load for two reasons. First, it slows down our data feed and any application that uses it. Second, we don't want to clog the Internet with unnecessary information. Each client is likely to be interested in only a small subset of the total universe of stocks. We need an efficient mechanism for controlling data transmission that minimizes load on the server, client, and the network.

To summarize, several key requirements must be met in designing what we will call the Network Pricing System, or NPS for short. The NPS must do the following:

- Use the Internet for data distribution

- Use the Internet for software distribution

- Allow third-party developer access

- Provide access control for users

- Transmit data efficiently

NPS Design and Architecture

In this section, we will explore the design issues in depth and explain the reasons behind our design choices.

NPS is designed as a three-tier application with a presentation tier, a business object tier, and a data source tier. Internally, our data comes from a Feed object. We won't concern ourselves at this stage with the details of how the Feed gets the stock price data that it distributes. Assume for now that it gets it from one of the major market data providers and that we have wrapped that data with a very simple CORBA IDL interface—each quote is simply an IDL struct. What we need to do is define an architecture for passing that data on to our customers in a way that satisfies our requirements. We'll explain some of the design issues and then introduce the objects that combine to make up the complete application.

Design Issues

While much of the design of NPS is relatively straightforward, there are a few issues that bear a closer look: filtering, security, and persistence.

Filtering

Let's start by looking at how we want to transmit the data. One of our requirements is that we make transmission reasonably efficient. The first design decision we made is that we definitely do NOT want to give our customers direct access to the full feed from our Feed source. We need to come up with a way of modifying the flow of data to tailor it to the needs of our clients. We need to filter the data.

There are two ways we can do this. We can have the client application do all the filtering, or we can do some of it on the server side. Client-side filtering requires all the data to be shipped across the network, so this is not a viable option. Server-side filtering requires us to implement a mechanism for controlling the flow of data to the client. This is done using filter objects. The filter objects will sit between the source channel and the client on the server side and filter the data that is sent to the client using user-specified criteria.

Security

Security is another issue that we need to address. Security is a broad term that covers a wide range of issues. Usually it refers to mechanisms for authentication, authorization, and encryption of data. For our purposes, we are concerned about only authentication because we want to block convenient access to the data to those who haven't paid for our service. We don't need a sophisticated mechanism: Once a user is authenticated as a legitimate customer, we will give him or her full access to the feed.

One way to do this is to ensure that the only reference NPS publishes in the CORBA namespace is for an authentication object that verifies that the user is really who he or she says he or she is before providing a reference to the true data feed object. Our implementation will use a simple password scheme to authenticate the user and rely on the passing of an authentication token in subsequent operations to verify that user's identity.

Authorization in this scenario is very simple: Any authenticated user is allowed full access to all the services NPS provides.

Because we are not delivering particularly sensitive data, there really is no need to encrypt it. The degradation in performance would not be worth it. Using an encryption mechanism in the authentication process would be advisable, but implementing that is beyond the scope of this book.

Persistence

Persistence is the final issue that we must address. How are we going to store the data that we need to make the application work? What is that data? The only data we really need to store is the database of user IDs and passwords, and user preferences. The market data will be provided by an outside data vendor and won't be saved for this application. For the simple implementation presented in this book, we'll use Java serialization to persist the user information into files, while making sure to use a generic interface internally to allow us the flexibility to upgrade to another implementation in the future. For example, it is easy to envision that our customer base will become large enough that we'll want to store the user ID database in a commercial relational or object-oriented database.

NPS Architecture

The overall architecture is illustrated here. The system we will be building consists of four separate CORBA objects. The relationship of these objects is shown in Figure 9.1. The objects are these:

FeedFactory

FilteredQuoteFeed

FeedChannel

QuoteReceiver

Figure 9.1 NPS architecture.

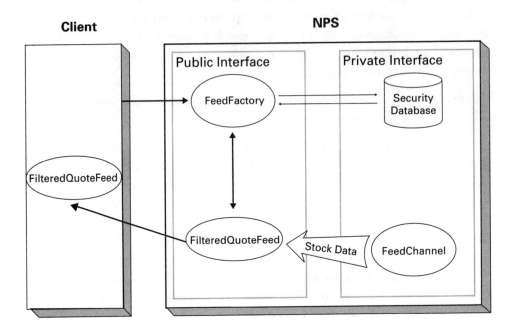

One FeedChannel manages access to multiple FilteredQuoteFeed objects. Each FilteredQuoteFeed object filters data from the FeedChannel according to the user's preferences. Only the FeedFactory and a single FilteredQuoteFeed object are accessible by each client. The QuoteReceiver is the client-side object that receives the quotes from the FilteredQuoteFeed. The interfaces to each of these objects and their functionality are explained in detail in the following sections.

Figure 9.2 shows a class diagram of the CORBA objects, as defined by their IDL interfaces.

FeedFactory

The FeedFactory generates and manages access to FilteredQuoteFeed objects, the sources of data for each client. The FeedFactory therefore does two things: It creates FilteredQuoteFeed objects, and it manages access to those objects via an authentication mechanism.

As shown in Figure 9.2, FeedFactory inherits from the Authenticator interface defined in the Auth module. Here is the IDL for the Authenticator.

Figure 9.2 NPS class diagram (UML).

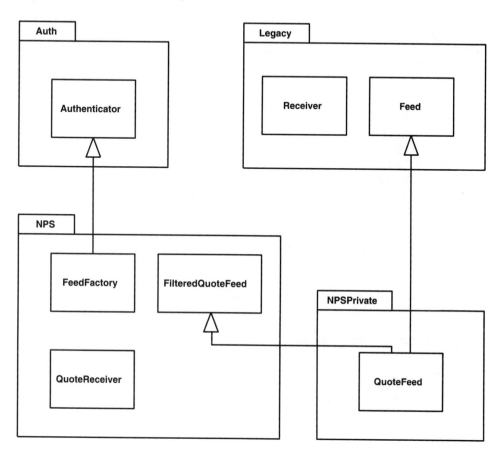

Auth.idl

```
module Auth
{
    // Authentication token
    typedef sequence<octet> AuthToken;

    // Packet to be passed to all "secured" servers
    struct AuthPacket {
        string userID;
        AuthToken token;
    };

    // Failure reason
    enum AuthReason {
```

```
     InvalidUser, InvalidPasswd, TimedOut, BadToken
};

// Exception for security errors
exception AuthFailure {
   string description;
   AuthReason reason;
};

// User profile
struct Profile {
   string userID;
   string fullName;
   double accountBalance;
};


// Abstract Authenticator interface to be specialized by
// objects that need to authenticate users.
interface Authenticator {

   AuthPacket login(in string user, in string passwd)
     raises(AuthFailure);

   void logout(in AuthPacket tok)
     raises(AuthFailure);

   boolean changePasswd(in AuthPacket tok, in string userID,
             in string passwd)
     raises(AuthFailure);

   boolean isAuthValid(in AuthPacket tok);
   };
};
```

Authenticator

The Authenticator interface is not meant to be used directly. It is intended to be inherited by other objects that will provide this functionality within the context of their own intended uses. It supports methods that allow clients to log in, change their passwords, and verify identities. Once a client logs in, the Authorize object returns an AuthPacket that contains the client's "credentials." All other methods require these credentials that contain the user's identity and access permissions. Note that there are no methods that allow clients to add new users and modify account information; these are administrative functions. Because the Authenticator will be a public interface we don't want to expose these operations. Administrative methods would be defined in a separate module containing the internal interfaces.

The AuthToken sequence is simply authentication data that the AuthenticationManager uses to verify the user's identity. Using a sequence of octets means that the data will be transmitted without modification. The AuthPacket simply encapsulates the authentication data with the username. It is this structure that is passed between client and server objects for authentication purposes.

The application-level functionality of the FeedFactory is provided by the FeedFactory interface, shown here (excerpted from the source file NPS.idl).

```
module NPS
{

  typedef string Filter;
  typedef sequence<Filter> FilterList;

  interface FeedFactory : Auth::Authenticator {
    FilteredQuoteFeed getFeed(in Auth::AuthPacket tok)
      raises(Auth::AuthFailure);
    FilterList getPreferences(in Auth::AuthPacket tok)
      raises(Auth::AuthFailure);
    void storePreferences(in Auth::AuthPacket tok,
              in FilterList prefs)
      raises(Auth::AuthFailure);
  };
}
```

The FeedFactory interface allows clients to obtain a reference to a FilteredQuoteFeed object after logging in. The FeedFactory creates the FilteredQuoteFeed object and returns its reference to the invoking client. The FeedFactory destroys the object when the user logs out. It also provides methods for storing and retrieving the user's preferences. For the purposes of this application, preferences are simply lists of stocks in which the user is interested.

Note that each method takes an AuthPacket authentication token. This allows the FeedFactory to authenticate the client on every operation. Without a valid token, no client can invoke any of the methods successfully. Every method of every other public object in our application takes an authentication token and verifies its validity with the Authenticator. It would be much more desirable to have this detail hidden from the interfaces. This is what the CORBA Security service does. Because we are not using that here, the explicit use of the authentication packet is sufficient for our purposes, at the cost of transparency and some measure of orthogonality in the interface specifications.

FilteredQuoteFeed and QuoteFilter

The FilteredQuoteFeed object is the source of the price quotes, as far as the user sees. Each client application acquires a reference to a FilteredQuoteFeed object after first logging in. This object is responsible for filtering the stock quotes sent to the client. Its IDL is shown here:

```
module NPS
{

  // data structures
  struct Quote {
    string symbol;
    string price;
    string fullName;
  } ;

  // client side receiver interface
  interface QuoteReceiver {
    void pushQuote(in Quote q);
    FilterList getFilters();
    void disconnect();
  };

  exception BadFilter {
    Filter f;
  };

  // Filtered quote feed source
  interface FilteredQuoteFeed {

    void addQuoteReceiver(in Auth::AuthPacket tok,
                inout QuoteReceiver recv)
      raises(BadFilter,Auth::AuthFailure);

    void disconnectQuoteReceiver(in Auth::AuthPacket tok,
                inout QuoteReceiver recv)
      raises(Auth::AuthFailure);

    void disconnectAndDestroy(in Auth::AuthPacket tok)
      raises(Auth::AuthFailure);

    FilterList getCurrentFilters(in Auth::AuthPacket tok)
```

```
        raises(Auth::AuthFailure);
    };
};
```

Each piece of data from our system will be a Quote struct that will contain the price information for a given stock. For simplicity, all the data is represented as strings. Data from our internal price feed is filtered to make sure that the client does not receive any unwanted information and to reduce the amount of data transmitted. The FilteredQuoteFeed does this using Filters. In this implementation, a Filter is simply a string that holds a particular stock name. A given client will then request the information only for the stocks named in its FilterList. A more sophisticated implementation might have defined Filters as full-blown objects with IDL interfaces and the ability to filter the data according to various rules.

Note that the QuoteReceiver arguments to the FilteredQuoteFeed::addQuoteReceiver and FilteredQuoteFeed::disconnectQuoteReceiver methods have been declared as **inout** parameters. They are actually meant to be used solely as **in** parameters; however, the early access release of Java IDL had problems when these were declared as **in** parameters.

QuoteReceiver

Stock data is distributed to clients via the QuoteReceiver interface. For a client application to receive price data, it must provide an object that implements this IDL interface. This object must also have a FilterList associated with it. The QuoteReceiver is then registered with the FilteredQuoteFeed and is ready to be used. The FilteredQuoteFeed queries the QuoteReceiver to get the list of stocks in which it is interested in using the getFilters() method. It then sends any price data that it receives for those stocks using the pushQuote() method.

As illustrated in the previous IDL class diagram, FilteredQuoteFeed is actually a superclass of QuoteFilter. In fact, FilteredQuoteFeed is never used directly. As with the Authenticator interface, the FilteredQuoteFeed interface is meant to be inherited. The main reason for doing this is that we want to hide the implementation details of our server. Because we are using a Legacy::Feed object as our primary source of data, our filters need to implement the Legacy::Receiver interface to be able to retrieve the data without polling. We don't want our clients to know about this implementation detail because we chose not to use the Legacy service in our external interfaces. We therefore create the QuoteFilter interface, which is both a Feed "consumer" and a FilteredQuoteFeed object. The IDL is shown here:

```
#include "NPS.idl"
#include "Legacy.idl"

module NPSPrivate
{

   interface QuoteFilter : Legacy::Receiver, NPS::FilteredQuoteFeed
{
   };

};
```

Note that this interface is defined in the NPSPrivate module. This is the only module that will not be published; it is for the our internal use only.

Feed

The final object to be discussed is the Feed. This can be thought of as an event channel that passes data of type Legacy::Quote on to any registered listener. Each QuoteFilter object registers with the Feed to receive its data via the Feed::register method. The details of this object will be described more fully in Chapter 10. The Receiver/Feed pair of interfaces have a relationship similar to the PushConsumer/PushSupplier interfaces of the CORBA Event Service. If the Java IDL package contained an implementation of the Event Service, we probably would have used that instead of inventing our own interfaces.

A Client Application

Now that we've looked at the design of the NPS system, let's look at the implementation of a client that uses the NPS data feed. This is a fairly simple client that allows the user to specify a list of stock symbols and receive updates as the prices of those stocks change over time. This is just one possible use for the NPS price feed. More sophisticated applications could be written that take advantage of the mechanisms and interfaces already provided.

The StockTracker applet presents two screens to the user. Upon start-up, the user is presented with a login screen, as shown in Figure 9.3.

Once the user has logged in, the applet presents the stock tracking screen, as illustrated in Figure 9.4. The stock tracking screen allows the user to add a new stock symbol to track, to delete a stock symbol from being tracked, or to log out from NPS.

Our client is a Java applet that uses Java IDL to access the objects discussed in the previous section. It consists of several main classes. These are StockTracker,

Figure 9.3 StockTracker applet login screen.

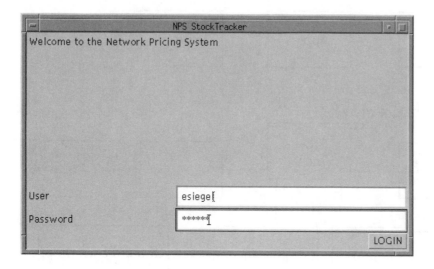

CommManager, QuoteReceiverImpl, TextRow, and TextTable, all in the package NPS. The relationships between these classes and others are illustrated in the class diagram in Figure 9.5.

Figure 9.4 StockTracker applet stock tracking screen.

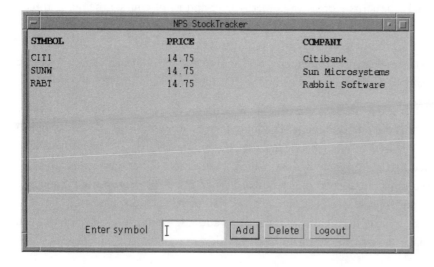

Figure 9.5 StockTracker applet class diagram (UML).

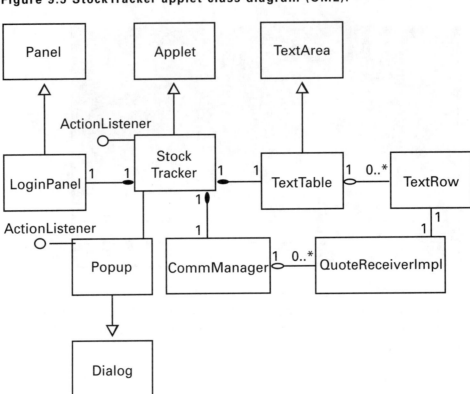

StockTracker inherits from java.applet.Applet and is, of course, the main applet class itself. It handles the composition of the GUI and the interaction with the user. Because most of the functionality of the user interface is provided through button actions, StockTracker also implements the ActionListener interface. This allows it to process events from the various buttons within the interface.

The StockTracker interface consists of two different views. One is the login view, and the other is the portfolio view. The login view is shown at start-up and provides a screen for the user to enter his or her user ID and password. The login view is implemented by the LoginPanel class, which, besides its GUI components, simply provides access to the user ID and password typed in by the user. If the login is successful, the portfolio screen is shown. This screen provides a display of all the stocks being monitored and allows the user to add additional stocks. A CardLayout layout manager is used to organize these two views.

When the StockTracker applet is initialized, one of the objects it creates after constructing the GUI is the CommManager. This object handles all interaction with the Java IDL- and CORBA-specific parts of our application. It allows us to separate the GUI from the communications layer.

The CommManager handles the creation and management of the QuoteReceiverImpl instances. These are the implementations of our client-side callback objects. Because they will be receiving requests from remote objects, they must themselves be server objects. One of these objects is created for every stock the user wishes to monitor.

TextTable is the main display area. It is here that the stock symbols and their prices are displayed. TextTable derives from TextArea and is responsible for keeping track of a list of TextRows.

TextRow is a very simple class that allows for the manipulation and formatting for display of multicolumn strings. It maintains a reference to its containing TextTable so that changes to the TextRow can be updated on the display.

At start-up, the applet first initializes itself and calls on the CommManager to initialize the necessary parts of the ORB. In its constructor, the CommManager performs several initialization actions. It first initializes the ORB using the standard Java IDL methods. It then creates a helper class to manage our callback objects, which will be acting as CORBA servers. The callback objects use the Java IDL transient server interfaces as described in Chapter 5.

Next, the CommManager tries to locate the FeedFactory server object. This is done using the CosNaming interface to the naming service. It uses the fundamental Java IDL narrow() idiom described in Chapter 5.

Here is the code for the CommManager constructor:

```
public CommManager(java.applet.Applet apl) {

    receivers = new Hashtable();

    // Save applet reference
    applet = apl;

    // Initialize ORB.
    java.util.Properties props = System.getProperties();
    props.put("org.omg.CORBA.ORBInitialHost", "freon.fsg.com");
    props.put("org.omg.CORBA.ORBInitialPort", "900");
```

```
// If this were an applet, it would be initialized like this:
//     orb = org.omg.CORBA.ORB.init(applet, props);

// But right now it's an app, so this is the right way to start:
String args[] = {};
orb = org.omg.CORBA.ORB.init(args, props);

org.omg.CORBA.Object objref = null;
try {

    // Get reference to root naming context
    objref = orb.resolve_initial_references("NameService");
    NamingContext ncRef = NamingContextHelper.narrow(objref);
    NameComponent nc = new NameComponent("QuoteFeedAdmin", "");
    NameComponent path[] = { nc };
    feedFactory = FeedFactoryHelper.narrow(ncRef.resolve(path));

} catch (Exception excp) {
    StockTracker.popErr("Initialization Failed! Try again later");
    System.err.println(
      "Error during initialization of FeedFactory");
    System.err.println("Exception: " + excp);
    excp.printStackTrace(System.err);
}


}
```

Once the user types in a user ID and password and presses the login button, the CommManager login() function is called. This function attempts to log the user into the FeedFactory using the previously obtained object reference. If successful, this returns a valid AuthPacket that is stored for use in future operations. The CommManager then tries to obtain a feed object and the user's previously stored preferences, if any. These preferences are held by the client for future use as well.

```
public void login(String userName, String password)
    throws Exception {
        System.out.println("Logging in with...");
        System.out.println("UserName: " + userName);
        System.out.println("Password: " + password);

        if(userName.length() == 0 || password.length() == 0) {
          System.out.println("No username or passwd");
          StockTracker.popErr("You must enter both a user name and password");
          throw (new Exception());
        }
```

```
try {
        packet = feedFactory.login(userName, password);
        feed = feedFactory.getFeed(packet);
    } catch(Exception excp) {
        StockTracker.popErr("Login failed.");
        System.err.println("Error occured attempting to login.");
        excp.printStackTrace(System.err);
        throw (new Exception("Login Failed"));
    }
    try {
        prefs = feedFactory.getPreferences(packet);
    } catch(Exception excp) {
        excp.printStackTrace();
    }
}
```

When the user adds a new stock to be monitored, the CommManager createReceiver() method is called. This creates a new QuoteReceiverImpl implementation class and connects it to the ORB as a server object. This object is then registered with the FilteredQuoteFeed object obtained earlier. Each Quote-ReceiverImpl contains a reference to its corresponding TextRow object, allowing it to update the display as soon as it receives any stock price updates.

```
public void createReceiver(String symbol, TextTable table)
    throws Exception {

  System.out.println(
        "Creating the receiver for: " + symbol + "...");
  try {
    // Create a new QuoteReceiver servant object
    // and bind it to the ORB as a server
    QuoteReceiverImpl quoteRecvImpl
       = new QuoteReceiverImpl(symbol, table);

    orb.connect(quoteRecvImpl);

    // register the new receiver with the Feed object
    try {
      feed.addQuoteReceiver(packet,quoteRecv);
    } catch (Auth.AuthFailure authExcp) {
      if(authExcp.reason==Auth.AuthReason.TimedOut ||
         authExcp.reason==Auth.AuthReason.BadToken) {
        // log in again?
      }
    }
```

```
    } catch(NPS.BadFilter bfExcp) {
      StockTracker.popErr("The symbol specified was unknown");
    } catch(Exception excp) {
      StockTracker.popErr("Failed to register quote filter.");
      System.err.println(
          "Something went wrong during quote creation");
      excp.printStackTrace(System.err);
    }
}
```

The QuoteReceiverImpl class provides implementations of the three methods defined in the QuoteReceiver IDL interface. PushQuote() updates the TextRow with the new data, getFilters() simply returns the symbol for the stock that this QuoteReceiver listens for, and disconnect() updates the TextRow to indicate this on the display.

```
public synchronized void pushQuote(Quote q)
    {
        row.setText(0,q.symbol);
        row.setText(1,q.price);
        row.setText(2,q.fullName);
        row.update();
    }

public synchronized String[] getFilters()
    {
        String[] fl=new String[1];
        fl[0]=symbol;
        return fl;
    }

public synchronized void disconnect()
    {
        row.setText(0,"disconnected");
        row.setText(1,"disconnected");
        row.setText(2,"disconnected");
        row.update();
    }
```

That's all the interesting parts of the StockTracker applet from the perspective of Java IDL and CORBA. Because this is not a book on Java GUI programming, we won't step through all the applet code in detail. However, here is the complete listing for the StockTracker client applet.

StockTracker.java

```java
package NPS;

import java.lang.*;
import java.util.*;
import java.awt.*;
import java.awt.event.*;

public class StockTracker extends java.applet.Applet
                    implements ActionListener
{

  // Application controller
  CommManager commMgr;

  // GUI components
  Button addButton;
  Button lButton;
  TextField symbol;
  TextTable table;
  LoginPanel lp;

  static Frame topFrame;

  CardLayout lyt;


  public void init() {

    // Need the frame for dialogs
    Component frm=this;
    while((frm!=null)&&!(frm instanceof Frame)) {
      frm=frm.getParent();
    }
    topFrame=(Frame)frm;

    super.init();

    lyt=new CardLayout();
    setLayout(lyt);

    lp=new LoginPanel(this);
    add("First",lp);

    Panel mainPan=new Panel();
```

```
            mainPan.setLayout(new BorderLayout(10,10));

            Panel p=new Panel();

            // Symbol entry and add button
            symbol=new TextField(8);
            addButton=new Button("Add");
            p.add(new Label("Enter symbol"));
            p.add(symbol);
            p.add(addButton);
            addButton.addActionListener(this);

            // Logout button
            p.add(new Label("          "));
            lButton = new Button("Logout");
            p.add(lButton);
            lButton.addActionListener(this);

            table=new TextTable();
            String [] hd={"SYMBOL","PRICE","COMPANY"};
            table.setHeader(hd);
            mainPan.add("South",p);
            mainPan.add("Center",table);

            add("Main",mainPan);

            lyt.first(this);

            // Create the comm manager
            commMgr = new CommManager(this);
        }

        public void actionPerformed(ActionEvent e) {
          String arg = e.getActionCommand();
          System.out.println("Received an action event: " + arg);
          if (arg == "LOGIN") {
            // Log the user into the Quote service
            try {
          commMgr.login(lp.getUserName(), lp.getPassword());
          commMgr.startFeed(table);
          lyt.show(this, "Main");
            }
            catch (Exception ex) {
            }
          }
          else if (arg == "Add") {
            System.out.println("Pressed Add");
```

```
      try {
    commMgr.createReceiver(symbol.getText(), table);
      }
      catch (Exception ex) {
    popErr("Failed to create receiver");
      }
    }
    else if (arg == "Logout") {
      System.out.println("Pressed Logout");
      commMgr.logout();
      lyt.first(this);
    }
  }

  public void destroy() {
    System.out.println("indestroy");
    super.destroy();
  }

  public static void popErr(String str) {
    Popup d=new Popup("Error",str,topFrame);
    System.err.println("in popup:"+str);
    d.show();
  }

}
```

CommManager.java

```
package NPS;

import java.lang.*;
import java.util.*;

import org.omg.CORBA.*;
import org.omg.CosNaming.*;

public class CommManager {

  java.applet.Applet applet;
  ORB orb;

  Auth.AuthPacket packet;
  FeedFactory feedFactory;
  FilteredQuoteFeed feed;
  String preferences[];
  Hashtable receivers;
```

```
public CommManager(java.applet.Applet apl) {

   receivers = new Hashtable();

   // Save applet reference
   applet = apl;

   // Initialize ORB.
   java.util.Properties props = System.getProperties();
   props.put("org.omg.CORBA.ORBInitialHost", "freon.fsg.com");
   props.put("org.omg.CORBA.ORBInitialPort", "900");

   // If this were an applet, it would be initialized like this:
   //    orb = org.omg.CORBA.ORB.init(applet, props);

   // But right now it's an app, so this is the right way to start:
   String args[] = {};
   orb = org.omg.CORBA.ORB.init(args, props);

   org.omg.CORBA.Object objref = null;
   try {

      // Get reference for the root naming context
      objref = orb.resolve_initial_references("NameService");
      NamingContext ncRef = NamingContextHelper.narrow(objref);
      NameComponent nc = new NameComponent("QuoteFeedAdmin", "");
      NameComponent path[] = { nc };
      feedFactory = FeedFactoryHelper.narrow(ncRef.resolve(path));

   } catch (Exception excp) {
      StockTracker.popErr("Initialization Failed! Try again later");
      System.err.println(
        "Error during initialization of FeedFactory");
      System.err.println("Exception: " + excp);
      excp.printStackTrace(System.err);
   }

}

public void login(String userName, String password)
   throws Exception {
      System.out.println("Logging in with...");
      System.out.println("UserName: " + userName);
      System.out.println("Password: " + password);

      if(userName.length() == 0 || password.length() == 0) {
        System.out.println("No username or passwd");
```

```
          StockTracker.popErr(
              "You must enter both a user name and password");
          throw (new Exception());
      }
      try {
        packet = feedFactory.login(userName, password);
      } catch(Exception excp) {
          System.err.println("Error occured attempting to login.");
          excp.printStackTrace(System.err);
          StockTracker.popErr("Login failed");
          throw (new Exception("Login Failed"));
      }

      System.err.println("packet = " + packet);

      try {
        feed = feedFactory.getFeed(packet);
      } catch(Exception excp) {
        System.err.println("Error occured attempting to getFeed.");
        excp.printStackTrace(System.err);
        StockTracker.popErr("Login failed");
        throw (new Exception("Login Failed"));
      }

      try {
        preferences = feedFactory.getPreferences(packet);
      } catch(Exception excp) {
        excp.printStackTrace();
      }
  }

public String[] startFeed(QuoteListener ql)
    throws Exception {
      System.err.println("Starting the feed...");
      System.err.println("Number of preferences: "
                          + preferences.length);
      for(int i = 0; i < preferences.length; i++) {
        createReceiver(preferences[i], ql);
        System.err.println(preferences[i]);
      }
      return preferences;
  }

public void createReceiver(String symbol, QuoteListener ql)
    throws Exception {
      System.out.println("Creating the receiver for: " + symbol
                          + "...");
```

```
        QuoteReceiverImpl quoteRecvImpl = null;
        QuoteReceiver quoteRecv = null;

        try {
          // Create a new QuoteReceiver servant object
          // and bind it the ORB as a server
          quoteRecvImpl = new QuoteReceiverImpl(symbol);
          orb.connect(quoteRecvImpl);

          // register the new receiver with the Feed object
          try {
            System.err.println("packet = " + packet);
            System.err.println("feed = " + feed);
            feed.addQuoteReceiver(packet,
                              new QuoteReceiverHolder(quoteRecvImpl));
          } catch (Auth.AuthFailure authExcp) {
            if(authExcp.reason == Auth.AuthReason.TimedOut ||
            authExcp.reason == Auth.AuthReason.BadToken) {
              // log in again?
              System.err.println("Login timed out!");
            }
          }
        } catch(NPS.BadFilter bfExcp) {
          StockTracker.popErr("The symbol specified was unknown");
        } catch(Exception excp) {
          System.err.println(
            "Something went wrong during quote creation");
          excp.printStackTrace(System.err);
          StockTracker.popErr("Failed to register quote filter.");
        }

        // register QuoteListener
        quoteRecvImpl.addQuoteListener(ql);

        // Save object reference
        receivers.put(symbol, quoteRecvImpl);
    }


    public void deleteReceiver(String sym, QuoteListener ql) {
      boolean found = false;
      QuoteReceiver qrecv = (QuoteReceiver) receivers.get(sym);

      if (qrecv != null) {
        receivers.remove(sym);
        try {
          feed.disconnectQuoteReceiver(packet,
```

```java
                                      new QuoteReceiverHolder(qrecv));
        System.err.println("removed " + sym);
      }
      catch (Auth.AuthFailure authExcp) {
        if(authExcp.reason == Auth.AuthReason.TimedOut ||
           authExcp.reason == Auth.AuthReason.BadToken) {

          // log in again?
          System.err.println("Login timed out!");
        }
      }
      catch(Exception excp) {
        System.err.println("Something went wrong");
        excp.printStackTrace(System.err);
        StockTracker.popErr("Failed disconnect " + sym);
      }
    }
    else {
      System.err.println("Failed to remove " + sym);
    }
}

public void logout() {

  // Disconnect all listeners
  for (Enumeration recvs = receivers.elements();
       recvs.hasMoreElements(); ) {
    QuoteReceiver qr = (QuoteReceiver) recvs.nextElement();
    try {
      feed.disconnectQuoteReceiver(packet,
                                   new QuoteReceiverHolder(qr));
      System.err.println("removed one");
    }
    catch (Auth.AuthFailure authExcp) {
      if(authExcp.reason == Auth.AuthReason.TimedOut ||
         authExcp.reason == Auth.AuthReason.BadToken) {

        // log in again?
        System.err.println("Login timed out!");
      }
    }
    catch(Exception excp) {
      System.err.println("Something went wrong");
      excp.printStackTrace(System.err);
    }
  }
```

```
      // Save the current selection
      String prefs[] = new String[receivers.size()];
      int i = 0;
      for (Enumeration names = receivers.keys();
           names.hasMoreElements(); ) {
        String sym = (String) names.nextElement();
        prefs[i] = sym;
        java.lang.Object obj = receivers.remove(sym);
        i++;
      }

      try {
        feedFactory.storePreferences(packet, prefs);
      }
      catch (Auth.AuthFailure authExcp) {
        if(authExcp.reason == Auth.AuthReason.TimedOut ||
           authExcp.reason == Auth.AuthReason.BadToken) {
          // log in again?
          System.err.println("Login timed out!");
        }
      }

      receivers.clear();
    }
}
```

QuoteReceiverImpl.java

```
package NPS;
import java.awt.*;

public class QuoteReceiverImpl extends _QuoteReceiverImplBase
{

  String symbol;
  boolean disconnected=false;
  TextRow row;

  public QuoteReceiverImpl(String s, TextTable table) {
    symbol=s;
    row = new TextRow(3);
    row.setParent(table);
    row.setText(0, symbol);
    table.addTextRow(row);
  }
```

```java
public synchronized void pushQuote(Quote q)
  {
    if(disconnected) {
  //throw new sunw.corba.SystemException();
    }
    row.setText(0,q.symbol);
    row.setText(1,q.price);
    row.setText(2,q.fullName);
    row.update();
  }

public synchronized String[] getFilters()
  {
    String[] fl=new String[1];
    fl[0]=symbol;
    return fl;
  }

public synchronized void disconnect()
  {
    row.setText(0,"disconnected");
    row.setText(1,"disconnected");
    row.setText(2,"disconnected");
    row.update();
  }


}
```

LoginPanel.java

```java
package NPS;

import java.awt.*;
import java.awt.event.*;


public class LoginPanel extends Panel {

  TextField userNameField;
  TextField passwdField;


  public LoginPanel(ActionListener listener) {

    Panel p;
```

```
p=new Panel();

GridBagLayout gbl = new GridBagLayout();
p.setLayout(gbl);
GridBagConstraints gbc = new GridBagConstraints();

// User label
gbc.weightx = 100;
gbc.weighty = 100;
gbc.gridx = 0;
gbc.gridy = 0;
gbc.gridwidth = 1;
gbc.gridheight = 1;
gbc.fill = GridBagConstraints.BOTH;
gbc.anchor = GridBagConstraints.EAST;
Label label = new Label("User");
gbl.setConstraints(label, gbc);
p.add(label);

// Password label
gbc.weightx = 100;
gbc.weighty = 100;
gbc.gridx = 0;
gbc.gridy = 1;
gbc.gridwidth = 1;
gbc.gridheight = 1;
gbc.fill = GridBagConstraints.BOTH;
gbc.anchor = GridBagConstraints.EAST;
label = new Label("Password");
gbl.setConstraints(label, gbc);
p.add(label);

// User field
gbc.weightx = 100;
gbc.weighty = 0;
gbc.gridx = 1;
gbc.gridy = 0;
gbc.gridwidth = 2;
gbc.gridheight = 1;
gbc.fill = GridBagConstraints.BOTH;
gbc.anchor = GridBagConstraints.WEST;
userNameField=new TextField(20);
gbl.setConstraints(userNameField, gbc);
p.add(userNameField);

// Password field
gbc.weightx = 100;
gbc.weighty = 0;
```

```
       gbc.gridx = 1;
       gbc.gridy = 1;
       gbc.gridwidth = 2;
       gbc.gridheight = 1;
       gbc.fill = GridBagConstraints.BOTH;
       gbc.anchor = GridBagConstraints.WEST;
       passwdField = new TextField(20);
       passwdField.setEchoChar('*');
       gbl.setConstraints(passwdField, gbc);
       p.add(passwdField);

       // Login Button
       gbc.weightx = 100;
       gbc.weighty = 100;
       gbc.gridx = 2;
       gbc.gridy = 2;
       gbc.gridwidth = 1;
       gbc.gridheight = 1;
       gbc.fill = GridBagConstraints.NONE;
       gbc.anchor = GridBagConstraints.EAST;
       Button button = new Button("LOGIN");
       gbl.setConstraints(button, gbc);
       p.add(button);
       button.addActionListener(listener);

       setLayout(new BorderLayout());
       add("North",new Label("Welcome to the Network Pricing System"));
       add("South",p);

     }

  public String getUserName() {
     return userNameField.getText();
  }

  public String getPassword() {
     return passwdField.getText();

  }
}
```

TextTable.java

```
package NPS;

import java.awt.*;
import java.util.*;
```

```
public class TextTable extends TextArea {

  int linelen=0;
  public Vector textLines=new Vector(5,5);

  public TextTable() {
    setEditable(false);
    setBackground(Color.white);
  }

  public void setHeader(String[] ar) {
    for(int i=0;i<ar.length;i++) {
      String s=ar[i];
      while(s.length()<20) {
    s+=" ";
      }
      linelen+=20;
      append(s);
    }
    append(" ");
    linelen++;
    setFont(new Font("courier",Font.PLAIN,14));
  }

  public void clear() {
    textLines=new Vector(5,5);
    String s=getText();
    setText(s.substring(0,linelen));
  }

  public synchronized void update(TextRow tr) {
    int i=textLines.indexOf(tr);
    String s="\n"+tr.getLine();
    System.out.println("updateing line "+i+" with "+s);
    //replaceItem(s,i);
    i++;
    replaceRange(s,(i*linelen),((i+1)*linelen));
    //    getParent().layout();
  }

  public void addTextRow(TextRow tr) {
    textLines.addElement(tr);
    append("\n"+tr.getLine());
    tr.setParent(this);
  }

}
```

TextRow.java

```java
package NPS;

public class TextRow {

  String[] text;
  protected TextTable parent;

  public TextRow(int cols) {
    text=new String[cols];
    for(int i=0;i<cols;i++) {
      text[i]=":\t";
    }
  }

  public void update() {
    if(parent!=null) {
      parent.update(this);
    }
  }

  public void setText(int c,String s) {
    text[c]=s;
  }

  public void setParent(TextTable p) {
    parent=p;
  }

  public String getLine() {
    String ret="";
    for(int i=0;i<text.length;i++) {
      ret +=text[i];
      for(int j=text[i].length();j<20;j++) {
    ret+=" ";
      }
    }
    return ret;
  }

}
```

Popup.java

```java
package NPS;
```

```
public class TextRow {

  String[] text;
  protected TextTable parent;

  public TextRow(int cols) {
    text=new String[cols];
    for(int i=0;i<cols;i++) {
      text[i]=":\t";
    }
  }

  public void update() {
    if(parent!=null) {
      parent.update(this);
    }
  }

  public void setText(int c,String s) {
    text[c]=s;
  }

  public void setParent(TextTable p) {
    parent=p;
  }

  public String getLine() {
    String ret="";
    for(int i=0;i<text.length;i++) {
      ret +=text[i];
      for(int j=text[i].length();j<20;j++) {
    ret+=" ";
      }
    }
    return ret;
  }

}
```

On to the Servers

That's all there is to the NPS StockTracker applet. We'll present the complete
implementations of the NPS server objects in Chapter 10.

Server Objects
for the Network
Pricing System

In Chapter 9, we presented the requirements analysis, design, and client implementation in Java and Java IDL for the Network Pricing System (NPS). In this chapter, we present the complete NPS Server object implementations.

Structure of the Network Pricing System Servers

The Network Pricing System defines three server objects that act as singletons—unique, well-known objects. These are the authorization manager, the original data feed, and the feed factory. Client programs deal only directly with the authorization manager. The feed factory creates multiple feed objects and attaches them to data feed objects. After login, clients request a feed from the authorization manager and receive a reference to one of these relatively short-lived objects. The runtime structure of the servers was presented in Figures 9.1 and 9.2.

The FeedFactory object is the one object outside users should be able to find. After initialization, a name in the naming service ("QuoteFeedAdmin") has a reference to this object. That reference must then be exported so outside users can find it.

The Network Pricing System maintains a database of users. This database could be kept in any appropriate manner and probably should be kept somewhere accessible by multiple services. To keep this sample implementation simple, the user data (passwords and auth packets) is kept using Java serialization. This data is kept in a collection of files, the interface to which is via the FeedFactory server object. Since there is a single FeedFactory object, this centralizes all checks for validity of all Auth packets architecturally, which may cause a bottleneck as the number of users increases. A way around this bottleneck would be to delegate the responsibility for AuthPacket checking to a separate interface, and to have multiple server instances available that implement that interface. Updates to the user database could remain centralized for some time, as logins, preference storage, and user creation are relatively infrequent operations compared to authorization checks.

This QuoteFilter object is a temporary object that users receive to do the filtering. The QuoteFilter interface derives from both `NPS::FilteredQuoteFeed` and `Legacy::Receiver`. This is because the QuoteFilter object is both a server for the users' client programs and a "client" of the Legacy Feed via the Receiver callback mechanism.

Because each QuoteFilter object exists only during the lifetime of a particular transient client and need not be accessible to anyone but the creating client, QuoteFilter objects never need to be registered into the namespace.

QuoteFilter objects are not persisted in this implementation because the Java IDL ORB only directly supports one activation model: essentially, start up the server by hand and leave it running. For an ORB that supports automatic activation and deactivation, we would persist the QuoteFilter objects across activations, but never beyond the lifetime of the user's client.

Quote Server Internal Data Structures

The data for the Feed object simply consists of a sequence of bins associating a filter with a list of consumers. We also keep track of the user for which this feed was created and the Authorization object from which to take hints.

The authorization object needs to keep track of user information and preferences. We simply define a simple data class with relevant fields and define a sequence to store. Note the use of the `transient` keyword to indicate a member that need not be persisted between user logins.

```
class UserData {
  String username;
  String passwd;
  String fullname;
  double account;
  String[] prefs;
  transient QuoteFilter feed;

  UserData(String u, String p, QuoteFilter qf) {
    username = u;
    passwd = p;
    feed = qf;
  }
}
```

FeedFactoryImpl

The FeedFactoryImpl class is the main implementation servant for the authorization piece of the application.

makePacket() is a utility function for making authorization packets. It is a hook where a variety of useful per-packet processing can take place. A future implementation might use this method to encrypt that packet's data. For now, all we do is place some useful information in the packet. Even though we could encode things such as user, time-out date, or a currency number, all we actually do here is place the array index of the user in the packet so we can easily find it later.

```
/***********************************************************/
// makePacket
/***********************************************************/
private AuthPacket makePacket(UserData us, int index) {
  AuthPacket pck;
  byte oc[] = new byte[1];
  oc[0] = (byte) index;
  return pck = new AuthPacket(us.username, oc);
}
```

createAccount creates space for the account in the database.

```
/***********************************************************/
// createAccount
/***********************************************************/
private synchronized
  UserData createAccount(String userName, String passwd)
{
  QuoteServer.trace("createAccount: add new account");
```

```
    // Add user
    UserData ud = new UserData(userName, passwd, null);
    users.addElement(ud);
    return ud;
}
```

getFeed() is a call for the authorization interface that is unique for this application. After the client logs in and gains an authorization packet, the client calls `getFeed()` to get a reference to a FilteredQuoteFeed object. Each user gets his or her own unique feed object that filters the feed information. In the sample implementation presented in this book, all feed objects reside in the same process. In a production application, feed objects would reside in multiple server processes, and the system would perform some load balancing between them.

```
/**************************************************************/
// getFeed
/**************************************************************/
public FilteredQuoteFeed getFeed(AuthPacket tok)
    throws Auth.AuthFailure {

    // Check auth packet
    if(!isAuthValid(tok)) {
        throw(new Auth.AuthFailure("Invalid Token",
                AuthReason.BadToken));
    }

    // Get index from auth packet
    int ind=0;
    if (tok.token.length == 1) {
        ind = tok.token[0];
    }
    QuoteServer.trace("getFeed: token " + ind);

    // Create a new feed object
    Authenticator auth = (Authenticator) this;
    QuoteFilterImpl fd = new QuoteFilterImpl(auth, tok);
    QuoteServer.trace("getFeed: Created feed...");

    // Register the new feed with the source channel
    // Note the use of ReceiverHolder for inout IDL parameter
    sourceChannel.register(new ReceiverHolder(fd));
    QuoteServer.trace("getFeed: registered new QuoteFilter");

    synchronized (this) {
        QuoteFilter feed = ((UserData) users.elementAt(ind)).feed;
```

```
    // If the user has an old feed here destroy it
    // User can only have one feed at a time.
    if(feed != null) {
      try {
        //simply destroy the stored reference
        feed.disconnectAndDestroy(adminTok);
      } catch(SystemException ex) {
        QuoteServer.trace("getFeed: Destroy of feed failed");
      }
    }

    // Store reference to new QuoteFeed
    ((UserData) users.elementAt(ind)).feed = fd;
  }
  QuoteServer.trace("getFeed: stored new QuoteFeed");

  return fd;
}


/*************************************************************/
// getPreferences
/*************************************************************/
public String[] getPreferences(AuthPacket tok)
  throws Auth.AuthFailure {

  // Authenticate user
  if(!isAuthValid(tok)) {
    throw new Auth.AuthFailure("bad Token", AuthReason.BadToken);
  }

  // Get index from auth packet
  int ind = 0;
  if (tok.token.length == 1) {
    ind = tok.token[0];
  }

  // Create filter list
  String fl[] = null;

  synchronized (this) {
    UserData ud = (UserData) users.elementAt(ind);
    if (ud.prefs == null) return new String[0];
    fl = new String[ud.prefs.length];
    for(int i = 0; i < fl.length; i++) {
      fl[i] = ud.prefs[i];
    }
  }
```

```
    return fl;
}

/*************************************************************/
//  storePreferences
/*************************************************************/
public void storePreferences(AuthPacket tok, String[] prefs)
      throws Auth.AuthFailure {

    // Authenticate user
    if(!isAuthValid(tok)) {
       throw new Auth.AuthFailure("bad Token", AuthReason.BadToken);
    }

    // Get index from auth packet
    int ind = 0;
    if (tok.token.length == 1) {
       ind = tok.token[0];
    }

    String [] newpref = new String[prefs.length];
    for (int i = 0; i < prefs.length; i++) {
       newpref[i] = prefs[i];
    }
    ((UserData) users.elementAt(ind)).prefs = newpref;

    return;
}
```

login() implements the simple NPS login process. Given a username and password, NPS looks up the username in the database and checks the stored password against the one presented by the client. If the password is wrong or if the user is not in the database, the login attempt is rejected with a BadPassword exception. We don't differentiate between the two to avoid giving too much information to a non-valid user. In a production system, adding a new user to the database requires a separate administrative action.

Because we envision making the sample implementation of NPS in this book available to everyone, we have made things a little easier to administer. If a user doesn't exist, we make a new account for the user given whatever password is passed in. In a production system, it would simply reject and we would use a different client program secured with an administrator password or perhaps add some logic that requires the client to register each new user by collecting credit card and billing information.

```
/*************************************************************/
// login
/*************************************************************/
public AuthPacket login(String user, String passwd)
    throws Auth.AuthFailure {

  AuthPacket pck;

  QuoteServer.trace("login: user " + user);

  // Go through list of current users and check password
  int cnt = users.size();
  UserData ud = null;

  for (int i = 0; i < cnt; i++) {
    ud = (UserData) users.elementAt(i);
    if(ud.username.equals(user)) {
      if(ud.passwd.equals(passwd)) {
        return makePacket(ud,i);
      }
      else {
        QuoteServer.trace("login: Bad Password: user " + user);
      throw new Auth.AuthFailure("Bad Password",
                                      AuthReason.InvalidPasswd);
      }
    }
  }

  // Add a new user if they don't exist
  ud = createAccount(user, passwd);
  QuoteServer.trace("login: create new user " + user);

  return makePacket(ud, users.size() - 1);
}
```

Logout is important in part because it frees up resources. The logout process invalidates the authorization packet and deletes the user feed object. The NPS user also wants to be sure to log out so that his or her account is no longer charged.

```
/*************************************************************/
// logout
/*************************************************************/
public void logout(AuthPacket tok) throws Auth.AuthFailure {
  // Check auth  packet
  if(!isAuthValid(tok)) {
```

```
              throw new Auth.AuthFailure("bad packet",
                                     AuthReason.BadToken);
       }

       // Get user index from packet
       int ind = 0;
       if (tok.token.length == 1) {
         ind = tok.token[0];
       }

       // remove the feed object associated with the user
       QuoteServer.trace("logout " + ind);
       synchronized (this) {
         ((UserData)
           users.elementAt(ind)).feed.disconnectAndDestroy(adminTok);
         ((UserData) users.elementAt(ind)).feed = null;
       }
       return;
    }


    /*************************************************************/
    // changePasswd
    /*************************************************************/
    public boolean changePasswd(AuthPacket tok,
                                String userID,
                                String passwd)
       throws Auth.AuthFailure {

       // Check auth packet
       if(!isAuthValid(tok)) {
         throw new Auth.AuthFailure("bad packet",
                                 AuthReason.BadToken);
       }

       // Get user index from packet
       int ind = 0;
       if (tok.token.length == 1) {
         ind = tok.token[0];
       }

       synchronized (this) {
         // double check user name and reassign passwd
         if (userID.equals(
               ((UserData) users.elementAt(ind)).username)) {
           ((UserData) users.elementAt(ind)).passwd = passwd;
           return true;
```

```
      }
    }
    return false;
}


/****************************************************************/
// isAuthValid
/****************************************************************/
public boolean isAuthValid(AuthPacket tok) {
    // Get user index from packet
    int ind = 0;
    if (tok.token.length == 1) {
      ind = tok.token[0];
    }

    QuoteServer.trace("isAuthValid: index = " + ind);

    // make sure index is in valid range
    if(ind >= 0 && ind < users.size()) {
      // make sure userID matches the index found
      if(((UserData)
            users.elementAt(ind)).username.equals(tok.userID)) {
        QuoteServer.trace("isAuthValid: Auth IS valid");
        return true;
      }
    }
    QuoteServer.trace("isAuthValid: Auth IS NOT valid");
    return false;
}
```

Finally, here is the constructor for the FeedFactoryImpl object. It logs itself in as the "Admin" user, initializes some internal state, and receives a reference to the legacy quote feed from its caller.

```
public FeedFactoryImpl(Legacy.Feed feed) {
      super();
      users = new Vector();
      // For now login as administrator here
      try {
        adminTok = login("Admin", "Password");
      } catch (AuthFailure e) {
        QuoteServer.trace("Admin login failure");
      }
      sourceChannel = feed;
    }
```

QuoteFilterImpl

The QuoteFilterImpl class is where the actual filtering takes place. Each user gets its own QuoteFilterImpl object and registers one or more receivers (consumers) with the object. The QuoteFilterImpl object asks each consumer which events it desires and only sends those to the consumer.

We maintain a list of bins, one bin for each type of event a consumer has requested. Each bin lists all consumers interested in that event. A consumer can exist in one or all bins.

Each QuoteFilterImpl object receives events from the legacy quote feed as a push. At each push, the object decides which consumers would be interested in the event and sends it. It looks for the bin reflecting the event and sends to all consumers listed there.

```
/***********************************************************/
// push
/***********************************************************/
public synchronized void push(Legacy.Quote qt) {

// make sure event is really a quote
 if (qt instanceof Legacy.Quote ) {

    NPS.Quote nqt = new NPS.Quote(qt.symbol,
                                  qt.price,
                                  qt.fullName);

    int cnt = consumers.size();
    // Go through list of current filters
    for (int i = 0; i < cnt; i++) {
      if (qt.symbol.equals(getConsumerFilter(i).filter)) {
        // if filter is in the list,
        // push to all consumers in the bin
        for (int j = 0;
             j < getConsumerFilter(i).receiverList.size();
             j++) {
          QuoteServer.trace("push:" + nqt.symbol
                            + " " + nqt.price);
          getConsumerFilter(i).getNthReceiver(j).pushQuote(nqt);
        }
      }
    }
  }
  return;
}
```

addQuoteReceiver is invoked when a new consumer is added. It requests the list of symbols to filter for that object. If a bin for that symbol doesn't exist, it makes one. Currently, if a symbol is specified twice, the object is added twice and so gets notified twice.

```
/*************************************************************/
// addQuoteReceiver
/*************************************************************/
public synchronized
    void addQuoteReceiver(AuthPacket tok,
                             QuoteReceiverHolder holder)
    throws NPS.BadFilter,Auth.AuthFailure {

  // Check auth packet
  if(tok.userID.equals(userPacket.userID) &&
     !authCenter.isAuthValid(tok)) {
    throw new Auth.AuthFailure("Invalid Packet",
                                 AuthReason.BadToken);
  }

  QuoteReceiver recv = holder.value;

  // get the list of symbols from filter consumer
  String[] filterList = recv.getFilters();

  int num = filterList.length;
  // Make sure the is a filter to add
  if (num == 0) {
    throw new NPS.BadFilter();
  }

  // For each symbol in new filter list,
  // add consumer to bin if bin for symbol exists.
  // If not, create new bin
  for (int i = 0; i<num; i++) {
    boolean found = false;
    // compare this filter with all bins
    for (int j = 0; j < consumers.size(); j++) {
      if(getConsumerFilter(j).filter.equals(filterList[i])) {
        // add consumer to bin
        getConsumerFilter(j).addReceiver(recv);
    QuoteServer.trace("adding to old filter list "
                       + filterList[i]);
    found = true;
    break;
      }
```

```
      }
      // If not found in any bin make new bin
      if (found == false) {
        ConsumerFilter newConsumerFilter
          = new ConsumerFilter(filterList[i], recv);
        consumers.addElement(newConsumerFilter);
        QuoteServer.trace("adding new filter "
                           + filterList[i]);
      }
    }

    return;
}
```

disconnectQuoteReceiver is invoked when a client wishes to be removed. The method finds occurrences of the object in every bin and removes it. It's important to disconnect a receiver since it's wasteful and problematic to send something across the wire if there is nothing to receive it. The receivers can't disconnect themselves since CORBA does not provide for the garbage collection of remote objects.

```
/*************************************************************/
// disconnectQuoteReceiver
/*************************************************************/
public synchronized
    void disconnectQuoteReceiver(AuthPacket tok,
                                      QuoteReceiverHolder holder)
    throws Auth.AuthFailure {

  // Check auth packet
  if(tok.userID.equals(userPacket.userID) &&
     !authCenter.isAuthValid(tok)) {
    throw new Auth.AuthFailure("bad packet",
                                AuthReason.BadToken);
  }

  QuoteReceiver recv = holder.value;

  // Find all occurences of consumer recv
  // remove each from the bin and call disconnect
  for (int j = 0; j < consumers.size(); j++) {
    Vector recvList = getConsumerFilter(j).receiverList;
    while (recvList.contains(recv)) {
    recv.disconnect();
    recvList.removeElement(recv);
    }
```

```
   }
  return;
}
```

disconnectAndDestroy() finds all clients and notifies them (`disconnect()`) and then destroys the QuoteFilterImpl object itself. If we were keeping track of sources, we would also go through all sources and notify them that we were disconnecting.

The name of this method is a bit misleading; it used to destroy, or clean up, certain unused resources in the ORB, but that isn't necessary for the Java IDL implementation. If we were to reimplement the QuoteServer in another language with another ORB, this would be a convenient place to perform such ORB-specific resource management.

```
/************************************************************/
// disconnectAndDestroy
/************************************************************/
public synchronized void disconnectAndDestroy(AuthPacket tok)
    throws Auth.AuthFailure {

  // Check auth packet
  // Make the packet is valid for the user this
  // feed object was made for
  if(tok.userID.equals(userPacket.userID) &&
     !authCenter.isAuthValid(tok)) {
    throw new Auth.AuthFailure("bad packet",
                               AuthReason.BadToken);
  }

  // Go through every bin and tell every consumer
  // that we are disconnecting
  int len = consumers.size();
  for (int i = 0; i < len; i++) {
    ConsumerFilter cf = getConsumerFilter(i);
    for (int j = 0; j < cf.receiverList.size(); j++) {
      try {
        cf.getNthReceiver(j).disconnect();
      } catch(SystemException ex) {
        // ignore disconnect exception; if it's gone, it's gone
      }
    }
  }
  return;
}
```

```
/****************************************************************/
// getCurrentFilters
/****************************************************************/
public String[] getCurrentFilters(AuthPacket tok)
      throws Auth.AuthFailure {

  // Check auth packet
  // Make the packet is valid for the user this
  // feed object was made for
  if(tok.userID.equals(userPacket.userID) &&
      !authCenter.isAuthValid(tok)) {
    throw new Auth.AuthFailure("bad packet",
                                    AuthReason.BadToken);
  }

  // Copy filters and return
  String filt[] = null;
  synchronized (this) {
    filt = new String[consumers.size()];
    for (int i = 0; i < consumers.size(); i++) {
      filt[i] = getConsumerFilter(i).filter;
    }
  }
  return filt;
}
```

QuoteServer class

Finally, the QuoteServer class itself provides housekeeping functions for the server objects. The `main()` method initializes the FeedFactoryImpl object and registers it in the CORBA namespace maintained by the Name Service. Also, the QuoteServer class provides a simple logging interface for error and status messages.

```
public class QuoteServer {

  static PrintWriter tracelog
    = new PrintWriter(System.out, true);
  static boolean tracing = false;
  static Legacy.Feed legacyRef = null;

  public static void trace(String msg) {
    if (tracing)
      tracelog.println(msg);
  }

  public static void setTraceLogFile(String file) {
```

```
    try {
        tracelog = new PrintWriter(new FileOutputStream(file),
                                        true);
    } catch (Exception e) {
        System.err.println("QuoteServer: could not open log file "
                                + file);
        System.err.println("Logging to standard output.");
        tracelog = new PrintWriter(System.out, true);
    }
}

public static void setTracing(boolean state) {
    tracing = state;
}

    public static void main(String args[]) {

        for (int i = 0; i < args.length; i++)
        if (args[i].toLowerCase().equals("-verbose"))
                setTracing(true);

        ORB orb = org.omg.CORBA.ORB.init(args, null);
        NamingContext ncRef = null;
        try {

            // Get reference for Naming Service root naming context
            org.omg.CORBA.Object objref
                    = orb.resolve_initial_references("NameService");
            ncRef = NamingContextHelper.narrow(objref);
        } catch (Exception e) {
            System.err.println("Error during ORB initialization");
            System.err.println("Exception: " + e);
            e.printStackTrace(System.err);
            System.exit(1);
        }

        NameComponent nc = new NameComponent("Legacy", "");
        NameComponent path[] = { nc };
        try {
            legacyRef = FeedHelper.narrow(ncRef.resolve(path));
        } catch (Exception ex) {
            System.err.println("Could not find LegacyQuoteFeed");
            System.err.println("Exception: " + ex);
            ex.printStackTrace(System.err);
            System.exit(2);
        }
```

```
// create instance FeedFactory instance
// and publish it in the namespace
nc = new NameComponent("QuoteFeedAdmin", "");
path[0] = nc;
try {
  FeedFactoryImpl feeder = new FeedFactoryImpl(legacyRef);
  orb.connect(feeder);
  ncRef.rebind(path, feeder);
} catch (Exception ex) {
  System.err.println("Could not create QuoteFeedAdmin");
  System.err.println("Exception: " + ex);
  ex.printStackTrace(System.err);
  System.exit(3);
}


try {
  java.lang.Object sync = new java.lang.Object();
  synchronized (sync) {
    sync.wait();
  }
} catch (InterruptedException err) {
  System.err.println("Interrupt - "+ err );
  err.printStackTrace(System.err);
  System.exit(4);
}
  }
}
```

Generating Stock Price Information to Demo NPS with Genquote

In a production version of a system like NPS, other server objects would be implemented to pass market data into the distribution objects presented earlier. Because we want people to be able to use the code presented in this book and can't afford to pay for a real-time market data feed for each of our readers, we present a quick-and-dirty implementation of a fake market data feed.

Because this implementation is so quick and dirty, we won't bother to do anything more than the bare minimum necessary to interface with the Java IDL infrastructure.

Genquote has a very sophisticated stock-pricing model: It starts things out near zero and increments the price of each stock somewhat until it reaches 500 or so.

Then, the market crashes and all the stocks reset to near zero for the next wave. This cycle repeats forever, or until someone kills the Genquote server.

Genquote is divided into two classes: FeedImpl, which provides the direct implementation for the Legacy.Feed interface, and Genquote, which provides a simple framework for the server program and then generates the sample quotes and sends them into the feed object for redistribution. Note the use of a separate thread for the quote generation task—we leave the main thread for the use of the Java IDL ORB since we don't know precisely how the ORB services incoming requests to object servers.

Genquote.java

```
/* Genquote -- a program to generate fake stock information.
                If this were a real system, this would
                be a CORBA wrapper for some external market data
                feed.

   Usage: java Genquote [-verbose]
   Options: -verbose    Run in verbose mode

*/

import java.io.*;
import org.omg.CORBA.*;
import org.omg.CosNaming.*;

import Legacy.*;

//
//
//
class Genquote implements Runnable {

    static boolean verbose = false;
    String symbols[] = { "IBM", "SGI", "SUNW", "NSCP", "RABT", "DEC", "CITI" };
    String names[] = { "International Business Machines",
            "Silicon Graphics",
            "Sun Microsystems",
            "Netscape",
            "Rabbit Software",
            "Digital Equipment",
            "Citibank"
    };
```

```
static FeedImpl feeder = null;

//
//
//
public static void main(String args[]) {

  for (int i = 0; i < args.length; i++)
    if (args[i].toLowerCase().equals("-verbose"))
      verbose = true;

  ORB orb = org.omg.CORBA.ORB.init(args, null);
  NamingContext ncRef = null;

  try {
    // Get reference for root naming context
    org.omg.CORBA.Object objref
      = orb.resolve_initial_references("NameService");
    ncRef = NamingContextHelper.narrow(objref);
  } catch (Exception e) {
    System.err.println("Error during ORB initialization");
    System.err.println("Exception: " + e);
    e.printStackTrace(System.err);
    System.exit(1);
  }

  NameComponent nc = new NameComponent("Legacy", "");
  NameComponent path[] = { nc };
  try {
    // create instance of feeder and publish in the namespace
    feeder = new FeedImpl();
    orb.connect(feeder);
    ncRef.rebind(path, feeder);
  } catch (Exception ex) {
    System.out.println("Could not create LegacyQuoteFeed");
    System.err.println("Exception: " + ex);
    ex.printStackTrace(System.err);
    System.exit(2);
  }

  // start a thread to send quotes at regular intervals
  Thread generator = new Thread( new Genquote() );
  generator.start();

  // wait for events...
  try {
    java.lang.Object sync = new java.lang.Object();
```

```
        synchronized (sync) {
          sync.wait();
        }
    } catch (InterruptedException err) {
        System.err.println("Interrupt - "+ err );
        err.printStackTrace(System.err);
        System.exit(3);
    }
  }

  //
  //
  //
  public void run() {
    Quote q = new Quote();
    double d = 1.0;

    try {
      while (true) { // loop forever
        for (int i = 0; i < symbols.length; i++) {
          // fill in stock quote structure
          q.symbol = symbols[i];
          q.fullName = names[i];
          q.price = "" + d;

          if (verbose)
            System.out.println(q.symbol + " " + q.fullName
                                 + " " + q.price);

          if ( feeder != null )
            feeder.sendQuote(q);

          Thread.sleep(1000);
        }

        // bump up generated price; oscillate between 0 and 500
        d += 0.25;
        if (d > 500.0)
        d = 0.0;
      }
    }
    catch ( InterruptedException err ){
        System.err.println("Interrupt - "+ err );
        err.printStackTrace(System.err);
    }
  }
}
```

FeedImpl.java

```java
//
//
//
import Legacy.*;

import org.omg.CORBA.*;
import java.util.*;

class FeedImpl extends _FeedImplBase {
  Hashtable receivers = new Hashtable();

  //
  //
  //
  public synchronized boolean register(ReceiverHolder holder)
{
     Receiver rec = holder.value;
     if ( ! receivers.containsKey(rec) )
       {
         receivers.put(rec,rec);
         return true;
       }
     else

       return false;
  }

  //
  //
  //
  public synchronized boolean unregister(ReceiverHolder holder)
{

     Receiver rec = holder.value;
     if ( receivers.containsKey(rec) )
       {
         receivers.remove(rec);
         return true;
       }
     else
       return false;
  }

  //
  //
  //
  public synchronized void sendQuote(Quote quote) {
```

```
    // iterate through the receivers and send the quote
    Enumeration stuff = receivers.elements();

    try {
      while ( stuff.hasMoreElements() ) {
        Receiver receiver = (Receiver)stuff.nextElement();
        receiver.push(quote);
      }
    } catch(Exception err) {
      // handle exceptions
    }
  }

}
```

Running the NPS Servers

The information in this section was current as of the Java IDL Early Access release. It may have changed by the time of the FCS release. Also, some of the details in this section are platform dependent. We've presented examples for the Sparc Solaris platform. Setting up for Wintel platforms is a matter of changing the slashes to backslashes.

First, make sure that the Java IDL Name service is running. If not, it can be started using the nameserv command in the bin directory of the Java IDL distribution. This may have to be done with special privileges such as root or Administrator since it will listen on a TCP/IP port, usually port 900. Note that at this point we can only use the Java IDL Name service—it's the only one that supports the proposed Initial References interface standard for bootstrapping.

Second, start up the Genquote server:

```
java -classpath NPS/class Genquote
```

You should replace NPS in the -classpath argument with the location of wherever you installed the NPS source distribution. You may have to use the -InitialPort and -InitialHost arguments depending on where and how the Java IDL Name service is running. For example, if the Java IDL name service were running on machine bozo.frobozz.com and listening to port 1050, the Genquote server would be started:

```
java -classpath NPS/class Genquote -InitialHost bozo.frobozz.com
-InitialPort 1050
```

If you want to see what it's doing as it runs, use the -verbose option:

```
java -classpath NPS/class Genquote -verbose
```

Finally, start up the quote server itself:

```
java -classpath NPS/class NPS.QuoteServer
```

QuoteServer also supports the -verbose option.

There's no graceful way to shut down these server implementations; just kill off their processes to stop them.

Once the servers are running, you can start up the client application like this:

```
java -classpath NPS/class NPS.StockTracker
```

That's all there is to the NPS servers. Its two-tier architecture shows how even a CORBA server can become a legacy interface, and also how such an interface can be used to support an evolving object model as requirements change within a business setting.

11

Summary

Where Have We Been?

Now that we've made it through the book, let's take a look back to see what we've covered. In this book, we've covered a number of basic areas such as distributed objects, Java, and CORBA, and we've learned a bit about how they fit together and how to build some simple distributed object systems with them.

One of the key points in discussing distributed objects is to distinguish between distributed object programming, which allows the methods of an object to be invoked across a network, and simple object-oriented programming, where all the objects are assumed to share the same address space, or at least reside on the same machine. Object orientation provides a useful framework for constructing individual computer programs; distributed objects provide an object-oriented approach to whole system design. CORBA takes distributed objects to the next step: It provides a systematic framework for integrating disparate legacy programs into well-architected, enterprise-wide systems.

Java provides a language and environment that not only can take advantage of a distributed object architecture, but also can provide this capability in a platform-independent way. It provides the perfect complement to CORBA, and it allows the creation of new systems that can migrate anywhere. CORBA provides the glue that binds Java programs together in a network.

Java IDL is an implementation of CORBA in Java, and it provides a small implementation of an Object Request Broker to support CORBA-compliant clients and servers. Since Java IDL uses IIOP for its transport, Java IDL clients and servers can interoperate with clients and servers developed and hosted using ORBs from different vendors such as Sun Microsystems, Iona, Visigenic, and BEA.

What Have We Learned?

In the chapters of this book that have provided example systems, we've tried to illustrate aspects of distributed object system construction that are both important and recurring. Themes that keep presenting themselves include client/server partitioning, multiuser support, authentication and security, integration of legacy systems (where legacy can mean anything from an IBM 3270 to an HTML-based Web page), and the distribution of asynchronous events and datastreams across a heterogeneous network. The Java, Java IDL, and CORBA combination provides a powerful toolkit to address most, if not all, of these problems in a way designed to be flexible and extensible as these Java/CORBA systems evolve over the next few years.

What Are the Next Steps?

In a book like this, we could not get much further than presenting the basics. Each of the topics we touched on could have been, and has been, explored in much greater depth elsewhere. We gave short shrift to important issues such as multithreaded programming, load balancing, transactions, performance, and system management in a Java/CORBA environment. We've certainly almost completely ignored such crucial areas as formal object design methodology and its more practical complement, the design patterns movement. In some cases, this was due to space and time constraints during the book preparation process. In others, we simply don't have enough experience as an industry to understand yet how these issues are going to play out, both in the development labs and in production systems.

Where Is CORBA Going?

CORBA itself has a challenging future. It is the critic's darling, offering a superior architecture to other distributed object systems. It is also a relatively slow-moving system, dependent as it is on the schedule of the OMG standardization process.

Technologies such as ActiveX, which is controlled by a single vendor despite the assignment of pieces of it to quasi-standards bodies such as The Open Group, can move a bit faster. CORBA may conquer the world, or it may go the way of other brilliant technologies that failed to catch on, such as Smalltalk, the Dvorak keyboard, Betamax, and possibly Apple Computer.

Like all standards bodies, the OMG stands a fighting chance when it is simply arbitrating between competing existing implementations. Picking a standard in such an environment can be messy, ugly, political work, but at least something usually gets done. Where the OMG standards appear to bog down is where the service does not represent some existing capability, but, as with the massive Security service that remains to be implemented, turns out to be too much of a committee effort.

CORBA is a somewhat strange standard in that while the common interfaces are well specified, the implementations are left to each vendor to reinterpret in its own way. While interoperability remains one of the primary watchwords for CORBA vendors, it can be interoperability only up to some semantic boundary, beyond which all is implementation specific. Up until now, this boundary has been the IIOP over-the-wire protocol. It is a good measure of the standard's success to see if interoperability between ORBs becomes a reality or remains a marketing idea.

Interoperability is also becoming more and more a central focus of CORBA activity. JavaSoft's Java IDL will put CORBA technology in easy reach of every Web browser on the Internet. Java IDL is an ORB-neutral technology, which means it takes advantage of only the basic CORBA services that any ORB might offer. One of the exciting features of Java IDL is that the OMG's Java mapping for IDL doesn't stop at the interface mapping itself, but goes on to specify some common mechanisms, such as the Portable Object Adapter, that standardize the interface between the ORB and the object's implementation. Thus, CORBA services written in Java stand a fighting chance of being ORB independent, as well as interoperable.

As end-user organizations move to implement CORBA-based systems as large-scale production systems, it's no longer enough for CORBA to be the new kid on the block with something interesting to say. It must develop a rich and nuanced feature set and a strong development community, and it must prove that it can be deployed in commercial-strength settings. Security and transactions become a much bigger part of the scene. Development environments must support CORBA objects directly. Even more important, integration with GUI tools and network management frameworks will become very, very much in demand. All of these areas are being addressed by the vendor community.

The Moving Target

There's no good place to end this book. The Java IDL and CORBA stories are still being written even as we go to press. None of these technologies has stopped moving long enough so that we could write about them in any detail—the evolution of Internet technologies simply happens too fast for print publishing to keep up. We expect the landscape to change dramatically between the time the last word of this book is set down and when the book turns up in stores for the first time: Java IDL will continue to evolve and the Java 1.2 JDK will become available sometime during the second half of 1997.

Writing a book like this can be an interesting experience. It is a collaboration of a team of engineers who worked on the design, implementation, and specification of Java IDL, the distributed object consultants at Fusion Systems Group, and the team at John Wiley & Sons. There were times during its production when contributors literally had to choose between pausing to write about the technology and moving the technology itself forward. Such is the nature of working so closely to the source of innovation in this industry. Some information was omitted because it would have been simply a historical curiosity by the time it saw print. In such an environment, we expect quick obsolescence, and we only hope that the experience of working through the information and examples in this book has provided the reader not only with the basic intellectual tools to follow the technology as it evolves, but also with a belief in and a fascination for the promise of open distributed object technology.

Keeping in Contact

We'd like to be able to keep up with our readers. Please send comments, corrections, and so on to javaidlbook@fsg.com. Information for this book will be maintained at the John Wiley & Sons Web site at www.wiley.com/compbooks/lewis/.

IDL/Java Language Mapping

This appendix is a condensation of the IDL/Java Language Mapping ratified by the Object Management Group. Section numbering corresponds to that in the ratified Mapping. Noncontiguous section numbering implies that sections have been omitted from this appendix. For example, Chapters 1 through 3 of the mapping have been omitted; the presentation here begins with Chapter 4. Within this appendix, Mapping chapters are referred to as sections.

The text of the specification reproduced corresponds to the specification as ratified on June 24, 1997 *(ftp://ftp.omg.org/pub/docs/orbos/97-03-01.pdf)*. Users of this appendix may wish to refer to the OMG Web site for updates *(http://www.omg.org)*.

Conventions

```
IDL appears using this font.
Java code appears using this font.
```

4.0 Overall Design Rationale

This section discusses some of the rationale behind the choices that were made for this mapping.

General issues are discussed in the Introduction. [. . . .]

4.1   Introduction

This specification strikes a balance between several different and often conflicting design centers.

An assumption is that CORBA is used in a multi-platform world. Distributed clients and servers will be developed using a variety of computing platforms and languages. The common denominator will be the IDL that describes the services being implemented. Consistency and uniformity between the various IDL language mappings will facilitate the learning and use of CORBA. Consequently, a conscious attempt has been made not to introduce gratuitous differences in the way standard CORBA IDL identifiers and Services are mapped into Java. E.G., the names of the standard CORBA system exceptions are mapped directly, rather than changing them to be more "Java friendly".

A strong attempt has also been made to make the mapping seem as natural and convenient to Java programmers, except when there are conflicts with the above two goals. E.g. IDL interface names map directly into Java interface names.

4.1.1   Goals

- Client-side and server-side source code portability

- ORB replaceability

- Binary compatibility between client stubs (and server skeletons) and ORBs.

4.1.2   Java Version

This specification is based upon the version of Java released by JavaSoft as JDK 1.0.2.

It does not rely upon or use features that are just starting to be released as part of the JDK 1.1beta program. While it is attractive to consider using that release because of its larger feature set, the fact remains that it will not be widely available until the end of 1997.

Because JDK 1.1 will be fully upwardly compatible with JDK 1.0.2, no changes to this mapping will be required in order for it be used with JDK1.1. After JDK 1.1 stabilizes and vendors gain some experience with it, the OMG may wish to add extensions to this mapping in order to take advantage of new Java features.

4.1.3   Reverse mapping issues

The submitters feel that it will be desirable in a future OMG RFP, possibly even the pending Call By Value RFP, to be able to implement a so-called reverse mapping from Java to IDL. Using it, it should be possible to generate OMG CORBA IDL that describes a Java interface. A desirable characteristic of such a mapping, is that it be idempotent so that the result of mapping a Java interface to IDL, and then mapping it back to Java (using this specification) results in the same Java interface. This specification was designed so as not to preclude this property.

4.1.4 *Java Stub and Skeleton ORB Interfaces*

This specification includes a specification for the interfaces between Java stubs and skeletons and the Java ORB runtime. The unique properties of Java and the way it is used within browsers makes the specification of these interfaces interesting and necessary for a number of reasons.

Many Java applications are run as applets in browsers. The applet is usually downloaded over the Internet or a LAN. If the applet communicates with a CORBA object using a static interface, then the stub for invoking operations must be downloaded as part of the applet. Similarly, a developer implementing a server, may wish to download the skeleton for a method. In both cases, it is highly desirable that the required amount of code to be downloaded be kept to a minimum, particularly in the case of a browser. Stubs (and skeletons) generated by compliant IDL compilers (or other compliant tools) which use these interfaces will be able to run in a browser environment which already contains an ORB which is compliant with this specification.

It is expected that support for these standardized interfaces will be "baked into" the popular Internet browsers and the JDK. Thus applets, either pure client or acting themselves as CORBA servers (along with their associated stubs and skeletons), can be created and compiled once, and be guaranteed to run in all these environments without the necessity of further downloads.

As a result of the adoption of this specification, third-party tool vendors will be able to generate applets that will work with any compliant Java ORB. Without this specification, tool vendors would be forced to generate ORB-specific stubs and skeletons for every environment in which they expect their applet to run.

Binary Compatibility Stubs and skeletons that implement this specification will not need to be recompiled when run with any ORB which supports the Java Stub/Skeleton ORB Interface. Thus CORBA client applets (applets that invoke operations on distributed CORBA objects) can be written, compiled once into Java bytecodes, downloaded, and run in any environment that includes an ORB supporting these interfaces.

Without the specification of these stub/skeleton to ORB interfaces, a CORBA client or server applet is not guaranteed to be compatible with any given Java ORB implementation. Stubs and skeletons that are not compatible with the resident Java ORB (because they use proprietary stub/skeleton ORB interfaces), must first have the compatible ORB downloaded, before they can be used. While in some environments, the time to download (and possibly cache) may be acceptable, in certain increasingly common situations such as those involving Internet browsers, the cost and increased complexity is unacceptable.

This issue is unique to Java, because for other languages (e.g. C++), there is no cross-platform binary compatibility at the language level. For those other languages, source code compatibility at the stub/skeleton signature level is sufficient since, in general, recompilation is necessary in order to move between platforms.

Value Added Extensions Specification of Java stub/skeleton ORB interfaces does not preclude ORB vendors from continuing to innovate and add value. Vendors are free to extend the stub/skeleton ORB interfaces, and use alternative ORB interfaces (proprietary or ORB-specific) in order to provide functionality not supported by these interfaces. However users will have a choice (with compliant tools) as to whether they wish to use these extensions or not.

The required ORB components can be downloaded if not already present, as would be the case even if these interfaces were not standardized.

4.2 Names

This is the first IDL language mapping specification which explicitly takes into account possible name collisions and provides rules for dealing with them.

The name collision rule was chosen so that it would only affect highly unlikely cases, and not disadvantage most users. It is expected to will be invoked only rarely. The alternative of always pre-pending underscores would have affected all programmers and forced them to use an unnatural mapping in order to avoid uncommon cases.

Collisions will normally only occur when the Java programmer has existing classes which use names corresponding to generated support classes, or are the same as a new IDL interface. Collisions will also occur if using an IDL interface named with a Java reserved word.

The emphasis here is on keeping the client-side mappings simple and natural. Hence the decision not to simply prepend underscores everywhere there would be a possibility of a name clash. On the server-side, a prepended underscore is used for such things as the implementation base class. Future extensions are expected to continue this policy.

4.3   Mapping of Module

Modules are a name-scoping mechanism in IDL. The corresponding name-scoping mechanism in Java is the Java package.

4.4   Mapping for Basic Types

OMG char could have been mapped to byte which would have avoided range checks at runtime. However, it was rejected because

- Java chars are more natural to Java programmers.

- According to the Java Language Specification, Section 5.1.3, conversions from byte to char are narrowing primitive conversions because bytes are signed quantities while chars are unsigned. Mapping IDL chars to byte would preclude the safe usage of any of the methods in java.lang.Character.

Mapping unsigned integer types to the next larger size does not scale all the way up to unsigned long long. Also, that is by no means a specification-preserving mapping. The most intuitive, under these circumstances, is to map IDL integer types to the correspondingly sized Java types.

4.5   Helper Classes

The helper classes have necessary methods that do not appear on the "regular" mapped classes. This is to make reverse mapping simpler.

4.6   Mapping for Constant

Java programmers typically use static final fields in classes or interfaces for constants. Thus, constants in IDL interfaces are best mapped to static final fields in corresponding Java interfaces.

   Constants declared at module scope or globally generates a class per IDL constant. **This is done so that global constants may be supported easily.** These classes are only required at compile time since the generated Java bytecode would not depend upon the constant classes at runtime and they can be optimized out by intelligent tools.

4.7   Mapping for Enum

The proposed mapping provides two representations for each case label in order to provide strong type checking as well as allow the use of the enumeration labels in switch statements.

4.8   Mapping for Struct

An alternate mapping was to have instance variables as private fields and have public accessor functions. Since the purpose of IDL structs is to define data that will be directly accessible, the fields are left exposed. Not having accessor methods also implies smaller generated code, and faster and more straightforward access.

4.9   Mapping for Union

An alternative mapping that would ensure strong-typing is to map the union to an abstract class and each of the branches to concrete subclasses. This was rejected because the use requires casts at runtime and there are too many classes generated.

4.10   Mapping for Sequence

Alternative choices included mapping bounded sequences to a class which had methods to access parts of the sequence. Such a mapping would have been specification-preserving as well as safer. However, that would not be natural to Java programmers who are used to accessing array components using the subscript operator ([]). It would also have made reverse mapping much more difficult.

4.11   Mapping for Array

An IDL array is mapped the same way as an IDL bounded sequence. In Java, the natural Java subscripting operator is applied to the mapped array. The bounds for the array are checked when the array is marshaled as an argument to an IDL operation. If you want the length of the array to be available in Java, bound the array with an IDL constant, which will be available through its mapping.

4.12   Mapping for Interface

Prepending "get" and "set" to the attribute methods was considered instead of overloading the attribute name. Doing this, however, often generates method names which have awkward capitalization or style. The overloaded style is consistent with the C++ and Smalltalk mappings.

4.13   Mapping for Exception

The exception hierarchies are set up so that only user-defined exceptions have to caught as a (large) convenience to Java programmers.

4.14   Mapping for the Any Type

Since predefined types do not map to Java classes, it was unnecessary to introduce Java classes for predefined types just to hold the insertion and extraction operations.

They are more naturally implemented and used by having insertion and extraction operations for predefined types on the Any class itself.

The static (for user-defined types) and non-static (for predefined types) asymmetry was a conscious decision. It was felt that statics on the Any class for insertion and extraction of predefined types would be tedious.

The read and write stream methods are mostly meant to provide support for the Java Stub and Skeleton portable ORB interfaces. It is not envisaged that they will be used by ordinary programmers.

4.15 Mapping for Certain Nested Types
Since the same IDL identifier would be used for both the class name and the package name (and this is illegal in Java) Package is appended to use as the package name.

4.16 Mapping for Typedef
Mapping for typedef is somewhat problematic since Java does not support the notion of typedef.

In general, typedef definitions are unwound to their basic types and thus avoid the tricky semantics of defining the exact meaning of the phrase "a typedef introduces a distinct IDL type".

4.17 Pseudo Interface Mapping
A conscious decision was made to map PIDL to Java public abstract classes that do not inherit nor extend from other classes or interfaces, rather than mapping them to Java interfaces. The primary reason was to support "interface" evolution of PIDL and not sacrifice the goal of allowing ORB implementations to be downloaded into a browser, even if it already has a "baked in" ORB. (The user may need to use a specific ORB implementation in order to take advantage of features that particular ORB implementation supports.)

As OMG specifications evolve, it is quite likely that new methods will be added to existing pseudo objects.If Java interfaces, rather than abstract classes were used, then adding a new method would not allow older ORBs to be downloaded. An example might be adding a new method to the Request pseudo object called useFedEx() to indicate that the request was to be guaranteed to get there by 10:00 AM the next morning. Let's assume that the next release of a Browser ships with support for this newly updated Request with the new useFedEx() method. Older ORB implementations, because they don't know about and hence don't implement the new method, will not load. By mapping the pseudo object to an abstract class, new methods can be added over time by giving the new methods default implementations which throw a NO_IMPLEMENT Java exception. Newer ORB implementations then override the default implementation with a real implementation. Old ORB implementations (and their users) never called the new method in the first place.

Our judgment is that the benefits of insuring upward compatibility in the face of future evolutionary change far outweighs the cost of mapping to abstract classes instead of interfaces.

5.0 Mapping IDL to Java

5.1 Introduction

This section describes the complete mapping of IDL into the Java language.

In most cases examples of the mapping are provided. It should be noted that the examples are code fragments that try to illustrate only the language construct being described. Normally they will be embedded in some module and hence will be mapped into a Java package.

5.2 Names

In general IDL names and identifiers are mapped to Java names and identifiers with no change. If a name collision could be generated in the mapped Java code, the name collision is resolved by prepending an underscore (_) to the mapped name.

In addition, because of the nature of the Java language, a single IDL construct may be mapped to several (differently named) Java constructs. The "additional" names are constructed by appending a descriptive suffix. For example, the IDL interface foo is mapped to the Java interface foo, and additional Java classes fooHelper and fooHolder.

In those exceptional cases that the "additional" names could conflict with other mapped IDL names, the resolution rule described above is applied to the other mapped IDL names. I.e., the naming and use of required "additional" names takes precedence.

For example, an interface whose name is fooHelper or fooHolder is mapped to _fooHelper or _fooHolder respectively, regardless of whether an interface named foo exists. The helper and holder classes for interface fooHelper are named _fooHelperHelper and _fooHelperHolder.

IDL names that would normally be mapped unchanged to Java identifiers that conflict with Java reserved words will have the collision rule applied.

5.2.1 Reserved Names

The mapping in effect reserves the use of several names for its own purposes. These are:

- The Java class **\<type>**Helper, where **\<type>** is the name of IDL user defined type.

- The Java class **\<type>**Holder, where **\<type>** is the name of an IDL defined type (with certain exceptions such as typedef aliases).

- The Java classes **\<basicJavaType>**Holder, where **\<basicJavaType>** is one of the Java primitive datatypes that is used by one of the IDL basic datatypes (Section 3.4.1.2, "Holder Classes).

- The nested scope Java package name **\<interface>**Package, where **\<interface>** is the name of an IDL interface (Section 3.15, "Mapping for Certain Nested Types).

- The keywords in the Java language:

abstract	default	if	private	throw
boolean	do	implements	protected	throws
break	double	import	public	transient
byte	else	instanceof	return	try
case	extends	int	short	void
catch	final	interface	static	volatile
char	finally	long	super	while
class	float	native	switch	
const	for	new	synchronized	
continue	goto	package	this	

The use of any of these names for a user defined IDL type or interface (assuming it is also a legal IDL name) will result in the mapped name having an (_) prepended.

5.3   Mapping of Module

An IDL module is mapped to a Java package with the same name. All IDL type declarations within the module are mapped to corresponding Java class or interface declarations within the generated package.

IDL declarations not enclosed in any modules are mapped into the (unnamed) Java global scope.

5.3.1 Example

```
// IDL
module Example {...}

// generated Java
package Example;
    ...
```

5.4 Mapping for Basic Types

5.4.1 Introduction

The following table shows the basic mapping. In some cases where there is a potential mismatch between an IDL type and its mapped Java type, the Exceptions column lists the standard CORBA exceptions that may be (or is) raised. See Section 2.13, "Mapping for Exception for details on how IDL system exceptions are mapped.

The potential mismatch can occur when the range of the Java type is "larger" than IDL. The value must be effectively checked at runtime when it is marshaled as an in parameter (or on input for an inout), e.g. Java chars are a superset of IDL chars.

Users should be careful when using unsigned types in Java. Because there is no support in the Java language for unsigned types, a user is responsible for ensuring that large unsigned IDL type values are handled correctly as negative integers in Java.

5.4.1.1 Future Support

In the future the "new" extended IDL types fixed, and possibly long double, are expected to be supported directly by Java. Currently there is no support for them in JDK 1.0.2, and as a practical matter, they are not yet widely supported by ORB vendors. They are expected to be mapped as follows:

IDL Type	Java type	Exceptions
long double	???	
fixed	java.math.BigDecimal	CORBA::DATA_CONVERSION

A future revision of this specification should make support of this mapping normative.

Figure 10.1 Microsoft Exchange server setup options.

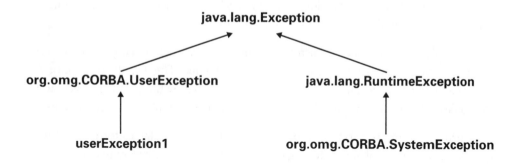

IDL Type	Java type	Exceptions
boolean	boolean	
char	char	CORBA::DATA_CONVERSION
wchar	char	
octet	byte	
string	java.lang.String	CORBA::MARSHAL
		CORBA::DATA_CONVERSION
wstring	java.lang.String	CORBA::MARSHAL
short	short	
unsigned short	short	
long	int	
unsigned long	int	
long long	long	
unsigned long long	long	
float	float	
double	double	

Additional details are described in the sections following.

5.4.1.2 Holder Classes

Support for out and inout parameter passing modes requires the use of additional "holder" classes. These classes are available for all of the basic IDL datatypes in the org.omg.CORBA package and are generated for all named user defined types except those defined by typedefs.

For user defined IDL types, the holder class name is constructed by appending Holder to the mapped (Java) name of the type.

For the basic IDL datatypes, the holder class name is the Java type name (with its initial letter capitalized) to which the datatype is mapped with an appended Holder, e.g. IntHolder. See Section 3.2, "Names" for a description of the implications on possible collisions with user defined names.

Each holder class has a constructor from an instance, a default constructor, and has a public instance member, value, which is the typed value. The default constructor sets the value field to the default value for the type as defined by the Java language: false for boolean, 0 for numeric and char types, null for strings, null for object references.

In order to support portable stubs and skeletons, holder classes for user defined types also have to implement the org.omg.CORBA.portable.Streamable interface.

The holder classes for the basic types are defined below. Note that they do not implement the Streamable interface. They are in the org.omg.CORBA package.

```Java
// Java
package org.omg.CORBA;
final public class ShortHolder {
    public short value;
    public ShortHolder() {}
    public ShortHolder(short initial) {
        value = initial;
    }
}

final public class IntHolder {
    public int value;
    public IntHolder() {}
    public IntHolder(int initial) {
        value = initial;
    }
}

final public class LongHolder {
    public long value;
    public LongHolder() {}
    public LongHolder(long initial) {
        value = initial;
    }
}

final public class ByteHolder {
    public byte value;
```

```
    public ByteHolder() {}
    public ByteHolder(byte initial) {
        value = initial;
    }
}

final public class FloatHolder {
    public float value;
    public FloatHolder() {}
    public FloatHolder(float initial) {
        value = initial;
    }
}

final public class DoubleHolder {
    public double value;
    public DoubleHolder() {}
    public DoubleHolder(double initial) {
        value = initial;
    }
}

final public class CharHolder {
    public char value;
    public CharHolder() {}
    public CharHolder(char initial) {
        value = initial;
    }
}

final public class BooleanHolder {
    public boolean value;
    public BooleanHolder() {}
    public BooleanHolder(boolean initial) {
        value = initial;
    }
}

final public class StringHolder {
    public java.lang.String value;
    public StringHolder() {}
    public StringHolder(java.lang.String initial) {
        value = initial;
    }
}
```

```
final public class ObjectHolder {
    public org.omg.CORBA.Object value;
    public ObjectHolder() {}
    public ObjectHolder(org.omg.CORBA.Object initial) {
        value = initial;
    }
}

final public class AnyHolder {
    public Any value;
    public AnyHolder() {}
    public AnyHolder(Any initial) {
        value = initial;
    }
}

final public class TypeCodeHolder {
    public TypeCode value;
    public typeCodeHolder() {}
    public TypeCodeHolder(TypeCode initial) {
        value = initial;
    }
}

final public class PrincipalHolder {
    public Principal value;
    public PrincipalHolder() {}
    public PrincipalHolder(Principal initial) {
        value = initial;
    }
}
```

The Holder class for a user defined type <foo> is shown below:

```
// Java
final public class <foo>Holder
    implements org.omg.CORBA.portable.Streamable {

    public <foo> value;
    public <foo>Holder() {}
    public <foo>Holder(<foo> initial) {}
    public void _read(org.omg.CORBA.portable.InputStream i)
        {...}
    public void _write(org.omg.CORBA.portable.OutputStream o)
        {...}
    public org.omg.CORBA.TypeCode _type() {...}
    }
```

5.4.1.3 Use of Java *null*

The Java null may only be used to represent the "null" object reference. For example, a zero length string, rather than null must be used to represent the empty string. Similarly for arrays.

5.4.2 Boolean

The IDL boolean constants TRUE and FALSE are mapped to the corresponding Java boolean literals true and false.

5.4.3 Character Types

IDL characters are 8-bit quantities representing elements of a character set while Java characters are 16-bit unsigned quantities representing Unicode characters. In order to enforce type-safety, the Java CORBA runtime asserts range validity of all Java chars mapped from IDL chars when parameters are marshaled during method invocation. If the char falls outside the range defined by the character set, a CORBA::DATA_CONVERSION exception shall be thrown.

The IDL wchar maps to the Java primitive type char.

5.4.4 Octet

The IDL type octet, an 8-bit quantity, is mapped to the Java type byte.

5.4.5 String Types

The IDL string, both bounded and unbounded variants, are mapped to java.lang.String. Range checking for characters in the string as well as bounds checking of the string shall be done at marshal time. Character range violations cause a CORBA::DATA_CONVERSION exception to be raised. Bounds violations cause a CORBA:: MARSHAL exception to be raised.

The IDL wstring, both bounded and unbounded variants, are mapped to java.lang.String. Bounds checking of the string shall be done at marshal time. Bounds violations cause a CORBA:: MARSHAL exception to be raised.

5.4.6 Integer Types

The integer types map as shown in Figure 5-1.

5.4.7 Floating Point Types

The IDL float and double map as shown in Figure 5-1.

5.4.8   Future Fixed Point Types

The IDL fixed type is mapped to the Java java.math.BigDecimal class. Size violations raises a CORBA::DATA_CONVERSION exception.

This is left for a future revision.

5.4.9   Future Long Double Types

There is no current support in Java for the IDL long double type. It is not clear at this point whether and when this type will be added either as a primitive type, or as a new package in java.math.*, possibly as java.math.BigFloat.

This is left for a future revision.

5.5   Helper Classes

All user defined IDL types have an additional "helper" Java class with the suffix Helper appended to the type name generated. Several static methods needed to manipulate the type are supplied. These include Any insert and extract operations for the type, getting the repository id, getting the typecode, and reading and writing the type from and to a stream.

For any user defined IDL type, <typename>, the following is the Java code generated for the type. In addition, the helper class for a mapped IDL interface also has a narrow operation defined for it.

```
// generated Java helper
public class <typename>Helper {
    public static void
        insert(org.omg.CORBA.Any a, <typename> t) {...}
    public static <typename> extract(Any a) {...}
    public static org.omg.CORBA.TypeCode type() {...}
    public static String id() {...}
    public static <typename> read(
                    org.omg.CORBA.portable.InputStream istream)
        {...}
    public static void write(
                    org.omg.CORBA.portable.OutputStream ostream,
                    <typename> value)
        {...}

    // only for interface helpers
    public static
        <typename> narrow(org.omg.CORBA.Object obj);
}
```

The helper class associated with an IDL interface also has the narrow method (see Section 2.12, "Mapping for Interface).

5.5.1 *Examples*

```
// IDL - named type
struct st {long f1; string f2;};

// generated Java
public class stHelper {
    public static void insert(org.omg.CORBA.Any any,
        st s) {...}
    public static st extract(Any a) {...}
    public static org.omg.CORBA.TypeCode type() {...}
    public static String id() {...}
    public static st read(org.omg.CORBA.InputStream is) {...}
    public static void write(org.omg.CORBA.OutputStream os,
        st s) {...}
}
// IDL - typedef sequence
typedef sequence <long> IntSeq;

// generated Java helper
public class IntSeqHelper {
    public static void insert(org.omg.CORBA.Any any,
                                      int[] seq);
    public static int[] extract(Any a){...}
    public static org.omg.CORBA.TypeCode type(){...}
    public static String id(){...}
    public static int[] read(
                         org.omg.CORBA.portable.InputStream is)
        {...}
    public static void write(
                         org.omg.CORBA.portable.OutputStream os,
                         int[] seq)
        {...}
}
```

5.6   Mapping for Constant

Constants are mapped differently depending upon the scope in which they appear.

5.6.1 *Constants Within An Interface*

Constants declared within an IDL interface are mapped to public static final fields in the Java interface corresponding to the IDL interface.

5.6.1.1 Example

```
// IDL
module Example {
        interface Face {
        const long aLongerOne = -321;
    };
};


// generated Java
package Example;
public interface Face {
    public static final int aLongerOne = (int) (-321L);
}
```

5.6.2 *Constants Not Within An Interface*

Constants not declared within an IDL interface are mapped to a public interface with the same name as the constant and containing a public static final field, named value, that holds the contant's value. Note that the Java compiler will normally inline the value when the class is used in other Java code.

5.6.2.1 Example

```
// IDL
module Example {
    const long aLongOne = -123;
    };

package Example;
public interface aLongOne {
    public static final int value = (int) (-123L);
}
```

5.7 Mapping for Enum

An IDL enum is mapped to a Java final class with the same name as the enum type which declares a value method, two static data members per label, an integer conversion method, and a private constructor as follows:

```
// generated Java
public final class <enum_name> {
    // one pair for each label in the enum
    public static final int _<label> = <value>;
    public static final <enum_name> <label> =
        new <enum_name>(_<label>);
```

```
    public int value() {...}
    // get enum with specified value
    public static <enum_name> from_int(int value);
    // constructor
    private <enum_name>(int) { ... }
}
```

One of the members is a public static final that has the same name as the IDL enum label. The other has an underscore (_) prepended and is intended to be used in switch statements.

The value method returns the integer value. Values are assigned sequentially starting with 0. Note: there is no conflict with the value() method in Java even if there is a label named value

There shall be only one instance of an enum. Since there is only one instance, equality tests will work correctly. I.E. the default java.lang.Object implementation of equals() and hash() will automatically work correctly for an enum's singleton object.

The Java class for the enum has an additional method from_int(), which returns the enum with the specified value.

The holder class for the enum is also generated. Its name is the enum's mapped Java classname with Holder appended to it as follows:

```
public class <enum_name>Holder implements
        org.omg.CORBA.portable.Streamable {
    public <enum_name> value;
    public <enum_name>Holder() {}
    public <enum_name>Holder(<enum_name> initial) {...}
    public void _read(org.omg.CORBA.portable.InputStream i)
        {...}
    public void _write(org.omg.CORBA.portable.OutputStream o)
        {...}
    public org.omg.CORBA.TypeCode _type() {...}
}
```

5.7.1 Example
```
// IDL
enum EnumType {a, b, c};

// generated Java
public final class EnumType {
    public static final int _a = 0;
```

```
public static final EnumType a = new EnumType(_a);

public static final int _b = 1;
public static final EnumType b = new EnumType(_b);

public static final int _c = 2;
public static final EnumType c = new EnumType(_c);

public int value() {...}
public static EnumType from_int(int value) {...};

// constructor
private EnumType(int) {...}


};
```

5.8   Mapping for Struct

An IDL struct is mapped to a final Java class with the same name that provides
instance variables for the fields in IDL member ordering and a constructor for all
values. A null constructor is also provided so that the fields can be filled in later.

The holder class for the struct is also generated. Its name is the struct's mapped
Java classname with Holder appended to it as follows:

```
final public class <class>Holder implements
        org.omg.CORBA.portable.Streamable {
    public <class> value;
    public <class>Holder() {}
    public <class>Holder(<class> initial) {...}
    public void _read(org.omg.CORBA.portable.InputStream i)
        {...}
    public void _write(org.omg.CORBA.portable.OutputStream o)
        {...}
    public org.omg.CORBA.TypeCode _type() {...}
}
```

5.8.1 *Example*

```
// IDL
struct StructType {
    long field1;
    string field2;
};
```

```
// generated Java
final public class StructType {
    // instance variables
    public int field1;
    public String field2;
    // constructors
    public StructType() {}
    public StructType(int field1, String field2)
        {...}
    }

final public class StructTypeHolder
        implements org.omg.CORBA.portable.Streamable {
    public StructType value;
    public StructTypeHolder() {}
    public StructTypeHolder(StructType initial) {...}
    public void _read(org.omg.CORBA.portable.InputStream i)
        {...}
    public void _write(org.omg.CORBA.portable.OutputStream o)
        {...}
    public org.omg.CORBA.TypeCode _type() {...}
```

5.9   Mapping for Union

An IDL union is mapped to a final Java class with the same name that has:

- a default constructor

- an accessor method for the discriminator, named discriminator()

- an accessor method for each branch

- a modifier method for branch

- a modifier method for each branch which has more than one case label

- a default modifier method if needed

The normal name conflict resolution rule is used (prepend an "_") for the discriminator if there is a name clash with the mapped uniontype name or any of the field names.

The branch accessor and modifier methods are overloaded and named after the branch. Accessor methods shall raise the CORBA::BAD_OPERATION system exception if the expected branch has not been set.

If there is more than one case label corresponding to a branch, the simple modifier method for that branch sets the discriminant to the value of the first case label. In addition, an extra modifier method which takes an explicit discriminator parameter is generated.

If the branch corresponds to the default case label, then the modifier method sets the discriminant to a value that does not match any other case labels.

It is illegal to specify a union with a default case label if the set of case labels completely covers the possible values for the discriminant. It is the responsibility of the Java code generator (e.g., the IDL complier, or other tool) to detect this situation and refuse to generate illegal code.

A default modifier method, named default() (_default() if name conflict) is created if there is no explicit default case label, and the set of case labels does not completely cover the possible values of the discriminant. It will set the value of the union to be an out-of-range value.

The holder class for the union is also generated. Its name is the union's mapped Java classname with Holder appended to it as follows:

```
final public class <union_class>Holder
            implements org.omg.CORBA.portable.Streamable {
    public <union_class> value;
    public <union_class>Holder() {}
    public <union_class>Holder(<union_class> initial) {...}
    public void _read(org.omg.CORBA.portable.InputStream i)
        {...}
    public void _write(org.omg.CORBA.portable.OutputStream o)
        {...}
    public org.omg.CORBA.TypeCode _type() {...}
}
```

5.9.1 Example

```
// IDL
union UnionType switch (EnumType) {
        case first: long win;
        case second: short place;
        case third:
        case fourth: octet show;
        default:   boolean other;
    };
```

```
// generated Java
final public class UnionType {
    // constructor
    public UnionType() {....}

    // discriminator accessor
    public <switch-type> discriminator() {....}

    // win
    public int win() {....}
    public void win(int value) {....}

    // place
    public short place() {....}
    public void place(short value) {....}

    // show
    public byte show() {....}
    public void show(byte value) {....}
    public void show(int discriminator, byte value){....}

    // other
    public boolean other() {....}
    public void other(boolean value) {....}
}


final public class UnionTypeHolder
        implements org.omg.CORBA.portable.Streamable {
    public UnionType value;
    public UnionTypeHolder() {}
    public UnionTypeHolder(UnionType initial) {...}
        public void _read(org.omg.CORBA.portable.InputStream i)
        {...}
    public void _write(org.omg.CORBA.portable.OutputStream o)
        {...}
    public org.omg.CORBA.TypeCode _type() {...}
}
```

5.10 Mapping for Sequence

An IDL sequence is mapped to a Java array with the same name. In the mapping, everywhere the sequence type is needed, an array of the mapped type of the sequence element is used. Bounds checking shall be done on bounded sequences when they are marshaled as parameters to IDL operations, and an IDL CORBA::MARSHAL is raised if necessary.

The holder class for the sequence is also generated. Its name is the sequence's mapped Java classname with Holder appended to it as follows:

```
final public class <sequence_class>Holder {
    public <sequence_element_type>[] value;
    public <sequence_class>Holder() {};
    public <sequence_class>Holder(
                        <sequence_element_type>[] initial) {...};
    public void _read(org.omg.CORBA.portable.InputStream i)
        {...}
    public void _write(org.omg.CORBA.portable.OutputStream o)
        {...}
    public org.omg.CORBA.TypeCode _type() {...}
}
```

5.10.1 Example

```
// IDL
typedef sequence< long > UnboundedData;
typedef sequence< long, 42 > BoundedData;

// generated Java
final public class UnboundedDataHolder
            implements org.omg.CORBA.portable.Streamable {
    public int[] value;
    public UnboundedDataHolder() {};
    public UnboundedDataHolder(int[] initial) {...};
    public void _read(org.omg.CORBA.portable.InputStream i)
        {...}
    public void _write(org.omg.CORBA.portable.OutputStream o)
        {...}
    public org.omg.CORBA.TypeCode _type() {...}
}


final public class BoundedDataHolder
            implements org.omg.CORBA.portable.Streamable {
    public int[] value;
    public BoundedDataHolder() {};
    public BoundedDataHolder(int[] initial) {...};
    public void _read(org.omg.CORBA.portable.InputStream i)
        {...}
    public void _write(org.omg.CORBA.portable.OutputStream o)
```

```
    {...}
    public org.omg.CORBA.TypeCode _type() {...}
}
```

5.11 Mapping for Array

An IDL array is mapped the same way as an IDL bounded sequence. In the mapping, everywhere the array type is needed, an array of the mapped type of the array element is used. In Java, the natural Java subscripting operator is applied to the mapped array. The bounds for the array are checked when the array is marshaled as an argument to an IDL operation and a CORBA::MARSHAL exception is raised if an bounds violation occurs. The length of the array can be made available in Java, by bounding the array with an IDL constant, which will be mapped as per the rules for constants.

The holder class for the array is also generated. Its name is the array's mapped Java classname with Holder appended to it as follows:

```
final public class <array_class>Holder
        implements org.omg.CORBA.portable.Streamable {
    public <array_element_type>[] value;
    public <array_class>Holder() {}
    public <array_class>Holder(
                        <array_element_type>[] initial) {...}
    public void _read(org.omg.CORBA.portable.InputStream i)
        {...}
    public void _write(org.omg.CORBA.portable.OutputStream o)
        {...}
    public org.omg.CORBA.TypeCode _type() {...}
}
```

5.11.1 Example

```
// IDL
const long ArrayBound = 42;
typedef long larray[ArrayBound];

// generated Java
final public class larrayHolder
        implements org.omg.CORBA.portable.Streamable {
    public int[] value;
    public larrayHolder() {}
    public larrayHolder(int[] initial) {...}
    public void _read(org.omg.CORBA.portable.InputStream i)
```

```
        {...}
    public void _write(org.omg.CORBA.portable.OutputStream o)
        {...}
    public org.omg.CORBA.TypeCode _type() {...}
}
```

5.12 Mapping for Interface

5.12.1 Basics

An IDL interface is mapped to a public Java interface with the same name, and an additional "helper" Java class with the suffix Helper appended to the interface name. The Java interface extends the (mapped) base org.omg.CORBA.Object interface.

The Java interface contains the mapped operation signatures. Methods can be invoked on an object reference to this interface.

The helper class holds a static narrow method that allows a org.omg.CORBA.Object to be narrowed to the object reference of a more specific type. The IDL exception CORBA::BAD_PARAM is thrown if the narrow fails.

There are no special "nil" object references. Java null can be passed freely wherever an object reference is expected.

Attributes are mapped to a pair of Java accessor and modifier methods. These methods have the same name as the IDL attribute and are overloaded. There is no modifier method for IDL readonly attributes.

The holder class for the interface is also generated. Its name is the interface's mapped Java classname with Holder appended to it as follows:

```
final public class <interface_class>Holder
        implements org.omg.CORBA.portable.Streamable {
    public <interface_class> value;
    public <interface_class>Holder() {}
    public <interface_class>Holder(
                        <interface_class> initial) {
        value = initial;
    public void _read(org.omg.CORBA.portable.InputStream i)
        {...}
    public void _write(org.omg.CORBA.portable.OutputStream o)
        {...}
    public org.omg.CORBA.TypeCode _type() {...}
```

```
}
```

Interface inheritance expressed in IDL is reflected directly in the Java interface hierarchy.

5.12.1.1   Example

```
// IDL
module Example {
    interface Face {
        long method (in long arg) raises (e);
        attribute long assignable;
        readonly attribute long nonassignable;
    }
}


// generated Java
package Example;

public interface Face extends org.omg.CORBA.Object {
    int method(int arg)
        throws Example.e;
    int assignable();
    void assignable(int i);
    int nonassignable();
}


public class FaceHelper {

    // ... other standard helper methods

    public static Face narrow(org.omg.CORBA.Object obj)
        {...}
}


final public class FaceHolder
        implements org.omg.CORBA.portable.Streamable {
    public Face value;
    public FaceHolder() {}
    public FaceHolder(Face initial) {...}
    public void _read(org.omg.CORBA.portable.InputStream i)
        {...}
    public void _write(org.omg.CORBA.portable.OutputStream o)
        {...}
    public org.omg.CORBA.TypeCode _type() {...}
}
```

5.12.2 Parameter Passing Modes

IDL in parameters which implement call-by-value semantics, are mapped to normal Java actual parameters. The results of IDL operations are returned as the result of the corresponding Java method.

IDL out and inout parameters, which implement call-by-result and call-by-value/result semantics, cannot be mapped directly into the Java parameter passing mechanism. This mapping defines additional holder classes for all the IDL basic and user-defined types which are used to implement these parameter modes in Java. The client supplies an instance of the appropriate holder Java class that is passed (by value) for each IDL out or inout parameter. The contents of the holder instance (but not the instance itself) are modified by the invocation, and the client uses the (possibly) changed contents after the invocation returns.

5.12.2.1 Example

```
// IDL
module Example {
   interface Modes {
       long operation(in long inArg,
                      out long outArg,
                      inout long inoutArg);
   };
};
```

```
// Generated Java
package Example;
public interface Modes {
    int operation(int inArg,
                    IntHolder outArg,
                    IntHolder inoutArg);
}
```

In the above, the result comes back as an ordinary result and the actual in parameters only an ordinary value. But for the out and inout parameters, an appropriate holder must be constructed. A typical use case might look as follows:

```
// user Java code

// select a target object
Example.Modes target = ...;

// get the in actual value
int inArg = 57;
```

```
// prepare to receive out
IntHolder outHolder =                 new IntHolder();

// set up the in side of the inout
IntHolder inoutHolder = new IntHolder(131);

// make the invocation
int result =target.operation(inArg, outHolder, inoutHolder);

// use the value of the outHolder
... outHolder.value ...

// use the value of the inoutHolder
... inoutHolder.value ...
```

Before the invocation, the input value of the inout parameter must be set in the holder instance that will be the actual parameter. The inout holder can be filled in either by constructing a new holder from a value, or by assigning to the value of an existing holder of the appropriate type. After the invocation, the client uses the

Figure 5-1 **Inheritance of Java Exception Classes**

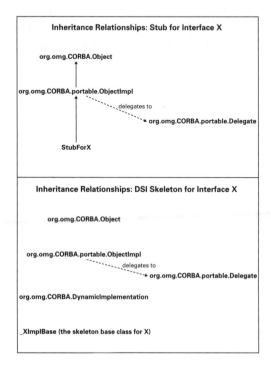

outHolder.value to access the value of the out parameter, and the inoutHolder.value to access the output value of the inout parameter. The return result of the IDL operation is available as the result of the invocation.

5.13 Mapping for Exception

IDL exceptions are mapped very similarly to structs. They are mapped to a Java class that provides instance variables for the fields of the exception and constructors.

CORBA system exceptions are unchecked exceptions. They inherit (indirectly) from java.lang.RuntimeException.

User defined exceptions are checked exceptions. They inherit (indirectly) from java.lang.Exception

5.13.1 User Defined Exceptions

User defined exceptions are mapped to final Java classes that extend org.omg.CORBA.UserException and are otherwise mapped just like the IDL struct type, including the generation of Helper and Holder classes.

If the exception is defined within a nested IDL scope (essentially within an interface) then its Java class name is defined within a special scope. See Section 3.15, "Mapping for Certain Nested Types for more details. Otherwise its Java class name is defined within the scope of the Java package that corresponds to the exception's enclosing IDL module.

5.13.1.1   Example

```
// IDL
module Example {
    exception ex1 { string reason; };
};

// Generated Java
package Example;
final public class ex1 extends org.omg.CORBA.UserException {
    public String reason;                      // instance
    public ex1() {...}                         // default constructor
    public ex1(String r) {...}                 // constructor
}

final public class ex1Holder
        implements org.omg.CORBA.portable.Streamable {
```

```
    public ex1 value;
    public ex1Holder() {}
    public ex1Holder(ex1 initial) {...}
    public void _read(org.omg.CORBA.portable.InputStream i)
        {...}
    public void _write(org.omg.CORBA.portable.OutputStream o)
        {...}
    public org.omg.CORBA.TypeCode _type() {...}
}
```

5.13.2 System Exceptions

The standard IDL system exceptions are mapped to final Java classes that extend org.omg.CORBA.SystemException and provide access to the IDL major and minor exception code, as well as a string describing the reason for the exception.Note there are no public constructors for org.omg.CORBA.SystemException; only classes that extend it can be instantiated.

The Java class name for each standard IDL exception is the same as its IDL name and is declared to be in the org.omg.CORBA package. The default constructor supplies 0 for the minor code, COMPLETED_NO for the completion code, and "" for the reason string. There is also a constructor which takes the reason and uses defaults for the other fields, as well as one which requires all three parameters to be specified. The mapping from IDL name to Java class name is listed in the table below:

Table 5-1 **Mapping of IDL Standard Exceptions**

IDL Exception	Java Class Name
CORBA::UNKNOWN	org.omg.CORBA.UNKNOWN
CORBA::BAD_PARAM	org.omg.CORBA.BAD_PARAM
CORBA::NO_MEMORY	org.omg.CORBA.NO_MEMORY
CORBA::IMP_LIMIT	org.omg.CORBA.IMP_LIMIT
CORBA::COMM_FAILURE	org.omg.CORBA.COMM_FAILURE
CORBA::INV_OBJREF	org.omg.CORBA.INV_OBJREF
CORBA::NO_PERMISSION	org.omg.CORBA.NO_PERMISSION
CORBA::INTERNAL	org.omg.CORBA.INTERNAL
CORBA::MARSHAL	org.omg.CORBA.MARSHAL

Table 5-1   *Continued*

IDL Exception	Java Class Name
CORBA::INITIALIZE	org.omg.CORBA.INITIALIZE
CORBA::NO_IMPLEMENT	org.omg.CORBA.NO_IMPLEMENT
CORBA::BAD_TYPECODE	org.omg.CORBA.BAD_TYPECODE
CORBA::BAD_OPERATION	org.omg.CORBA.BAD_OPERATION
CORBA::NO_RESOURCES	org.omg.CORBA.NO_RESOURCES
CORBA::NO_RESPONSE	org.omg.CORBA.NO_RESPONSE
CORBA::PERSIST_STORE	org.omg.CORBA.PERSIST_STORE
CORBA::BAD_INV_ORDER	org.omg.CORBA.BAD_INV_ORDER
CORBA::TRANSIENT	org.omg.CORBA.TRANSIENT
CORBA::FREE_MEM	org.omg.CORBA.FREE_MEM
CORBA::INV_IDENT	org.omg.CORBA.INV_IDENT
CORBA::INV_FLAG	org.omg.CORBA.INV_FLAG
CORBA::INTF_REPOS	org.omg.CORBA.INTF_REPOS
CORBA::BAD_CONTEXT	org.omg.CORBA.BAD_CONTEXT
CORBA::OBJ_ADAPTER	org.omg.CORBA.OBJ_ADAPTER
CORBA::DATA_CONVERSION	org.omg.CORBA.DATA_CONVERSION
CORBA::OBJECT_NOT_EXIST	org.omg.CORBA.OBJECT_NOT_EXIST
CORBA::TRANSACTIONREQUIRED	org.omg.CORBA.TRANSACTION REQUIRED
CORBA::TRANSACTION ROLLEDBACK	org.omg.CORBA.TRANSACTION ROLLEDBACK
CORBA::INVALIDTRANSACTION	org.omg.CORBA.INVALID TRANSACTION

The definitions of the relevant classes are specified below.

```
// from org.omg.CORBA package
package org.omg.CORBA;
public final class CompletionStatus {
    // Completion Status constants
    public static final int     _COMPLETED_YES = 0,
                                _COMPLETED_NO = 1,
                                _COMPLETED_MAYBE = 2;
    public static final CompletionStatus COMPLETED_YES =
        new CompletionStatus(_COMPLETED_YES);
    public static final CompletionStatus COMPLETED_NO =
```

```
            new CompletionStatus(_COMPLETED_NO);
        public static final CompletionStatus COMPLETED_MAYBE =
            new CompletionStatus(_COMPLETED_MAYBE);
        public int value() {...}
        public static final CompletionStatus from_int(int) {...}
        private CompletionStatus(int) {...}
}

abstract public class
    SystemException extends java.lang.RuntimeException {
        public int minor;
        public CompletionStatus completed;
        // constructor
        protected SystemException(String reason,
                                  int minor,
                                  CompletionStatus status) {
            super(reason);
            this.minor = minor;
            this.status = status;
        }
    }

final public class
    UNKNOWN extends org.omg.CORBA.SystemException {
    public UNKNOWN() ...
    public UNKNOWN(int minor, CompletionStatus completed) ...
    public UNKNOWN(String reason) ...
    public UNKNOWN(String reason, int minor,
                        CompletionStatus completed)     ...
}

...

// there is a similar definition for each of the standard
// IDL system exceptions listed in the table above
```

5.14 Mapping for the Any Type

The IDL type Any maps to the Java class org.omg.CORBA.Any. This class has all the necessary methods to insert and extract instances of predefined types. If the extraction operations have a mismatched type, the CORBA::BAD_OPERATION exception is raised.

In addition, insert and extract methods which take a holder class are defined in order to provide a high speed interface for use by portable stubs and skeletons.

There is an insert and extract method defined for each primitive IDL type as well as a pair for a generic streamable to handle the case of non-primitive IDL types. Note that to preserve unsigned type information unsigned methods (which use the normal holder class) are defined where appropriate.

The insert operations set the specified value and reset the any's type if necessary.

Setting the typecode via the type() accessor wipes out the value. An attempt to extract before the value is set will result in a CORBA::BAD_OPERATION exception being raised. This operation is provided primarily so that the type may be set properly for IDL out parameters.

```
package org.omg.CORBA;

abstract public class Any {

abstract public boolean equal(org.omg.CORBA.Any a);
// type code accessors
abstract public org.omg.CORBA.TypeCode type();
abstract public void type(org.omg.CORBA.TypeCode t);


// read and write values to/from streams
//          throw excep when typecode inconsistent with value
abstract public void read_value(
    org.omg.CORBA.portable.InputStream is,
    org.omg.CORBA.TypeCode t) throws org.omg.CORBA.MARSHAL;
abstract public void
    write_value(org.omg.CORBA.portable.OutputStream os);

abstract public org.omg.CORBA.portable.OutputStream
          create_output_stream();
abstract public org.omg.CORBA.portable.InputStream
          create_input_stream();


// insert and extract each primitive type

abstract public short          extract_short()
    throws org.omg.CORBA.BAD_OPERATION;
abstract public void           insert_short(short s);

abstract public int            extract_long()
    throws org.omg.CORBA.BAD_OPERATION;
abstract public void           insert_long(int i);

abstract public long           extract_longlong()
```

```
        throws org.omg.CORBA.BAD_OPERATION;
abstract public void          insert_longlong(long l);

abstract public short         extract_ushort()
      throws org.omg.CORBA.BAD_OPERATION;
abstract public void          insert_ushort(short s);

abstract public int           extract_ulong()
      throws org.omg.CORBA.BAD_OPERATION;
abstract public void          insert_ulong(int i);

abstract public long          extract_ulonglong()
      throws org.omg.CORBA.BAD_OPERATION;
abstract public void          insert_ulonglong(long l);

abstract public float         extract_float()
      throws org.omg.CORBA.BAD_OPERATION;
abstract public void          insert_float(float f);

abstract public double        extract_double()
      throws org.omg.CORBA.BAD_OPERATION;
abstract public void          insert_double(double d);

abstract public boolean       extract_boolean()
      throws org.omg.CORBA.BAD_OPERATION;
abstract public void          insert_boolean(boolean b);

abstract public char          extract_char()
      throws org.omg.CORBA.BAD_OPERATION;
abstract public void          insert_char(char c)
      throws org.omg.CORBA.DATA_CONVERSION;

abstract public char          extract_wchar()
      throws org.omg.CORBA.BAD_OPERATION;
abstract public void          insert_wchar(char c);

abstract public byte          extract_octet()
      throws org.omg.CORBA.BAD_OPERATION;
abstract public void          insert_octet(byte b);

abstract public org.omg.CORBA.Any extract_any()
      throws org.omg.CORBA.BAD_OPERATION;
abstract public void          insert_any(org.omg.CORBA.Any a);

abstract public org.omg.CORBA.Object  extract_Object()
```

```
                throws org.omg.CORBA.BAD_OPERATION;
    abstract public void            insert_Object(
                                        org.omg.CORBA.Object o);
    //          throw excep when typecode inconsistent with value
    abstract public void            insert_Object(
                                        org.omg.CORBA.Object o,
                                        org.omg.CORBA.TypeCode t)
                                            throws org.omg.CORBA.MARSHAL;


    abstract public String          extract_string()
        throws org.omg.CORBA.BAD_OPERATION;
    abstract public void            insert_string(String s)
        throws org.omg.CORBA.DATA_CONVERSION, org.omg.CORBA.MARSHAL;


    abstract public String          extract_wstring()
        throws org.omg.CORBA.BAD_OPERATION;
    abstract public void            insert_wstring(String s)
        throws org.omg.CORBA.MARSHAL;


    // insert and extract typecode

    abstract public org.omg.CORBA.TypeCode extract_TypeCode()
        throws org.omg.CORBA.BAD_OPERATION;
    abstract public voidinsert_TypeCode(
                                        org.omg.CORBA.TypeCode t);


    // insert and extract Principal

    abstract public org.omg.CORBA.Principal extract_Principal()
        throws org.omg.CORBA.BAD_OPERATION;
    abstract public void insert_Principal(
                                        org.omg.CORBA.Principal p);


    // insert non-primitive IDL types

    abstract public void insert_Streamable(
                        org.omg.CORBA.portable.Streamable s);

}
```

5.15 Mapping for Certain Nested Types

IDL allows type declarations nested within interfaces. Java does not allow classes to
be nested within interfaces. Hence those IDL types that map to Java classes and
that are declared within the scope of an interface must appear in a special "scope"
package when mapped to Java.

IDL interfaces that contain these type declarations will generate a scope package to contain the mapped Java class declarations. The scope package name is constructed by appending Package to the IDL type name.

5.15.1 Example

```
// IDL
module Example {
    interface Foo {
        exception e1 {};
    };
};
```

```
// generated Java
package Example.FooPackage;
final public class e1 extends org.omg.CORBA.UserException
    {...}
```

5.16 Mapping for Typedef

Java does not have a typedef construct.

5.16.1 Simple IDL types

IDL types that are mapped to simple Java types may not be subclassed in Java. Hence any typedefs that are type declarations for simple types are mapped to the original (mapped type) everywhere the typedef type appears.

The IDL types covered by this rule are described in Section 3.4, "Mapping for Basic Types.

Helper classes are generated for all typedefs.

5.16.2 Complex IDL types

Typedefs for non arrays and sequences are "unwound" to their original type until a simple IDL type or user-defined IDL type (of the non typedef variety) is encountered.

Holder classes are generated for sequence and array typedefs only.

5.16.2.1   Example

```
// IDL
struct EmpName {
```

```
        string firstName;
        string lastName;
};
typedef EmpName EmpRec;

// generated Java
//        regular struct mapping for EmpName
//        regular helper class mapping for EmpRec

final public class EmpName {
    ...
}

public class EmpRecHelper {
    ...
}
```

6.0   Mapping Pseudo-Objects to Java

6.1   Introduction

Pseudo objects are constructs whose definition is usually specified in "IDL", but whose mapping is language specified. A pseudo object is not (usually) a regular CORBA object. Often it exposed to either clients and/or servers as a process, or a thread local, programming language construct.

For each of the standard IDL pseudo-objects, either a specific Java language construct is specified or it is specified as a pseudo interface.

This mapping is based on the revised version 1.1 C++ mapping.

This specification has chosen the option allowed in the IDL specification section 4.1.3 to define Status as void and has eliminated it for the convenience of Java programmers.

6.1.1   Pseudo Interface

The use of pseudo interface is a convenient device which means that most of the standard language mapping rules defined in this specification may be mechanically used to generate the Java. However, in general the resulting construct is not a CORBA object. Specifically it is:

- not represented in the Interface Repository

- no helper classes are generated

- no holder classes are generated

- mapped to a Java public abstract class that does not extend or inherit from any other classes or interfaces

Note: The specific definition given for each piece of PIDL may override the general guidelines above. In such a case, the specific definition takes precedence.

All of the pseudo interfaces are mapped as if they were declared in:

```
module org {
    module omg {
        module CORBA {

                          . . .
```

That is, they are mapped to the org.omg.CORBA Java package.

6.2   Certain Exceptions

The standard CORBA PIDL uses several exceptions, Bounds, BadKind, and InvalidName.

No holder and helper classes are defined for these exceptions, nor are they in the interface repository., However so that users can treat them as "normal exceptions" for programming purposes, they are mapped as normal user exceptions.

They are defined within the scopes that they are used. A Bounds and BadKind exception are defined in the TypeCodePackage for use by TypeCode. A Bounds exception is defined in the standard CORBA module for use by NVList, ExceptionList, and ContextList. An InvalidName exception is defined in the ORBPackage for use by ORB.

```
// Java

package org.omg.CORBA;

final public class Bounds
    extends org.omg.CORBA.UserException {
    public Bounds() {...}
}
package org.omg.CORBA.TypeCodePackage;

final public class Bounds
```

```
      extends org.omg.CORBA.UserException {
      public Bounds() {...}
}
final public class BadKind
      extends org.omg.CORBA.UserException {
      public BadKind() {...}
}

package org.omg.CORBA.ORBPackage;

final public class InvalidName
      extends org.omg.CORBA.UserException {
      public InvalidName() {...}
}
```

6.3   Environment

The Environment is used in request operations to make exception information available.

```
// Java code

package org.omg.CORBA;

public abstract class Environment {
   void exception(java.lang.Exception except);
   java.lang.Exception exception();
   void clear();
}
```

6.4   NamedValue

A NamedValue describes a name, value pair. It is used in the DII to describe arguments and return values, and in the context routines to pass property, value pairs.

In Java it includes a name, a value (as an any), and an integer representing a set of flags.

```
typedef unsigned long Flags;
typedef string Identifier;
const Flags ARG_IN = 1;
const Flags ARG_OUT = 2;
const Flags ARG_INOUT = 3;
const Flags CTX_RESTRICT_SCOPE = 15;

pseudo interface NamedValue {
```

```
        readonly attribute Identifier name;
        readonly attribute any value;
        readonly attribute Flags flags;
};

// Java

package org.omg.CORBA;

public interface ARG_IN {
    public static final int value = 1;
}
public interface ARG_OUT {
    public static final int value = 2;
}
public interface ARG_INOUT {
    public static final int value = 3;
}

public interface CTX_RESTRICT_SCOPE {
    public static final int value = 15;
}


public abstract class NamedValue {
    public abstract String name();
    public abstract Any value();
    public abstract int flags();
}
```

6.5   NVList

A NVList is used in the DII to describe arguments, and in the context routines to describe context values.

In Java it maintains a modifiable list of NamedValues.

```
pseudo interface NVList {
    readonly attribute unsigned long count;
    NamedValue add(in Flags flags);
    NamedValue add_item(in Identifier item_name, in Flags flags);
    NamedValue add_value(in Identifier item_name,
                          in any val,
                          in Flags flags);
    NamedValue item(in unsigned long index) raises
(CORBA::Bounds);
    void remove(in unsigned long index) raises (CORBA::Bounds);
};
```

```java
// Java

package org.omg.CORBA;

public abstract class NVList {
    public abstract int count();
    public abstract NamedValue add(int flags);
    public abstract NamedValue add_item(String item_name, int flags);
    public abstract NamedValue add_value(String item_name, Any val,
                              int flags);
    public abstract NamedValue item(int index)
                    throws org.omg.CORBA.Bounds;
    public abstract void remove(int index) throws org.omg.CORBA.Bounds;
}
```

6.6   ExceptionList

An ExceptionList is used in the DII to describe the exceptions that can be raised by IDL operations.

It maintains a list of modifiable list of TypeCodes.

```
pseudo interface ExceptionList {
    readonly attribute unsigned long count;
    void add(in TypeCode exc);
    TypeCode item (in unsigned long index) raises (CORBA::Bounds);
    void remove (in unsigned long index) raises (CORBA::Bounds);
};
```

```java
// Java

package org.omg.CORBA;

public abstract class ExceptionList {
    public abstract int count();
    public abstract void add(TypeCode exc);
    public abstract TypeCode item(int index)
                throws org.omg.CORBA.Bounds;
    public abstract void remove(int index)
                throws org.omg.CORBA.Bounds;
}
```

6.7   Context

A Context is used in the DII to specify a context in which context strings must be resolved before being sent along with the request invocation.

```
pseudo interface Context {
    readonly attribute Identifier context_name;
```

```
    readonly attribute Context parent;
    Context create_child(in Identifier child_ctx_name);
    void set_one_value(in Identifier propname, in any propvalue);
    void set_values(in NVList values);
    void delete_values(in Identifier propname);
    NVList get_values(in Identifier start_scope,
                      in Flags op_flags,
                      in Identifier pattern);
};
```

```
// Java

package org.omg.CORBA;

public abstract class Context {
    public abstract String context_name();
    public abstract Context parent();
    public abstract Context create_child(String child_ctx_name);
    public abstract void set_one_value(String propname,
                                       Any propvalue);
    public abstract void set_values(NVList values);
    public abstract void delete_values(String propname);
    public abstract NVList get_values(String start_scpe, int op_flags,
                                      String pattern);
}
```

6.8 ContextList

```
pseudo interface ContextList {
    readonly attribute unsigned long count;
    void add(in string ctx);
    string item(in unsigned long index) raises (CORBA::Bounds);
    void remove(in unsigned long index) raises (CORBA::Bounds);
};
```

```
// Java

package org.omg.CORBA;

public abstract class ContextList {
    public abstract int count();
    public abstract void add(String ctx);
    public abstract String item(int index)
        throws org.omg.CORBA.Bounds;
    public abstract void remove(int index)
        throws org.omg.CORBA.Bounds;
}
```

6.9   Request

```
pseudo interface Request {
    readonly attribute Object target;
    readonly attribute Identifier operation;
    readonly attribute NVList arguments;
    readonly attribute NamedValue result;
    readonly attribute Environment env;
    readonly attribute ExceptionList exceptions;
    readonly attribute ContextList contexts;

    attribute Context ctx;

    any add_in_arg();
    any add_named_in_arg(in string name);
    any add_inout_arg();
    any add_named_inout_arg(in string name);
    any add_out_arg();
    any add_named_out_arg(in string name);
    void set_return_type(in TypeCode tc);
    any return_value();

    void invoke();
    void send_oneway();
    void send_deferred();
    void get_response();
    boolean poll_response();
};


// Java

package org.omg.CORBA;

public abstract class Request {
    public abstract Object target();
    public abstract String operation();
    public abstract NVList arguments();
    public abstract NamedValue result();
    public abstract Environment env();
    public abstract ExceptionList exceptions();
    public abstract ContextList contexts();

    public abstract Context ctx();
    public abstract void ctx(Context c);

    public abstract Any add_in_arg();
    public abstract Any add_named_in_arg(String name);
```

```
    public abstract Any add_inout_arg();
    public abstract Any add_named_inout_arg(String name);
    public abstract Any add_out_arg();
    public abstract Any add_named_out_arg(String name);
    public abstract void set_return_type(TypeCode tc);
    public abstract Any return_value();

    public abstract void invoke();
    public abstract void send_oneway();
    public abstract void send_deferred();
    public abstract void get_response();
    public abstract boolean poll_response();
}
```

6.10 ServerRequest and Dynamic Implementation

```
pseudo interface ServerRequest {
    Identifier op_name();
    Context ctx();
    void params(in NVList parms);
    void result(in Any res);
    void    except(in Any ex);
} ;
```

```
// Java

package org.omg.CORBA;

public abstract class ServerRequest {
    public abstract String op_name();
    public abstract Context ctx();
    public abstract void params(NVList parms);
    public abstract void result(Any a);
    public abstract void except(Any a);
```

The DynamicImplementation interface defines the interface such a dynamic server is expect to implement. Note that it inherits from the base class for stubs and skeletons (see Section 8.5.2, "Portable ObjectImpl").

```
// Java

package org.omg.CORBA;

public abstract class DynamicImplementation
        extends org.omg.CORBA.portable.ObjectImpl {
    public abstract void invoke(org.omg.CORBA.ServerRequest request);
}
```

6.11 TypeCode

The deprecated parameter and param_count methods are not mapped.

```
enum TCKind {
    tk_null, tk_void,
    tk_short, tk_long, tk_ushort, tk_ulong,
    tk_float, tk_double, tk_boolean, tk_char,
    tk_octet, tk_any, tk_TypeCode, tk_Principal, tk_objref,
    tk_struct, tk_union, tk_enum, tk_string,
    tk_sequence, tk_array, tk_alias, tk_except,
    tk_longlong, tk_ulonglong, tk_longdouble,
    tk_wchar, tk_wstring, tk_fixed
};


// Java

package org.omg.CORBA;

public final class TCKind {
    public static final int _tk_null = 0;
    public static final
        TCKind tk_null = new TCKind(_tk_null);
    public static final int _tk_void = 1;
        TCKind tk_void = new TCKind(_tk_void);
    public static final int _tk_short = 2;
        TCKind tk_short = new TCKind(_tk_short);
    public static final int _tk_long = 3;
        TCKind tk_long = new TCKind(_tk_long);
    public static final int _tk_ushort = 4;
        TCKind tk_ushort = new TCKind(_tk_ushort);
    public static final int _tk_ulong = 5;
        TCKind tk_ulong = new TCKind(_tk_ulong);
    public static final int _tk_float = 6;
        TCKind tk_float = new TCKind(_tk_float);
    public static final int _tk_double = 7;
        TCKind tk_double = new TCKind(_tk_double);
    public static final int _tk_boolean = 8;
        TCKind tk_boolean = new TCKind(_tk_boolean);
    public static final int _tk_char = 9;
        TCKind tk_char = new TCKind(_tk_char);
    public static final int _tk_octet = 10;
        TCKind tk_octet = new TCKind(_tk_octet);
    public static final int _tk_any = 11;
        TCKind tk_any = new TCKind(_tk_any);
    public static final int _tk_TypeCode = 12;
        TCKind tk_TypeCode = new TCKind(_tk_TypeCode);
```

```
    public static final int _tk_Principal = 13;
        TCKind tk_Principal = new TCKind(_tk_Principal);
    public static final int _tk_objref = 14;
        TCKind tk_objref = new TCKind(_tk_objref);
    public static final int _tk_stuct = 15;
        TCKind tk_stuct = new TCKind(_tk_stuct);
    public static final int _tk_union = 16;
        TCKind tk_union = new TCKind(_tk_union);
    public static final int _tk_enum = 17;
        TCKind tk_enum = new TCKind(_tk_enum);
    public static final int _tk_string = 18;
        TCKind tk_string = new TCKind(_tk_string);
    public static final int _tk_sequence = 19;
        TCKind tk_sequence = new TCKind(_tk_sequence);
    public static final int _tk_array = 20;
        TCKind tk_array = new TCKind(_tk_array);
    public static final int _tk_alias = 21;
        TCKind tk_alias = new TCKind(_tk_alias);
    public static final int _tk_except = 22;
        TCKind tk_except = new TCKind(_tk_except);
    public static final int _tk_longlong = 23;
        TCKind tk_longlong = new TCKind(_tk_longlong);
    public static final int _tk_ulonglong = 24;
        TCKind tk_ulonglong = new TCKind(_tk_ulonglong);
    public static final int _tk_longdouble = 25;
        TCKind tk_longdouble = new TCKind(_tk_longdouble);
    public static final int _tk_wchar = 26;
        TCKind tk_wchar = new TCKind(_tk_wchar);
    public static final int _tk_wstring = 27;
        TCKind tk_wstring = new TCKind(_tk_wstring);
    public static final int _tk_fixed = 28;
        TCKind tk_fixed = new TCKind(_tk_fixed);

    public int value() {...}
    public static TCKind from_int(int value) {...}
    private TCKind(int value) {...}
}
pseudo interface TypeCode {

    exception Bounds {};
    exception BadKind {};

    // for all TypeCode kinds
    boolean equal(in TypeCode tc);
    TCKind kind();

    // for objref, struct, union, enum, alias, and except
```

```
        RepositoryID id() raises (BadKind);
        RepositoryId name() raises (BadKind);

        // for struct, union, enum, and except
        unsigned long member_count() raises (BadKind);
        Identifier member_name(in unsigned long index)
            raises (BadKind, Bounds);

        // for struct, union, and except
        TypeCode member_type(in unsigned long index)
            raises (BadKind, Bounds);

        // for union
        any member_label(in unsigned long index) raises (BadKind, Bounds);
        TypeCode discriminator_type() raises (BadKind);
        long default_index() raises (BadKind);

        // for string, sequence, and array
        unsigned long length() raises (BadKind);
        TypeCode content_type() raises (BadKind);

    }

// Java

package org.omg.CORBA;

public abstract class TypeCode {

    // for all TypeCode kinds
    public abstract boolean equal(TypeCode tc);
    public abstract TCKind kind();

    // for objref, struct, unio, enum, alias, and except
    public abstract String id() throws TypeCodePackage.BadKind;
    public abstract String name() throws TypeCodePackage.BadKind;

    // for struct, union, enum, and except
    public abstract int member_count() throws TypeCodePackage.BadKind;
    public abstract String member_name(int index)
            throws TypeCodePackage.BadKind;

    // for struct, union, and except
    public abstract TypeCode member_type(int index)
            throws TypeCodePackage.BadKind,
```

```
                    TypeCodePackage.Bounds;

    // for union
    public abstract Any member_label(int index)
            throws TypeCodePackage.BadKind,
                            TypeCodePackage.Bounds;
    public abstract TypeCode discriminator_type()
            throws TypeCodePackage.BadKind;
    public abstract int default_index() throws TypeCodePackage.BadKind;

    // for string, sequence, and array
    public abstract int length() throws TypeCodePackage.BadKind;
    public abstract TypeCode content_type() throws TypeCodePackage.BadKind;
}
```

6.12 ORB

The UnionMemeberSeq, EnumMemberSeq, and StructMemberSeq typedefs are real IDL and bring in the Interface Repository. Rather than tediously list its interfaces, and other assorted types, suffice it to say that it is all mapped following the rules for IDL set forth in this specification in Section 3.0, "Mapping IDL to Java.

StructMember[], UnionMember[], EnumMember[]

```
pseudo interface ORB {

    exception InvalidName {};

    typedef string ObjectId;
    typedef sequence<ObjectId> ObjectIdList;

    ObjectIdList list_initial_services();
    Object resolve_initial_references(in ObjectId object_name)
        raises(InvalidName);
    string object_to_string(in Object obj);
    Object string_to_object(in string str);

    NVList create_list(in long count);
    NVList create_operation_list(in OperationDef oper);
    NamedValue create_named_value(in String name, in Any value,
                        in Flags flags);
    ExceptionList create_exception_list();
    ContextList create_context_list();

    Context get_default_context();
```

```
Environment create_environment();

void send_multiple_requests_oneway(in RequestSeq req);
void send_multiple_requests_deferred(in RequestSeq req);
boolean poll_next_response();
Request get_next_response();

// typecode creation
    TypeCode create_struct_tc           (in RepositoryId id,
                                         in Identifier name,
                                         in StructMemberSeq members);

    TypeCode create_union_tc            (in RepositoryId id,
                                         in Identifier name,
                                         in TypeCode discriminator_type,
                                         in UnionMemberSeq members);

    TypeCode create_enum_tc             (in RepositoryId id,
                                         in Identifier name,
                                         in EnumMemberSeq members);

    TypeCode create_alias_tc            (in RepositoryId id,
                                         in Identifier name,
                                         in TypeCode original_type);

    TypeCode create_exception_tc        (in RepositoryId id,
                                         in Identifier name,
                                         in StructMemberSeq members);

    TypeCode create_interface_tc        (in RepositoryId id,
                                         in Identifier name);

    TypeCode create_string_tc           (in unsigned long bound);

    TypeCode create_wstring_tc          (in unsigned long bound);

    TypeCode create_sequence_tc         (in unsigned long bound,
                                         in TypeCode element_type);

    TypeCode create_recursive_sequence_tc(in unsigned long bound,
                                         in unsigned long offset);

    TypeCode create_array_tc            (in unsigned long length,
                                         in TypeCode element_type);
```

```
    Current get_current();

// Additional operations for Java mapping

    TypeCode get_primitive_tc(in TCKind tcKind);
    Any create_any();
    OutputStream create_output_stream();
    void connect(Object obj);
    void disconnect(Object obj);
// additional  methods for ORB initialization go here, but only
//   appear  in the mapped Java (seeSection 8.8, "ORB Initialization" )

// Java signatures
//    public static ORB init(Strings[] args, Properties props);
//    public static ORB init(Applet app, Properties props);
//    public static ORB init();
// abstract protected void set_parameters(String[] args,
//                                     java.util.Properties props);
// abstract protected void set_parameters(java.applet.Applet app,
//                                     java.util.Properties props);

}


// Java

package org.omg.CORBA;

public abstract class ORB {

    public abstract String[] list_initial_services();
    public abstract org.omg.CORBA.Object resolve_initial_references(
        String object_name)
        throws org.omg.CORBA.ORBPackage.InvalidName;

    public abstract String object_to_string(org.omg.CORBA.Object obj);
    public abstract org.omg.CORBA.Object string_to_object(String str);

    public abstract NVList create_list(int count);
    public abstract NVList create_operation_list(OperationDef oper);
    public abstract NamedValue create_named_value(String name,
                                    Any value,
                                    int flags);
    public abstract ExceptionList create_exception_list();
    public abstract ContextList create_context_list();

    public abstract Context get_default_context();
```

```
public abstract Environment create_environment();

public abstract void send_multiple_requests_oneway(Request[] req);
public abstract void sent_multiple_requests_deferred(Request[] req);
public abstract boolean poll_next_response();
public abstract Request get_next_response();

// typecode creation

public abstract TypeCode create_struct_tc(
                                String id,
                                String name,
                                StructMember[] members);
public abstract TypeCode create_union_tc(
                                String id,
                                String name,
                                TypeCode discriminator_type,
                                UnionMember[] members);
public abstract TypeCode create_enum_tc(
                                String id,
                                String name,
                                EnumMember[] members);
public abstract TypeCode create_alias_tc(
                                String id,
                                String name,
                                TypeCode original_type);
public abstract TypeCode create_exception_tc(
                                String id,
                                String name,
                                StructMember[] members);
public abstract TypeCode create_interface_    tc    (
                                String id,
                                String name);
public abstract TypeCode create_string_tc(int bound);
public abstract TypeCode create_wstring_tc(int bound);
public abstract TypeCode create_sequence_tc(
                                int bound,
                                TypeCode element_type);
public abstract TypeCode create_recursive_sequence_tc(
                                int bound,
                                int offset);
public abstract TypeCode create_array_tc(
                                int length,
                                TypeCode element_type);

public abstract Current get_current();
```

```
// additional methods for IDL/Java mapping

public abstract TypeCode get_primitive_tc(TCKind tcKind);
public abstract Any create_any();
public abstract org.omg.CORBA.portable.OutputStream
    create_output_stream();
public abstract void connect(        org.omg.CORBA.Object obj);
public abstract void disconnect(        org.omg.CORBA.Object obj);
// additional static methods for ORB initialization

public static ORB init(Strings[] args, Properties props);
public static ORB init(Applet app, Properties props);
public static ORB init();
abstract protected void set_parameters(String[] args,
                                    java.util.Properties props);
abstract protected void set_parameters(java.applet.Applet app,
                                    java.util.Properties props);

}
```

6.13 CORBA::Object

The IDL Object type is mapped to the org.omg.CORBA.Object and org.omg.CORBA.ObjectHelper classes as shown below.

The Java interface for each user defined IDL interface extends org.omg.CORBA.Object, so that any object reference can be passed anywhere a org.omg.CORBA.Object is expected.

```
// Java
package org.omg.CORBA;
public interface Object {
    boolean _is_a(String Identifier);
    boolean _is_equivalent(Object that);
    boolean _non_existent();
    int _hash(int maximum);
    org.omg.CORBA.Object _duplicate();
    void _release();
    ImplementationDef _get_implementation();
    InterfaceDef _get_interface();
    Request _request(String s);
    Request _create_request(Context ctx,
                                    String operation,
                                    NVList arg_list,
                                    NamedValue result);
    Request _create_request(Context ctx,
```

```
                                    String operation,
                                    NVList arg_list,
                                    NamedValue result,
                                    ExceptionList exclist,
                                    ContextList ctxlist);

}
```

6.14 Current

```
pseudo interface Current {
}


// Java
public abstract class Current
        extends org.omg.CORBA.portable.ObjectImpl {
}
```

6.15 Principal

```
pseudo interface Principal {
attribute sequence<octet> name;
}


// Java
public abstract class Principal {
    public abstract byte[] name();
    public abstract void name(byte[] name);
}
```

7.0 Server-Side Mapping

7.1 Introduction

This section discusses how implementations create and register objects with the ORB runtime.

The material in this section may change as a result of future OMG work on the Portable Object Adaptor being considered through the Portability RFP.

7.2 *Transient Objects*

For this initial specification only a minimal API to allow application developers to implement transient ORB objects is described. There may be changes due to the Portability work, but they are not expected to be major.

7.3 Servant Base Class

For each IDL interface **<interface_name>** the mapping defines a Java class as follows:

```
// Java

public class _<interface_name>ImplBase implements <interface_name> {
}
```

7.3.1 Servant Class

For each interface, the developer must write a servant class. Instances of the servant class implement ORB objects. Each instance implements a single ORB object, and each ORB object is implemented by a single servant.

Each object implementation implements ORB objects that supports a most derived IDL interface. If this interface is <interface_name>, then the servant class must extend _<interface_name>ImplBase.

The servant class must define public methods corresponding to the operations and attributes of the IDL interface supported by the object implementation, as defined by the mapping specification for IDL interfaces. Providing these methods is sufficient to satisfy all abstract methods defined by _**<interface_name>**ImplBase.

7.3.2 Creating A Transient ORB Object

To create an instance of an object implementation, the developer instantiates the servant class.

7.3.3 Connecting a Transient ORB Object

Object implementations (object references) may be explicitly connected to the ORB by calling the ORB's connect() method (seeSection 6.12, "ORB").

An object implementation may also be automatically and implicitly connected to the ORB if it is passed as a (mapped IDL) parameter to a (mapped) IDL operation that is itself not implemented as a local (Java) object. I.e., it has to be marshaled and sent outside of the process address space. Note, a vendor is free to connect such an object implementation "earlier" (e.g. upon instantiation), but it must connect the implementation to the ORB when it is passed as described above.

Note that calling connect() when an object is already connected has no effect.

7.3.4 Disconnecting a Transient ORB Object

The servant may disconnect itself from the ORB by invoking the ORB's disconnect() method (see Section 6.12, "ORB"). After this method returns, incoming requests will be rejected by the ORB by raising the CORBA::OBJECT_NOT_EXIST exception. The effect of this method is to cause the ORB object to appear to be destroyed from the point of view of remote clients.

Note that calling disconnect() when the object is not connected has no effect.

Note however, that requests issued using the servant directly (e.g. using the implementation's this pointer) do not pass through the ORB; these requests will continue to be processed by the servant.

8.0   Java ORB Portability Interfaces

8.1   Introduction

The APIs specified here provide the minimal set of functionality to allow portable stubs and skeletons to be used with a Java ORB. The interoperability requirements for Java go beyond that of other languages. Because Java classes are often downloaded and come from sources that are independent of the ORB in which they will be used, it is essential to define the interfaces that the stubs and skeletons use. Otherwise, use of a stub (or skeleton) will require: either that it have been generated by a tool that was provided by the ORB vendor (or is compatible with the ORB being used), or that the entire ORB runtime be downloaded with the stub or skeleton. Both of these scenarios are unacceptable.

8.1.1   Design Goals

The design balances several goals:

- *Size* Stubs and skeletons must have a small bytecode footprint in order to make downloading fast in a browser environment and to minimize memory requirements when bundled with a Java VM, particularly in specialized environments such as set-top boxes.

- *Performance* Obviously, the runtime performance of the generated stub code must be excellent. In particular, care must be taken to minimize temporary Java object creation during invocations in order to avoid Java VM garbage collection overhead.

- *Reverse Mapability* The design does not require adding methods to user-defined types such as structures and exceptions to ensure that stubs and skeletons generated by IDL to Java compilers and reverse Java to IDL mapping tools are interoperable and binary compatible.

A very simple delegation scheme is specified here. Basically, it allows ORB vendors maximum flexibility for their ORB interfaces, as long as they implement the interface APIs. Of course vendors are free to add proprietary extensions to their ORB runtimes. Stubs and skeletons which require proprietary extensions will not necessarily be portable or interoperable and may require download of the corresponding runtime.

8.1.2 Portability Package
The APIs needed to implement portability are found in the org.omg.CORBA .portable package.

The portability package contains interfaces and classes that are designed for and intended to be used by ORB implementors. It exposes the publicly defined APIs that are used to connect stubs and skeletons to the ORB.

8.2 Architecture
The stub and skeleton portability architecture allows the use of the DII and DSI as its portability layer. The mapping of the DII and DSI PIDL have operations that support the efficient implementation of portable stubs and skeletons.

All stubs shall inherit from a common base class org.omg.CORBA.portable.ObjectImpl. The class is responsible for delegating shared functionality such as is_a() to the vendor specific implementation. This model provides for a variety of vendor dependent implementation choices, while reducing the client-side and server "code bloat".

All DSI-based skeletons inherit from org.omg.CORBA.DynamicImplementation.

8.3 Streamable APIs
The Streamable Interface API provides the support for the reading and writing of complex data types. It is implemented by static methods on the Helper classes. They are also used in the Holder classes for reading and writing complex data types passed as out and inout parameters.

```
package org.omg.CORBA.portable;

public interface Streamable {
    void _read(org.omg.CORBA.portable.InputStream istream);
    void _write(org.omg.CORBA.portable.OutputStream ostream);
    org.omg.CORBA.TypeCode _type();
}
```

8.4   Streaming APIs

The streaming APIs are Java interfaces that provide for the reading and writing of all of the mapped IDL types to and from streams. Their implementations are used inside the ORB to marshal parameters and to insert and extract complex datatypes into and from Anys.

The streaming APIs are found in the org.omg.CORBA.portable package.

The ORB object is used as a factory to create an output stream. An input stream may be created from an output stream.

```
package org.omg.CORBA;

interface ORB {
        OutputStream                        create_output_stream();
};



package org.omg.CORBA.portable;

public abstract class InputStream {
    public abstract boolean     read_boolean();
    public abstract char        read_char();
    public abstract char        read_wchar();
    public abstract byte        read_octet();
    public abstract short       read_short();
    public abstract short       read_ushort();
    public abstract int         read_long();
    public abstract int         read_ulong();
    public abstract long        read_longlong();
    public abstract long        read_ulonglong();
    public abstract float       read_float();
    public abstract double      read_double();
    public abstract String      read_string();
    public abstract String      read_wstring();
    public abstract void        read_boolean_array(boolean[] value,
                                            int offset, int length);
```

```
        public abstract void          read_char_array(char[] value,
                                                  int offset, int length);
        public abstract void          read_wchar_array(char[] value,
                                                  int offset, int length);
        public abstract void          read_octet_array(byte[] value,
                                                    int offset, int length);
        public abstract void          read_short_array(short[] value,
                                                  int offset, int length);
        public abstract void          read_ushort_array(short[] value,
                                                  int offset, int length);
        public abstract void          read_long_array(int[] value,
                                                  int offset, int length);
        public abstract void          read_ulong_array(int[] value,
                                                  int offset, int length);
        public abstract void          read_longlong_array(long[] value,
                                                  int offset, int length);
        public abstract void          read_ulonglong_array(long[] value,
                                                  int offset, int length);
        public abstract void          read_float_array(float[] value,
                                                  int offset, int length);
        public abstract void          read_double_array(double[] value,
                                                  int offset, int length);
        public abstract org.omg.CORBA.Object          read_Object();
        public abstract org.omg.CORBA.TypeCode         read_TypeCode();
        public abstract org.omg.CORBA.Any              read_any();
        public abstract org.omg.CORBA.Principal        read_Principal();
}


public abstract class OutputStream {
    public abstract InputStream create_input_stream();
    public abstract void write_boolean       (boolean value);
    public abstract void write_char          (char value);
    public abstract void write_wchar         (char value);
    public abstract void write_octet         (byte value);
    public abstract void write_short         (short value);
    public abstract void write_ushort        (short value);
    public abstract void write_long          (int value);
    public abstract void write_ulong         (int value);
    public abstract void write_longlong      (long value);
    public abstract void write_ulonglong     (long value);
    public abstract void write_float         (float value);
    public abstract void write_double        (double value);
    public abstract void write_string        (String value);
    public abstract void write_wstring       (String value);
    public abstract void write_boolean_array (boolean[] value,
                                          int offset, int length);
```

```
        public abstract void write_char_array(char[] value,
                                               int offset, int length);
        public abstract void write_wchar_array(char[] value,
                                               int offset, int length);
        public abstract void write_octet_array(byte[] value,
                                               int offset, int length);
        public abstract void write_short_array(short[] value,
                                               int offset, int length);
        public abstract void write_ushort_array(short[] value,
                                               int offset, int length);
        public abstract void write_long_array(int[] value,
                                               int offset, int length);
        public abstract void write_ulong_array(int[] value,
                                               int offset, int length);
        public abstract void write_longlong_array(long[] value,
                                               int offset, int length);
        public abstract void write_ulonglong_array(long[] value,
                                               int offset, int length);
        public abstract void write_float_array(float[] value,
                                               int offset, int length);
        public abstract void write_double_array(double[] value,
                                               int offset, int length);
        public abstract void write_Object(org.omg.CORBA.Object value);
        public abstract void write_TypeCode(org.omg.CORBA.TypeCode value);
        public abstract void write_any (org.omg.CORBA.Any value);
        public abstract void write_Principal(org.omg.CORBA.Principal value);
}
```

8.5 Portability Stub Interfaces

8.5.1 Stub Design

The stub class is implemented on top of the DII..

8.5.2 Portable ObjectImpl

The ObjectImpl class is the base class for stubs and skeletons. It provides the basic delegation mechanism.

The method _ids() returns an array of repository ids that an object implements. The string at the zero index shall represent the most derived interface. The last id, for the generic CORBA object (i.e. "IDL:omg.org/CORBA/Object:1.0"), is implied and not present.

```
package org.omg.CORBA.portable;

abstract public class ObjectImpl implements
```

```java
                                    org.omg.CORBA.Object {
    private Delegate __delegate;

    public Delegate _get_delegate() {
        if (__delegate == null) {
            throw new org.omg.CORBA.BAD_OPERATION();
        }
        return _delegate;
    }

    public void _set_delegate(Delegate delegate) {
        __delegate = delegate;
    }

    public abstract String[] _ids() {...}

// methods for standard CORBA stuff

    public org.omg.CORBA.ImplementationDef
                                    _get_implementation() {
        return _get_delegate().get_implementation(this);
    }

    public org.omg.CORBA.InterfaceDef
                                    _get_interface() {
        return _get_delegate().get_interface(this);
    }

    public org.omg.CORBA.Object _duplicate() {
        return _get_delegate().duplicate(this);
    }

    public void _release() {
        _get_delegate().release(this);
    }

    public boolean _is_a(String repository_id) {
        return _get_delegate().is_a(this, repository_id);
    }

    public boolean _is_equivalent(org.omg.CORBA.Object rhs) {
        return _get_delegate().is_equivalent(this, rhs);
    }

    public boolean _non_existent() {
```

```
        return _get_delegate().non_existent(this);
    }

    public int _hash(int maximum) {
        return _get_delegate().hash(this, maximum);
    }

    public org.omg.CORBA.Request _request(String operation) {
        return _get_delegate().request(this, operation);
    }

    public org.omg.CORBA.Request _create_request(
                        org.omg.CORBA.Context ctx,
                String operation,
                org.omg.CORBA.NVList arg_list,
                org.omg.CORBA.NamedValue result) {
        return _get_delegate().create_request(this, ctx,
                                operation, arg_list, result);
    }

    public Request _create_request(
                        org.omg.CORBA.Context ctx,
                String operation,
                org.omg.CORBA.NVList arg_list,
                org.omg.CORBA.NamedValue result,
                  org.omg.CORBA.ExceptionList exceptions,
                org.omg.CORBA.ContextList contexts) {
        return _get_delegate().create_request(this, ctx, operation,
                        arg_list, result,exceptions, contexts);
    }

}
```

8.6   Delegate

The delegate class provides the ORB vendor specific implementation of CORBA object.

```
// Java

package org.omg.CORBA.portable;

public abstract class Delegate {

    public abstract org.omg.CORBA ImplementationDef get_implementation(
```

```
                                  org.omg.CORBA.Object self);
    public abstract org.omg.CORBA.InterfaceDef get_interface(
                                  org.omg.CORBA.Object self);
    public abstract org.omg.CORBA.Object duplicate(
                                  org.omg.CORBA.Object self);
    public abstract void release(org.omg.CORBA.Object self);
    public abstract boolean is_a(org.omg.CORBA.Object self,
                                  String repository_id);
    public abstract boolean non_existent(org.omg.CORBA.Object self);
    public abstract boolean is_equivalent(org.omg.CORBA.Object self,
                                  org.omg.CORBA.Object rhs);
    public abstract int hash(org.omg.CORBA.Object self
                                  int max);
    public abstract org.omg.CORBA.Request request(org.omg.CORBA.Object self,
                                  String operation);
    public abstract org.omg.CORBA.Request create_request(
                                  org.omg.CORBA.Object self,
                                  org.omg.CORBA.Context ctx,
                                  String operation,
                                  org.omg.CORBA.NVList arg_list,
                                  org.omg.CORBA.NamedValue result);
    public abstract org.omg.CORBA.Request create_request(
                                  org.omg.CORBA.Object self,
                                  org.omg.CORBA.Context ctx,
                                  String operation,
                                  org.omg.CORBA.NVList arg_list,
                                  org.omg.CORBA.NamedValue result,
                                  org.omg.CORBA.ExceptionList excepts,
                                  org.omg.CORBA.ContextList contexts);
}
```

8.7 Skeleton

The skeleton uses the DynamicImplementation (seeSection 6.10, "ServerRequest and Dynamic Implementation").

See Section 7.2.2, "Servant Class" for more information.

8.8 ORB Initialization

The ORB class represents an implementation of a CORBA ORB. Vendors specific ORB implementations can extend this class to add new features.

There are several cases to consider when creating the ORB instance. An important factor is whether an applet in a browser or an stand-alone Java application is being used.

In any event, when creating an ORB instance, the class names of the ORB implementation are located using the following search order:

- check in Applet parameter or application string array, if any

- check in properties parameter, if any

- check in the System properties

- fall back on a hardcoded default behavior

8.8.1 Standard Properties

The OMG standard properties are defined in the following table.

Table 8-2   Standard ORB properties

Property Name	Property Value
org.omg.CORBA.ORBClass	class name of an ORB implementation
org.omg.CORBA.ORB SingletonClass	class name of the singleton ORB implementation

8.8.2 ORB Initialization Methods

There are three forms of initialization as shown below. In addition the actual ORB implementation (subclassed from ORB) must implement the set_parameters() methods so that the initialization parameters will be passed into the ORB from the initialization methods.

```
// Java

package org.omg.CORBA;

abstract public class ORB {

    // Application init

    public static ORB init(String[] args,
                                    java.util.Properties props) {
        // call to: set_parameters(args, props);
        ...
        }
```

```
    // Applet init

    public static ORB init(java.applet.Applet app,
                                    java.util.Properties props) {
        // call to: set_parameters(app, props);
        ...
        }

    // Default (singleton) init

    public static ORB init()
        {...}

    // Implemented by subclassed ORB implementations
    //     and called by init methods to pass in their params

    abstract protected void set_parameters(String[] args,
                                    java.util.Properties props);
    abstract protected void set_parameters(Applet app,
                                    java.util.Properties props);

}
```

8.8.2.1 Default initialization

The default initialization method returns the singleton ORB. If called multiple times it will always return the same the Java object.

The primary use of the no-argument version of ORB.init() is to provide a factory for TypeCodes for use by Helper classes implementing the type() method, and to create Any instances that are used to describe union labels as part of creating a union TypeCode. These Helper classes may be baked-in to the browser (e.g. for the interface repository stubs or other wildly popular IDL) and so may be shared across untrusted applets downloaded into the browser. The returned ORB instance is shared across all applets and therefore must have sharply restricted capabilities so that unrelated applets can be isolated from each other. It is not intended to be used directly by applets. Therefore, the ORB returned by ORB.init(), if called from a Java applet, may only be used to create Typecodes. An attempt to invoke other "regular" ORB operations shall raise a system exception.

If called from an application a fully functional ORB object is returned.

8.8.2.2 Application initialization

The application initialization method should be used from a stand-alone Java application. It is passed a array of strings which are the command arguments and a list of Java properties. Either the argument array or the properties may be null.

It returns a new fully functional ORB Java object each time it is called.

8.8.2.3 Applet initialization

The applet initialization method should be used from an applet. It is passed "the applet" and a list of Java properties. Either the applet or the properties may be null.

It returns a new fully functional ORB Java object each time it is called.

9.0 Changes to CORBA 2.0

9.1 Request PIDL

It appears that there an error was introduced in the PIDL defining Request by the C+1.1 Revision that is now part of CORBA 2.0. Overloaded versions of the add arg routines were added without modifying the PIDL. Since IDL does not support overloading the new operations would have to have new names in the PIDL. The Java mapping is specified as if this were the case and also added the new operations to the PIDL (see Section 6.9, "Request").

9.2 Certain Exceptions

The CORBA 2.0 specification is ambiguous as to which scope the Bounds, BadKind, and InvalidName are declared.

This specification places Bounds and BadKind in the TypeCode scope. It also places a different Bounds in the CORBA module, as well as placing InvalidName in the ORB module.

10.0 Missing Items

The following topics are completely missing from this specification, pending completion of the Server-side Portability RFP by the OMG:

* Portable Object Adaptor

- possible new PIDL and other required mappings

- dynamic any type management

What's on the
Programming with Java IDL Web Site?

The *Programming with Java IDL* Web Site has a number of things to make your exploration of Java IDL easier and more fruitful. It's at www.wiley.com/compbooks/lewis.

There's a description of the book, a nice picture of the cover, the book's table of contents and a sample chapter. None of which is of any interest to you since if you are reading this you've got the book in your hands and don't need millions of dollars' worth of electronic infrastructure just to see the stuff. But it's there, in case you ever want to recommend us to a friend or colleague who isn't standing next to you.

Of somewhat more interest to our faithful readers is the source code and executables for the extended examples presented in this book. The short ones you can type in for yourself; it's good practice. We'll make available at least the source for the famous "Hello, World!" Java applet, Java IDL applet, and Java IDL server objects from Chapter 6, as well as the complete example Network Pricing System Java IDL applet from Chapter 9 and servers from Chapter 10. We're still debating whether or how much of the InterPoll applet and server source or executables will be on the site; at the very least we'll have copies of as much of the source as it appears in the book.

We've put together a small yet high-quality collection of links and resources for the authors' favorite CORBA and Java Web sites and other repositories of Internet-accessible free information.

If, heaven forbid, some error crept through our rigorous team of authors, reviewers, editors, experts, family members, and other assorted hangers-on, first of all, we apologize. Even better, we'll make an effort to provide corrections and minor updates as we find them. Actually, there's likely to be at least some updates since Java IDL has not been quite finalized as this book goes to press, so please check the Web site before investing a lot of time investigating any problems you might have with the code in the book.

For hardware and software requirements and installation and use instructions for the examples, please see the Web site.

User Assistance and Information

The software accompanying this book is being provided as is without warranty or guarantee of support of any kind. For questions or comments regarding the example programs or the contents of this book, please send e-mail to:

javaidlbook@fsg.com.

To place additional orders or to request information about other Wiley products, please call (800) 879-4539.

Index